Relativism
and the Study of Man

The William Volker Fund Series in the Humane Studies

Relativism
AND THE STUDY OF MAN

Edited by

HELMUT SCHOECK AND JAMES W. WIGGINS

Papers by

LEONARD CARMICHAEL

J. V. LANGMEAD CASSERLEY

BRUNO LEONI

JAMES C. MALIN

LUDWIG VON MISES

MARIO A. PEI

HELMUT SCHOECK

LEO STRAUSS

JOHN W. TIETZ

ELISEO VIVAS

RICHARD M. WEAVER

CONWAY ZIRKLE

D. VAN NOSTRAND COMPANY, INC.

PRINCETON, NEW JERSEY

TORONTO

NEW YORK

LONDON

D. VAN NOSTRAND COMPANY, INC.
120 Alexander St., Princeton, New Jersey *(Principal office)*
24 West 40 Street, New York 18, New York

D. VAN NOSTRAND COMPANY, LTD.
358, Kensington High Street, London, W. 14, England

D. VAN NOSTRAND COMPANY (Canada), LTD.
25 Hollinger Road, Toronto 16, Canada

PRINTED IN THE UNITED STATES OF AMERICA

Contributors

LEONARD CARMICHAEL, Secretary, Smithsonian Institution. He is editor and coauthor of numerous books in the field of psychology. Selected titles include *Ontogenetic Development* 1951), *Manual of Child Psychology* (1954), *The Selection of Military Manpower* (1951), and *Reading and Visual Fatigue* (1947).

J. V. LANGMEAD CASSERLEY, Professor of Philosophical Theology, Seabury Western Theological Seminary. Selected works include *Morals and Man in the Social Sciences* (1951), *The Christian in Philosophy* (1951), *Graceful Reason* (1954), and *Retreat from Christianity in the Modern World* (1952).

BRUNO LEONI, Dean, School of Political Sciences, Professor of Legal Theory and Theory of the State, University of Pavia. Dr. Leoni, who was a Fulbright Research Scholar in the United States in 1953, is editor of *Il Politico,* where several of his studies have appeared. Selected titles include "The 'Actuality' of Federalism," "Possibilità di applicazione delle matematiche alle discipline economiche," and "The Meaning of 'Political' in Political Decisions."

JAMES C. MALIN, Professor of History, University of Kansas. His books include *The Contriving Brain and the Skillful Hand* (1955), *On the Nature of History* (1954), *The Grassland of North America* (1957), and *Essays on Historiography* (1946).

LUDWIG VON MISES, Professor of Economics, New York University. His works include *Theory and History* (1957), *The*

Theory of Money and Credit (1953), *Socialism* (1951), and *Human Action* (1949).

MARIO A. PEI, Professor of Romance Philology, Columbia University. His publications include *One Language for the World* (1958), *All About Language* (1954), *The Story of English* (1952), and *The Story of Language* (1949).

HELMUT SCHOECK, Professor of Sociology, Emory University. His books include *Was heisst politisch unmoeglich* (1959), *U.S.A.: Motive und Strukturen* (1958), *Soziologie* (1952), and *Nietzsches Philosophie des Menschlich-Allzumenschlichen* (1948).

LEO STRAUSS, Robert Maynard Hutchins Distinguished Service Professor, Department of Political Science, University of Chicago. Selected works include *Thoughts on Machiavelli* (1958), *Natural Right and History* (1953), *Persecution and the Art of Writing* (1952), and *On Tyranny: An Interpretation of Xenophon's Hiero* (1948).

JOHN W. TIETZ, Professor of Education (retired), New York University. Among his publications are articles in the field of education and *Biological Foundations of Education* (coauthor, 1931).

ELISEO VIVAS, John Evans Professor of Moral and Intellectual Philosophy, Northwestern University. His publications include *Creation and Discovery* (1955), *The Problems of Aesthetics* (coeditor, 1953), *The Moral Life and the Ethical Life* (1950), and *D. H. Lawrence* (1960).

RICHARD M. WEAVER, Professor of English, University of Chicago. His works include *Composition: A Course in Writing and Rhetoric* (1957), *The Ethics of Rhetoric* (1953), and *Ideas Have Consequences* (1948).

CONWAY ZIRKLE, Professor of Botany, University of Pennsylvania. His books include *Evolution, Marxian Biology, and the Social Scene* (1959), *Death of a Science in Russia* (1949), and *The Beginnings of Plant Hybridization* (1935).

Preface

In recent years an increasing number of writers have focused their attention on the problem produced by the extension of methodological relativism beyond its legitimate domain into the realm of human values, and particularly toward the determination of broad policy questions implicitly or explicitly involving conflicting values. Some of these authors have drawn attention to the consequences of this extension of relativistic assumptions in areas of human life ranging from personal morality and integrity to societal survival.

The present volume is an outgrowth of a Symposium on Relativism, which brought together a small group of scholars, from some ten academic disciplines, to consider certain aspects of the problem. Each participant prepared and circulated a paper prior to the sessions of the group. In a cloistered setting, each had the opportunity to benefit from formal and informal discussion and criticism of his own and other papers. A few discussions were continued through correspondence after the conclusion of the Symposium. The revisions of the papers, following the conference, ranged from slight to incisive.

Each essay in this volume represents the independent work of its author. The views expressed are his own, and no collective conclusion was intended by either the editors or the writers.

After, and possibly as a result of, lively and frank disagreements posed by differences of approach or interpretation, a number of basic convergences did appear. These may be recognized by the reader.

The editors are grateful to all the participants in the Symposium for their personal contributions to an unusual intellectual experience.

Contents

1

Absolutes, Relativism, and the Scientific Psychology of Human Nature

Leonard Carmichael

> Nor did I think your edicts were so strong
> That any mortal man could override
> The gods' unwritten and undying laws;
> Their life is not today and yesterday
> But always, and none knows from
> where they came.
> I would not pay the price before the gods
> Of breaking these for fear of any man.
>
> Sophocles [1]

Human values depend on our physical make-up, on the way our brain, belly, and members act, and on the demands made by the needs, appetites, and impulses they give rise to.

Bernard Berenson [2]

Taxonomy, or the classification of animals and plants according to their natural relationships, is an important branch of biology. Today taxonomy does not play quite so large a role in the total family of the biological sciences as it did one hundred years ago. A good many present-day philosophers and students of

1

concepts seem to be rather like old-fashioned taxonomists in dealing with ideas. They see a concept such as relativism come home in a philosopher's collecting bag, and, as intellectual taxonomists, they are not satisfied until they have classified and labeled it, and then all too often they just put it on the shelf with other clearly marked and preserved concepts.

It is not difficult to defend the importance of biological taxonomy; it is easy also to advocate philosophical taxonomy; but it is harder to make a positive case for doing nothing further with ideas once they have been neatly labeled as part of this or that system of philosophy and then, as it were, just locked up in a book. Surely in this symposium we should be more than taxonomic in our dealing with the role of the great revolutionary idea of relativism and the study of man and the currently less popular and yet also clearly labeled and important idea that there are unchanging absolutes. It seems especially worthwhile at this time to think about these concepts in the context of modern science and scholarship rather than to limit ourselves to the history of technical philosophy. It is distinctly worth knowing what Plato, Aristotle, St. Thomas Aquinas, Descartes, Hobbes, Kant, Newton, Locke, Hamilton, Shaftesbury, Hegel, James, Dewey, and others have made of these concepts in the past. But the mere history of their ideas is not enough. Many people today —more, it may be, than in earlier, more static periods—are actively seeking stable guide lines in their own lives. This means that a re-examination of some of the arguments for the existence of unchanging absolutes in the rules of human social conduct now has a new urgency.

These introductory sentences may have been written merely as a defense against what will be the justifiable charge that the arguments presented in this paper have been formulated before by others and are indeed but a few of the old, well-rubbed coins of the history of thought. There are, however, recent discoveries in regard to human nature in anthropology, biology, and psychology that bear on these ideas. It is mainly in the light of these scientific facts that the concepts of the relative and of the absolute will be examined very briefly in this paper.

In spite of these more or less brave words, it is not safe to omit all definitions. A quick glance at any of the standard histories of philosophy shows in how many senses the concepts of relativity, relativism, and the relative as well as of the absolute have been used down through the years. Central in these definitions is the idea that relativism is opposed to the proposition that anything is fixed, absolute, and invariable. The notion of the absolute, on the contrary, is to be thought of as having reference to a fixed, unchanging reality not imparted by other varying realities.

Those who consider relativism as having sprung entirely from very recent mathematical and physical thinking and as stemming back no farther than Einstein should not forget the long history of the term "relativity" in philosophy. Even in scientific psychology it may be noted that Wilhelm Wundt himself used the concept when he stressed the fact that every phase of consciousness is influenced by every other phase of the experience of the moment.[3] This same investigator, in considering Weber's Law, temperature adaptation, and contrast colors, specifically pointed to the importance of relativity in psychology. Thus, this term has been generally used even in experimental psychology for more than three quarters of a century.

It may be presumed, however, that in the present symposium, when the term "relativism" is considered in connection with the study of man, the ideas to be discussed are those primarily related to human value systems. Our task here, therefore, is to think of the contrasts between the relative and the absolute in ethics, in esthetics, and in other normative fields.

Herbert Spencer spoke of absolute ethics as a final permanent code of conduct that would describe the behavior of fully evolved men in a fully evolved society.[4] What Spencer meant by a fully evolved man or a fully evolved society is not clear; but these concepts need to be further considered because it is becoming increasingly evident that mankind may in some ways be thought of as fully evolved. Human beings have not basically changed in bodily make-up, at least since recorded history began. There is no reason to believe, indeed, that there were not the same individual differences among men as well as similar average capacities in sensory acuity, reaction time, and intelligence when the Sumerians first began inscribing clay tablets as there are now. It may be emphasized that this does not mean that all men of any generation are alike now or that they were all alike in any previous age. Rather, it seems that the range of human capacities in any period of historical time is similar to the range in other periods, at least in regard to many inborn characteristics. This begins to suggest that while man may not yet—biologically speaking—be "fully evolved," man is certainly not now rapidly changing. Therefore, such a relatively unchanging man may be described in Spencer's sense if one uses the modern scientific techniques of physiology and psychology in studying the characteristics of individuals in well-selected samples of modern populations.

If, then, human beings are fully evolved in Spencer's sense, or at least not rapidly evolving, one may look to see what these essentially unchanging human beings have discovered in ethics and esthetics and other value areas as they have lived together in very different social orders through some thousands of years.

First of all, however, let us look at man's biological make-up. It sometimes seems that the two greatest marvels of living forms are, first, the mechanisms by means of which new species of plants and animals are created, that is, the fact of biological novelty, and, second, that once created, some species of organisms persist essentially unchanged through literally millions of generations, that is, the fact of biological conservatism. The chromosomes of the reproductive cells of animals and plants are minute, complex, very specific chemical packets. It seems almost incredible that such small, unstable systems can maintain themselves unchanged from parent to offspring from generation to generation through almost endless eons of time. But this is the case. For example, great geological changes have taken place since Devonian times, but the coelacanth fishes have remained unaltered for at least 30 million years, while some mountains have risen and been worn away. *Limulus,* the familiar horseshoe crab of our beaches, is at least 160 million years old. Here indeed is a true unreconstructed conservative. Many of the genera of fossil ants preserved in amber are as much as 60 million years old, and only a few of these genera are now extinct. This biological stability determined by chromosomal make-up is not of body structure alone. No entomologist can doubt that the behavior and indeed even, in the case of such organisms as the ants, the social organization of their colonies are today what they were millions of years ago when these organisms first appeared with their present specific and unchanging structures and functions. The growth of social organizations in animals has recently been given new meaning in the studies of Tinbergen and his associates.[5] If values arise out of bodily make-up, as the quotation from Berenson at the start of this paper suggests, and if fixed types of interindividual response have life-saving and other biologically important functions, then certainly, at least in these ant societies, we can say that there have been fixed and absolute values of a sort for many millions of years.

K. D. Roeder, one of the foremost present-day experimental students of the physiology of the insect nervous system, has recently pointed out that the knowledge of the form, character, and the limited number of the neurons of the insect nervous system helps us to understand the complex, but largely fixed, behavior patterns of these typically short-lived organisms.[6]

The human nervous system is much more complex than the best insect nervous system, and man's brain is peculiarly effective in making learning and individual environmental adaptations possible. Even the human brain, however, has very definite inborn limitations of function, and these characteristics fix the possible capacities that may be considered by one who would understand not only what man can do, but also, and most importantly, what man cannot do.

We are sometimes blind to these all-important conservative and essentially unchanging factors in the structures and functions underlying human nature because we think of man's almost unlimited ability to put words, symbols, and concepts together in new ways and to build ever better and more complex tools. But behind this very facility with symbols and tools are the age-old limitations imposed upon men by the inborn make-up of human sense organs, brain, and muscles. It is upon these fixed and genetically determined biological structures that what is now called human "species-specific behavior" depends.

It is worth remembering that as man has certainly changed little in his basic physical respects for at least thirty-five thousand years, there are many constants in human adaptive responses. There is little reason to believe—to make this conservatism more vivid—that the physical and physiological make-up of a good modern jet pilot is much, if any, different from that of a good hunter of Paleolithic times. There has always been, as just noted, in each generation, then and now, variability between human individuals in height, weight, strength, problem-solving ability, and other physiological and psychological characteristics. The earliest tools and machines we know of that were built by men have much the same average dimensions and shape they would have if they were being newly built for people today. The handles of Bronze Age swords fit our hands much as they did those of their first users.

To take but one of many other possible examples of similar factors important in esthetics, it may be noted that visual capacities and other sensory limitations have not changed during the centuries of truly human life on this globe. Thus, absolute sensitivity to light, the ability to discriminate brightness patterns, visual acuity, depth perception, and even induced colors of the type now being so well described by E. H. Land [7] have been human constants down through the generations. This means that what we see now as visual balance, as dynamic symmetry, and as the representation of movement in a drawing must be much the same as these percepts were when men first experimented with the graphic arts. Recently discovered cave drawings bring home the truth of this observation.

The principle of empathy, to take another example, in its most inclusive sense summarizes the way in which unchanging human sense organs, brain, and muscles determine our reaction to and our evaluation of what we see and feel as well as the very way in which we perceive. [8] By feeling ourselves into so-called external reality, we recognize many qualities such as depth, strain, rhythm, texture, calmness, and repose in sights and sounds. The great arts of architecture, sculpture, painting, music, poetry, and the dance are in part, at least, built upon these fixed relationships between the unchanging character of the physics of radiant energy (light) and of material vibrations (sound) and the reactions of living, behaving organisms.[9] Hence, each art acquires canons that determine the relationships that are and that are not evaluated as good or bad in human visual or auditory patterns in time and space. Once such values are discovered, only a changing romantic whimsy or caprice can pretend that they are not fixed and immutable so long as human brains and human senses remain unchanged. Thus, it seems that esthetic theory must make a place for certain absolutes that are determined by the fixed factors of human nature.

Drugs that were known to the ancients still have much the same physiological and psychological effects on modern man as they had when first described. Tobacco was presumably valued for its pleasing effects by pre-Columbian Indians just as it is by modern smokers. Wine and spirits have changed little during the years in the way in which they affect human central nervous systems and thus conversation. The truth of the old adage, *in vino veritas*, is fixed. Plant-derived narcotics have worked as they do now on central nervous systems down through the centuries. This does not mean that when opium was first discovered in poppies man knew, as he does now, how to use it and what its good as well as its bad psychological and social effects are.

These examples seem to show that by long trial and error the human race has gradually discovered (and let it be emphasized that the word properly used here seems to be *discovered* and not *invented*) some real absolutes in regard to the best individual and social uses of tobacco, alcohol, narcotics, and other drugs.

The preceding statements have given only a few of the quite literally thousands of possible examples of the essentially fixed characteristics of behavior that are related to our age-old human nature. In recent years specific studies have been made of some of these unchanging characteristics. A good many of the results of these studies that bear upon good and bad ways of performing tasks have been brought together in books such as a large handbook prepared to be used by the constructors of new weapons and industrial machines.[10] Thus, newly invented devices or designs may be made to fit the range and the averages of human body size and of physiological and psychological capacity. The tensile strength and melting point of metals are absolutes that the engineer cannot neglect in constructing a new space vehicle. If such a vehicle is to carry a man, some unchanging characteristics of the human frame and of human mental life must also be recognized as anatomically, physiologically, and psychologically fixed limits, for some of these capacities cannot be changed by courses of instruction or periods of adaptation.

What has all this to do with values? The sage historian of art, the late Bernard Berenson, already quoted at the beginning of this paper, in his *Aesthetics and History* points to the answer when he says: "There is, in fact, a relative absolute in art, which is determined by our psycho-physiological condition and our mental preparation." This is a profound and significant statement, which seems to have relevance not only in esthetics, but also in ethics and in all other human normative fields. One who wishes to consider a philosophically wise behavioristic approach to the way values arise in human beings may read S. C. Pepper's *The Sources of Value*.[11]

Studies of this sort suggest the possibility that because of man's conservative and essentially unchanging and inborn anatomical, physiological, and psychological characteristics, some of the legal, ethical, esthetic, and other value scales of mankind, once they are discovered, may also be considered to be fixed and unchanging.

Customs related to birth, puberty, marriage, child-rearing, food-providing and eating, illness, death, and other standard events of every human life and culture have had many different superficial forms in various ages and societies. This does not suggest that all these patterns of behavior are equally satisfactory in what may be thought of as an absolute sense. Few now doubt that the scientific discovery of the nature and cause of many infectious diseases has, as it were, established certain absolutes that must be socially enforced, such as vaccination to prevent smallpox. Vaccination is thus absolutely better than are the incantations of a witch doctor in preventing this disease. Is there any reason to suppose that in a more subtle way men have not also discovered certain preferred ways of dealing, for example, with the social contract of marriage?

This thesis—and, as suggested at the outset, there is no claim that it is a novel one—is that because man has an unchanging and an age-old, genetically determined anatomical, physiological, and psychological make-up, there is reason to believe that at least some of the "values" that he recognizes as good or bad have been discovered or have emerged as human individuals have lived together for thousands of years in many societies. Is there any reason to suggest that these values, once identified and tested, may not be thought as essentially fixed and unchanging? For example, the wanton murder of one adult by another for the purely personal amusement of the person committing the murder, once it is recognized as a general wrong, is likely always to be so recognized. Such a murder has disadvantageous individual and social effects. Or to take a milder example from esthetics, man is always likely to recognize in a special way the balance in design of two complementary colors because he is born with specially constituted human eyes, a human brain, and human muscles.

It may also be suggested that mankind, especially since the invention of language, mathematics, and other forms of oral and written symbolism, has gradually discovered that some types of political, economic, and social relationships work better than others. Some individual patterns of behavior, such as those summarized by such words as "courage," "temperance," "justice," "wisdom," "charity," and "friendliness," at least in some specific and identifiable circumstances, can be seen to be preferred *absolutely* to their opposites.

We may now go back to the idea that since man is no longer biologically evolving, at least in a rapid way, it is conceivable that a permanent code of preferred human conduct may gradually be discovered and described.

This idea of biological fixity may imply that as man's scientific discoveries, technology, and inventions rapidly alter the patterns of human social living, the old and fixed absolutes of inborn

human nature are to be thought of not as changing, but as reactions that are displayed in many new contexts. For example,
if unnecessary cruelty to animals is bad, and if it is so absolutely,
then it is bad for an unlettered peasant to kick a stray dog or
for a space scientist to send a mammal into orbit without proper
humane controls. If pornographic drawings are undesirable, so
also is pornographic television.

If we assume, therefore, that there are, in the sense just outlined, some absolutes or "relative-absolutes" in ethics, in esthetics,
and in other normative fields and that these values are so well
established that they need no longer be questioned as advantageous for the human race, then this is a fact that is most important
for education. For it is only by instruction that the human race
can make sure that these discovered rules of proper behavior are
to govern the lives of as many people as possible in each generation. The surest way to accomplish this result is by formal education in the home, the church, and, above all, in the school. Thus,
accepted values can be handed down in human society. In this
way the young of the human race can be taught how to make
correct judgments in solving the new problems of their own
personal lives on the basis of fixed rules concerning what is good
or true or beautiful.

The desirability of this practical inculcation of knowledge
about absolutes by education raises a most urgent problem. How
can "the elders" be sure that the absolutes they themselves recognize are indeed established and are not mere invented human
dogmas, passing fashions, or a *Zeitgeist* in flux? No one wishes to
see absolutes where they are not; as Santayana says of his hero
in *The Last Puritan,* one cannot demand some absolute and special sanction for mere natural preferences.[12] The educational and
social philosophers and sociologists who say that all instruction
can be or should be "value-free" thus take an easy, but not
necessarily a correct, way when they advocate closing our eyes
to mankind's most important problems. In other words, an educational philosophy that would exclude values and deal only with
"facts" is in danger of losing its main nutriment for real human
lives. When this problem is clearly seen, few can doubt that

Wolfgang Köhler is profoundly correct when he says: "At the bottom of all human activities are 'values,' the conviction that some things 'ought to be' and others not."

The mere mention of the problem of ethical absolutes in education would nevertheless have set on edge the essentially romantic and almost completely relativistic teeth of John Dewey and many of the "new" educational reformers of the last generation. The very idea that an argument can be made for fixed values would also be very hard for those social anthropologists who like to tell us with superior smiles that all social standards are relative. Those who say that it is just as "good" to grow up in a fine hut in a native village in New Guinea and there to learn the tribal rites of the group as it is to develop as a native New Englander in a fine house in Milton, Massachusetts, to attend Phillips Exeter Academy and to graduate from Harvard naturally dislike to think that there are fixed and discoverable values.

The idea, also, that there are some established esthetic values in the arts is likewise hard for those who now like to say that a fashionable nonobjective painter who reports that he experiences great emotional satisfaction as he paints is necessarily as satisfactory an artist as was Titian.

If we accept the suggestions so far presented in this paper that there may be some absolutes in human conduct that can be discovered, we must have the courage to apply this knowledge in deciding the content of the education that we wish to furnish for the children of this or any other age. No human being can learn everything. Also, all members of each generation are not alike in abilities or in interests. That which children should learn in school must, therefore, be selected and decided in some way. To "let the child decide," especially in early developmental years, is an odd doctrine that almost seems to refute itself.

If, on the contrary, there are some absolutes, it is clear that they should be taught to as many members of each generation as possible. It is hard to believe that even linguistic and mathematical skills are more important than are correct ideas about what is true, good, or beautiful in human social living. It seems almost self-evident that a strong society, therefore, must teach both facts and values.

The idea that standards of good and bad in social living and of esthetics in man's attitudes toward art must always undergo continuous change from century to century and from locality to locality is an easy doctrine for many present-day writers to accept. According to this view, the student of society records and describes the behavior of groups and the values that such groups accept. Some such students like to think of themselves as purely scientific and objective sociologists. Somehow they feel that they alone of all people can step back from their own group-inculcated evaluations and see facts as clear and free of value. This view has many consequences in everyday life. According to this popular relativistic attitude, for example, judges sitting on the bench make the law each day. Hence, it is assumed that human beings must invent new laws as social theories progress or as man's technology changes or even as fashions alter. Judges do not, thus, as an older view holds, attempt to discover what the eternally valid law is that must be applied to each new specific case.

It may be worth pausing for a moment to suggest that these two theories of the law are a good test for anyone to use in regard to his own thinking about the advantages of a relativistic or the absolute approach to the understanding of codes of human conduct. The relativist says, "Of course there was no television law before television was invented." The believer in absolutes says, on the contrary, that after the invention of television it was necessary for wise judges to discover how the old absolute codes or rules of justice could be applied in this new field.

One of the dangers of a fully relativistic approach to the determination of what is good, true, or beautiful is that the problem itself is too often dismissed from court by those who hold this view. All that one who is a consistent relativist need do is to say, "My personal emotions and those feelings that I attribute to my neighbors are the judge of what is good or true or beautiful for me at this time and in this place, and I need and wish for no other sanction." Such a relativist may then continue: "In our

mechanized age and here in New York, for a person of my education, such and such may now be considered as good or bad, but,
of course, this was not true here in the eighteenth century nor
would it be now for a Bushman in the Kalahari Desert of Africa."

To put this in another way, one who adopts a completely relativistic approach to ethical or esthetic questions either accepts his
own feelings as law or may come to assert that a statistically
analyzed poll of the beliefs of a well-selected sample of individuals
is to be taken as a temporary norm. Or such relativists may assert
that a complete and adequate statistical study of the actual behavior of other individuals selected by some "sampling technique" in a given society at a specific time may indicate not only
what people now do, but, amazingly enough, what they ought to
do. Relativism thus all too easily substitutes what statisticians
call "measures of central tendency" for old discovered and established absolutes of what people "ought to do" in social living.
A carefully conducted and statistically verified study of the sex
life of human beings in a modern American city may show that
few people achieve in full measure the ideal moral position held
by the most generally approved time-tested, legal, and religiously
established codes of human sexual life. From the standpoint of
the relativist, this may seem to disprove the existence of absolutes
in this field of behavior. From the standpoint of one who believes
that absolutes have been discovered and that they are fixed, the
problem of our day in sex behavior is how to be effective in the
teaching of the highest established code of such behavior. Thus
the believer in absolutes hopes that gradually more and more
people may bring what they actually do into harmony with what
society has discovered that they ought to do.

Human ethical and esthetic standards must be known and accepted individually as guides in decision-making by individuals
if values are to play a realistic role in life. It is, however, not
always enough for such individuals to learn rules of conduct by
rote. A sensitive and informed "wisdom of the sentiments" is
sometimes needed to determine that which is absolutely right or
wrong in complex, novel human problems. Education that transmits the best that the human race has discovered in the past is one

of the ways in which such wisdom can be given to individuals, but only to those individuals who have the inborn interests and abilities to acquire it.

The truly great literature of civilization has provided some people in many generations of men and women with the sort of wisdom that is needed in the subtle selection of proper courses of action in solving the often truly novel problems that arise in each life. By the study of such books the student, if he has the required intellectual capacity and emotional sensitivity, comes to know the thoughts of great men and their solutions to recurring human problems. Some complex decisions in humanly important matters are thus better carried out by those who know what Socrates thought and did than they could be by persons without this knowledge. One great aim of education is seen as the teaching of the results of man's gradual discovery of absolute values down through the ages. To use old theological language, people thus learn what sins are and how men have in the past resisted them.

If the able members of each generation are thus exposed to some of the best thoughts of good and able men and women of successive periods of the past, one method of uncovering absolutes is presented, and in this way the learner also gains measuring scales or mental maps for his own use.

One old difficulty in the use of technical language in the field of values may be illustrated by this idea of the *mental map* which has become a favorite concept of some modern psychologists. Such maps or "value scales" are "subjective" in that they depend on learning and are in what the older psychologists called "conscious experience." But such maps are also "objective" in that they may be common to many sensitive and well-educated members of a generation and because they are based upon fixed, externally derived data.

How to develop such good standard maps or measuring rods to be used in human normative fields by many members of each generation is, as has been noted, a practical educational problem of general significance. The formal study of such writers as Homer, Dante, Shakespeare, Molière, Milton, and Goethe is one tested way that may be used in establishing such self-accepted standards. It is not just the result of custom that such works of literature are studied in good programs of education, but rather that this sort of learning has a deep human need at its base. Moreover, if the study of such tested books is introduced with the classicist's critical aim of discovering moral absolutes, the result may be, at its best, the establishment or the strengthening in the learner of an ability to make choices in the basic problems of his own life by reference to established standards. The same may be said of the ethical education provided by the playing rules of competitive sports when such games are conducted in accordance with the best traditions of what is called "good sportsmanship."

This is not the place to evaluate psychoanalytic theory. It is interesting to note, however, that it seems almost a paradox of our day that Freudian psychology, which has such wide acceptance in the writings of many modern relativistic thinkers, has, at its core, certain absolute elements so far as human nature is concerned. One has but to study the psychoanalytic use of the ideas of the id, the ego, and the superego to recognize this clearly. The id is considered as rooted deeply in man's inborn biological nature, and the superego is a socially determined "map" or conscience. This set of psychoanalytic concepts seems to become invalid if some "absolutes" of human nature and society are not assumed.

Many people, however, have given up an intellectual belief in unchanging absolutes because they cannot convince themselves that there is any authority that can establish such fixed rules in ethics, esthetics, or the other human normative fields. The argument being presented here would deny that a failure to have at any time an infallible, ethical "litmus paper," as it were, or any simple test of what is absolutely good or bad is proof that there are no fixed good or bad ways in human action. As has been pointed out, some of man's physiological and psychological capacities are essentially fixed. The physical universe is governed by law and not by caprice. Therefore, it seems reasonable to expect that fixed normative scales to be used in making evaluations possible in man's social life can gradually be discovered and applied. We do not turn aside from what we know about astronomy at any time because there is a great deal we do not know or because so much that we once thought we knew is no longer recognized as true. May not the same argument be accepted in our thinking about ethical and esthetic judgments? To achieve real standards of morality and taste thus requires a truly liberal education. To know what is absolutely true or beautiful demands study and research. As Edith Hamilton says of one great period in human history: "But in Athens, in Platonic Athens, at least, the idea that each man must be a research worker in the truth if he were ever to attain any share in it, seemed rather to attract than to repel." [13]

Other approaches besides the study of great literature and works of art in the discovery of unchanging standards that are as they are because of man's fixed biological and psychological make-up may be found in the study of codes of law and the so-called "wisdom literatures" of different cultures and of different ages as well as in the collection of ancient aphorisms and proverbs of mankind. S. N. Kramer has recently translated a code of the Sumerian king of Ur-Nammu of about 2050 B.C.[14] This may well be the oldest written law code yet discovered. In a sun-baked tablet this scholar found that the ancient ruler of Ur provided for the protection of his citizens from the unscrupulous men who would steal oxen and sheep not belonging to them. This king also saw to it that the orphan did not fall prey to the wealthy or the widow to the powerful. He also protected the man with one shekel so that he would not be imposed upon by the man with many shekels. Is it not possible to say that this early legal system is a beginning of the codification of the discoveries of certain absolutes of conduct that have survival value in social living? Lists of hundreds of proverbs have been compiled. In many of these sentences, founded as they are in common human experience, one sees guidelines to much that is not "relative" in human living.

The question may very properly be raised concerning the role of religion in a world that recognizes or does not accept ethical absolutes. First of all, one who is interested in this question may begin with an evaluation and ask, "Are all religions equally true or false?" It is said that in the late Professor John Dewey's seminar at Columbia University, no one ever heard any phrase except, "Religion used to say that . . ." Today, this general negative attitude toward all religion seems strangely old-fashioned, but it must be admitted that even those who believe that there are ethical and other absolutes must still face the question of determining whether religious teachings can be absolutely true, and then if the answer is in the affirmative, the question must then be answered as to which religion is best.

The present author is not attempting in this paper to set forth any final "positivistic" argument concerning religion. It would be bad, however, to omit the fact that in the history of the race, religious ideas and ideals have played a large role in man's acceptance or rejection of certain ethical ideas as absolutes.

Some relativists, in thinking about religion, may still cynically say, "Why choose between mythologies?" But the individual who accepts the teaching of any church "as true" must in childhood or later life learn to know what the rules and ideals of his church are. Thus, education becomes most important in religious life and for the believer in a particular religious system in establishing his ethical attitudes. It may be noted, also, that many of those who accept religious ideas and commandments as absolutes find satisfaction in the belief that the basic teachings of their religion have not been discovered by human individuals, but are rather divine revelations to man.

Religious upholders of a belief in absolutes can thus turn to well-organized churches such as Judaism, the Roman Catholic Church, the Eastern Orthodox churches, the Anglican churches, the Lutheran churches, the Presbyterian churches, and some religions in eastern and other traditions and find in the teaching of each a more or less organized guide to individual and social living based upon an acceptance of unquestioned absolutes supernaturally established. Even some who on positivistic grounds reject the idea of supernatural knowledge and of absolutes fixed by this so-called type of knowledge may recognize that the results of such beliefs are socially advantageous. Few can doubt, for example, that an effort to take the Ten Commandments as absolute and unchanging divinely established rules of conduct is better for social living than would be the acceptance of a life to be lived without a knowledge of these rules or of a life lived by one who would oppose these rules.

Sometimes we forget how much of our legal structure and of the now almost intuitively accepted ethical standards of modern social living or even the structure of our own superegos, if we like this terminology, was first clearly set forth in the writings of Christian philosophers such as Saint Augustine and Saint Thomas. Roman Catholic moral philosophy today, following in this great tradition, clearly defines the absolutes of present-day conduct and specifically lists the actions that are good and those that are sinful. This is done in such a way that ordinary church members can know when they are doing what they should do or when they are committing sins.

A similar dogmatic and absolutist view of ethical standards has been taken by many Protestant theologians and philosophers, such as the Quaker moralist Jonathan Dymond. This writer, in his *Essays on the Principles of Morality,* bases his view of the moral upon a study of what he calls "the Will of God as presented in the Bible." [15] One has but to glance at a more modern book in the same vein, such as Mary Ward's *Lessons on Morality,*[16] to see how an authoritarian ethic may be taken as establishing that which is good and bad in a fixed way by a reference to Biblical teaching. Here what is considered as *the* established truth in regard to approved and disapproved behavior in such matters as property rights, bankruptcy, the duties of heirs, honesty of speech, amusements, suicide, civil obedience, the function of punishment, and many other specific human problems is presented in categorical form. The rules these authors and many others like them give are held as unquestioned absolutes because they are considered as founded on the unchanging will of God. Here again the positivist meets a problem. It is hard for him to say that the society is not better, by most tests he accepts, which acknowledges these absolutes and does its human best to live up to them than is a society that does not know these rules or that adopts courses of action that are at variance with them because they are supposed to have no authoritative basis.

It may thus be asked if this very fact of the apparent social utility of these so-called "absolutes" may not lend some operational or pragmatic support to the idea that there are, in fact, basic social laws that have been discovered and that, when established, may best be thought of as fixed and immutable? If this view is accepted, it may be expected that just as new basic and true relationships are continually being discovered by the physical and biological sciences, so may new absolute values be discovered as new insights appear in ethical judgments in modern social living. Thus, some old examples of absolutes may come to seem "uncouth" without invalidating the absolutes themselves.

In this paper no single topic has been treated in sufficient detail to organize all, or even most of, the arguments pro and con that may be raised in connection with the positions that have been examined. It may now be noted briefly that for some true believers in absolutes, certain of the positivistic arguments given here are quite unnecessary and beside the point. Such modern thinkers as Jacques Maritain would say much more about inspired understanding and a truly mystical approach to the knowledge of absolutes and of the eternal verities than has been presented here.[17] In fact, now and in the past, at least some of those who believe in ethical absolutes have asserted that the whole notion is so clearly right and so basically sound that all nature cries out that this point of view must be and is deeply and eternally true. The present paper, therefore, may be thought of by such people to be a mere limping and pragmatic approach of a positivistic or operational view that sees absolutes as important in the understanding of the basis of a stable and ordered society. Many religious people, as just noted, hold that such eternal truths are better apprehended in more immediate, nonpositivistic or nonoperational ways by the mystical approach to what they think of as eternal truth. The present writer is not equipped to evaluate this mystical philosophy or its results, but he does feel that its existence should be noted.

It is interesting, also, to remember that not only in the establishment of ethical norms but also in what has been called the cult of estheticism there have been those who advance the role of mysticism in relation to the appreciation of esthetic values that are considered as absolutely fixed. R. A. Parker has recently described this view as follows: "The ecstasy of art could never be communicated by the unregenerate—appreciation could come only by mystical, never by rational, criticism." He further speaks of the "aesthetic moment," "the sense of union, not with God as the religious mystic experiences it, but with the divinity in the work of art; that fusion of subjective and objective when the work of art is no longer outside the observer but becomes one with the initiated; that aesthetic moment, which is comparable to the mystic vision or ecstasy of a Saint Theresa." [18]

In this brief paper, therefore, an effort has been made to point out a few naturalistic, pragmatic, and positivistic arguments that may be advanced for the recognition of absolutes in human normative fields. This presentation has a limited objective. It is similar to that used by Irving Babbitt in one of his books in which he defended classicism against romanticism by saying "the remedy for the partial positivism that is the source of this [romantic] unsoundness is a more complete positivism." [19]

It may be irrelevant by some rules of logic, but surely today the uncertainty and turmoil of the social and political world make the assumption of a complete relativistic anarchy of values and rules of life seem less attractive than it did in the academic rooms of those writers who knew only the order and peace of the Victorian world. Then the fact, if not the theory, of stability dominated the life of the intellectual advocates of relativism who could talk about their new liberation from absolutes while they enjoyed the comfort of a world that still largely assumed them.

Now we see that a series of atomic blasts might write an all too final end to all concepts, relative and absolute, that depend on the living protoplasm of human brains. It may thus again be worth active intellectual effort to examine, in detail, the arguments for the existence of absolutes in human social living. The knowledge that such absolutes exist and what they are, if clearly demonstrated, might do much to rescue mankind from the ethical and esthetic chaos of our day.

NOTES

(The dates are those of the editions of the works used, not in all cases the first publication date.)

1. See C. M. Bowra, *The Greek Experience* (Cleveland: World Publishing Co., 1957).
2. Bernard Berenson, *Aesthetics and History* (Garden City: Doubleday Anchor Books, 1954).
3. Wilhelm Wundt, *Outlines of Psychology* (Leipzig: Wilhelm Engleman, 1897).
4. Herbert Spencer, *Principles of Ethics,* Part I, "The Data of Ethics" (New York: D. Appleton & Co., 1897).
5. N. Tinbergen, *Social Behavior in Animals* (London: Methuen, 1953).
6. K. D. Roeder, "A Physiological Approach to the Relation Between Prey and Predator," in *Studies in Invertebrate Morphology* (Washington: Smithsonian Institution, 1959), pp. 287-306.
7. E. H. Land, "Experiments in Color Vision," *Sci. Amer.,* Vol. CC, No. 5 (May, 1959), pp. 84-99.
8. Wolfgang Köhler, *The Place of Value in a World of Facts* (New York: Liveright, 1938).
9. Geoffrey Scott, *The Architecture of Humanism: A Study in the History of Taste* (Garden City: Doubleday Anchor Books, 1954).
10. *Handbook of Human Engineering Data* (2nd ed.; Tufts College, Institute of Applied Experimental Psychology, 1952), Department of the Navy, Special Devices Center, Technical Report No. 199-1-2.
11. S. C. Pepper, *The Sources of Value* (Berkeley: University of California Press, 1958), pp. xiv + 372.
12. George Santayana, *The Last Puritan: A Memoir in the Form of a Novel* (New York: Scribner's, 1936).
13. Edith Hamilton, *The Greek Way to Western Civilization* (New York: Mentor Books, 1942).
14. S. N. Kramer, *History Begins at Sumer* (Garden City: Doubleday Anchor Books, 1959).
15. Jonathan Dymond, *Essays on the Principles of Morality* (1st ed., 1829; New York: C. C. Francis & Co., 1842).
16. Mary Ward, *Lessons on Morality* (Westtown, Pennsylvania: Privately published, 1907).

17. Jacques Maritain, *The Degrees of Knowledge* (New York: Scribner's, 1959).
18. R. A. Parker, *The Transatlantic Smiths* (New York: Random House, 1959).
19. Irving Babbitt, *Rousseau and Romanticism* (New York: Meridian Press, 1955).

2

Human Evolution and Relativism

CONWAY ZIRKLE

I

Today almost every scientist whose interests extend beyond the range of his technical researches is a relativist of one kind or another. To a professional scientist, this needs no explanation; it is only what he would expect. When we view the phases through which our expanding sciences are passing, we find that they contain a vast amount of information and that this information is still growing exponentially just as it has been growing for the past three hundred years. While we have not yet learned to know ourselves, we are getting a better idea as to what sort of creatures we actually are. And this knowledge helps to explain what might otherwise be a paradox. The more our knowledge increases—the greater the achievements in which our species can take a legitimate pride—the greater becomes the modesty of the scientists who are responsible for the increase. Today our better scientists know so much about themselves that they have become acutely aware of their many limiting deficiencies.

Since the ambitious attempts of Sir Isaac Newton, nearly three centuries ago, almost no good scientist has ever fallen into the *hubris* of assailing the absolute. Scientists have learned enough to be convinced of their all-encompassing ignorance, and this knowledge compels them to be modest as individuals and, consequently, relativists in their philosophy. When they examine the universe and then contemplate themselves, they are almost forced to conclude that the absolute will always elude them. One of the greatest discoveries in all science occurred when the scientists learned, after much hard experience, that science itself has its limitations. Very few scientists believe that science will ever reach the ultimate or that it will ever encompass the All.

Hence, the majority of our scientists label themselves "relativists," and this seems to have given relativism a prestige it might not otherwise have had. Today science enjoys an enormous vogue, and any concept that scientists endorse or that can be labeled "scientific" is, more often than not, accepted uncritically and in complete ignorance of the evidence on which it is based. Thus, relativism was bound to become a most respectable philosophy and, inevitably, sooner or later to permeate the disciplines that aspire to be sciences. Certainly it was inevitable that many who had little understanding of what relativism implies should call themselves relativists but remain absolutists and, from long habit, continue to assume that whatever they believed was absolutely true.

The vogue of relativism naturally has some humorous aspects, and perhaps we should get what fun we can from it, because its consequences are not all humorous. Once relativism had spread outward from the sciences and permeated fields where it was not subject to the checks and balances of scientific skepticism, it quickly developed into a faith—one, moreover, that is very comforting to those of our contemporaries who have wandered away from their adolescent convictions but who still need the anchorage of a faith. As a faith, relativism makes unpleasant conclusions easy to avoid, and the gambit of the avoidance reaction can be learned by almost anyone. If the ultimate truth is forever beyond our grasp, which is a tenet of relativism, why is not one belief as good as another? Is there any real need for us to consider seriously any aspect of things in general that might lacerate our feelings? Why face any of the so-called facts that we do not like? (Ultimately they may turn out not to be facts!) Since we lack absolute co-ordinates, should not a belief, a cultural complex, or a moral or ethical system be judged on its own terms, and is not one of them just as good as another? These questions show the evasive value of relativism, and we can see from them how easily the belief can be distorted to a point where it can obscure a great deal of valid information.

It is true that our scientists no longer hope to attain the absolute, but they can and do approach the approximate; the nearer they come to what we, for want of a better word, call the "truth," the more reliable their information becomes. That truth exists, of course, is a hitherto unprovable postulate, but the proposition that it does not exist cannot be established on relativistic grounds. Scientists must assume that somewhere and at some time there is something very like the "truth." Otherwise there would be no difference between science and quackery.

Relativism in science is a comparatively recent doctrine, although the factors that have given it its present approved status can be traced back to the Renaissance. Earlier, during the Middle Ages, the very concept of relativism would have been puzzling because then the search for the absolute was the preoccupation of most of the scholars, philosophers, and theologians. Their efforts and ambitions were admirable, of course, and, in the light of what they knew, quite reasonable. Many of the paths they traversed in their search for the ultimate, however, led nowhere, while others circled back to their starting points. Fortunately, these attempts to reach absolute certainty can now be weighed in the balance, and we can discover just where they are wanting. Some of them, we realize, were worse than useless, and others were based on scholarly conventions that were harmfully deceptive. We have, for example, become completely disillusioned with the claims and supposed contributions of dogma, and we have learned, as scientists, to discard every "truth" that is based solely on dogmatic grounds. Even the more modest contributions of our best scientific research methods, while extraordinarily fruitful in specific instances, may, at times, lead us into error. In fact, falling into error has always been a major human activity.

II

Let us, for the time being, admit our cosmic insignificance and recognize the limitations of even the best intellects that the primates have ever produced. Let us remain complete relativists in all our science, but let us also be optimistic enough to hope that we may approach the "truth" even though we may never reach it. Even so, we are still faced with a number of questions that no conscientious scientist can avoid. How good are our approximations? Do they promote our understanding? How well will they serve us? How effective are they in improving our well-being? What happens to us when we ignore what knowledge we have and seek refuge in more comforting beliefs? How far can we renounce what little we know and still avoid disaster? Granting that all of our notions fall short of the "truth," are the notions of everyone then equally valid? Can we construct coordinates of any kind that will allow us to evaluate meaningfully the notions of different individuals, of different groups, nations, races, philosophies, or religions? To what philosophical and practical use can we put our limited understanding? What criteria can we use for judgment or for reaching even provisional conclusions?

Needless to say, we can expect no meaningful answers from those who consider themselves relativists but who think automatically in absolute terms. Fortunately for the physical and biological sciences, these folk generally labor in other vineyards where their labors have little effect on the sciences proper. The overflow of relativism into peripheral fields, however, does cause some popular confusion. Often, hidden in obscure background assumptions, is the tacit concept that, inasmuch as we can never really know anything positively, we can never discriminate intelligently between alternatives. In the last analysis, we may have to admit that one idea, concept, culture, ethical system, or philosophy is as "true" as another. Some who call themselves relativists have even reached the absolute conclusion that there are *no* universal principles of behavior, certainly none that apply—or should apply—to all human cultures, and that no single behavior pattern is better fitted than another for ameliorating human life or even for preserving the human species.

While we may have to admit that the welfare of our species is unimportant in any cosmic scale of values and that on such a scale all the differences among all human standards and cultures may be too small to be of any moment, it does not follow that our species is unimportant when measured by a human, planetary standard. Nor does it follow that we have learned nothing valid about the world around us that can be used for promoting our own small ends and aims. While we can avoid the excesses of the pseudo relativists, who have failed to grasp the implications of relativism, and easily identify and discard their errors, we should be careful not to assume that the mistakes of relativists have made absolutism more reasonable. No matter how silly individual relativists may be, their mistakes do not justify us in retreating into the traditional conventions. We still cannot assume that the values we have lived by in the past are permanent values, although the mere fact that we are alive shows that we can label them provisionally as "good."

We are, in truth, a successful species, and our behavior patterns have served us well in the past—including the patterns whose rationale we do not understand. Even our automatic actions are generally fit, as are most of the acts that, for some unknown reason, give us pleasure. We may—and perhaps we have to— exercise what judgment we have toward advancing the welfare of our kind and endeavor to live pleasant and profitable lives, and we may direct our culture and perhaps our future evolution along the paths we find attractive. These paths do not necessarily lead to salvation, but, to the extent that our species is adapted— to the extent that we and our desires are fit—leading pleasant and profitable lives should advance our fortunes and the fortunes of our species.

III

If our standards come from directives handed down from Olympus, and if our ethical ideals are based upon our acceptance of these directives, then our course of action is clear. We must adapt ourselves to the commandments and live according to them as well as we can. If, on the other hand, our standards are derived from the past accomplishments and aspirations of our own species, we should find them useful and accept them gratefully, but with a recognition of their human origin and human imperfections. We may even make it a point of honor to preserve and improve the standards and ideals that we received from our ancestors and pass them on to our descendants. If we accept (provisionally, of course) the human origin of our better thought-of behavior patterns, it brings the moral and ethical standards of mankind directly into the field of human evolution.

Evolution in general and human evolution in particular are subjects of such complexity that we can refer to them only briefly and consider but one or two of their more elementary aspects. All living organisms have structures and carry on activities. Nearly all the activities are on the physiological level and are pursued quite unconsciously. Animals that move around, however, expend a little of their energy in activities called behavior patterns, which, while they have a physiological basis, we find it convenient to consider apart from physiology *sensu stricto*. These behavior patterns have been preserved and developed by nature to just the extent to which they aid the behaving organism to survive and reproduce. Whenever they decrease the chances of survival or reproduction, they are sooner or later discarded by nature. All gregarious animals—and nature has decided that gregariousness is fit for many of the higher forms—have to act in groups, and thus they must evince some social behavior. Among the higher animals, groups are effective units for natural selection, but this is true only when the egotism of the individuals in the group is checked and balanced by the altruism that is necessary for the effective functioning of the group. Since human beings live in groups, some altruism must become a necessary part of the human behavior that nature has preserved and declared to be, up to the present, fit.

It is possible now for us to bring our moral and ethical systems into the picture of human evolution, and we can account for their existence by assuming that they have aided us to survive, although this does not mean that they are perfect or that their precepts have an absolute value. Our adaptation is far from perfect, and our evolution still continues. Indeed, we know enough about evolution to know that, if once we became perfectly adapted to the set of mundane conditions in which we live, evolution would cease, and we would both stabilize and stagnate. But, as we know, human beings are not stable. It is only a truism to state that almost everything about us is in flux and our evolutionary progress consists in a continuing adjustment to continuous change. It follows naturally that we are in part maladjusted, and because of our incomplete adaptation our evolution continues. (Whether we approve or disapprove of the course of our evolution is a very different question, but this question will not be considered here.)

Granting the fact of our evolution, the least we can expect of the ethical or moral standards that we label "good" is that they enable us to survive. Still we may not find this minimum requirement very satisfying. Mere existence may be very dreary. We have the ambition not only to live, but to pursue happiness. Now it is true that, to the extent that we are adapted—to the extent of our fitness—our pursuit of happiness is a means of aiding our personal survival and the survival of the species. But, as our adaptation is not perfect, doing what makes us happy is not always the same as doing what is good. Fortunately, our species has a considerable margin of safety, and we can sin—to a reasonable extent, of course—and still survive. We can also make mistakes and live to make more mistakes. And when we look at our past history, particularly the history of our past philosophies and our past notions of what constituted the good, the true, and the beautiful, we can indeed be happy that our species had this margin. Not all groups, philosophies, and religions, however, had a great enough margin of safety, and those that did not are now extinct. We may, *pace* the historians, learn a little from history. Thus, before we try to evaluate some of the better thought-of notions that our contemporaries hold, it might be well to examine some of the better thought-of notions of earlier times and measure, as well as we can, their effects on the survival of those who held them. It should be emphasized that this is only a preliminary examination and a partial evaluation of these notions.

Let us examine first a few of the codes and cultures with which we are most familiar, those that come loosely under the rubric "Western civilization." By survival standards these cultures have been pre-eminently successful. The Europeans who created and developed them not only succeeded in maintaining themselves in their home continent, but in colonizing and controlling the two Americas, Australia, Siberia, and South Africa and, for a while at least, in dominating and in establishing their ideals, if not their standards, over most of the world. We should point out, however, that "Western civilization" is based on a cluster of subcultures and that many of the subcultures overlap and interact, but are not always compatible with one another. The Western nations have, as a rule and in spite of some lamentable relapses into fanaticism, been more tolerant of cultural variations than have other nations. Their basic behavior patterns have been more flexible, and this may have been a major source of their strength. As a rule, they have tolerated any minority that they considered "harmless." Thus, by observing how the minorities behaved and what happened to them, they have been able to learn how certain notions actually work out without having to commit their whole culture to an experiment.

Competition between the Western subcultures can be considered a part of the struggle for existence in that this intracultural conflict allows nature to select from among the competing behavior patterns those that are more fitted for survival. Weird as many of the notions are that well-meaning believers have practiced and proclaimed as absolute truth, they have really done society very little damage because, thus far, their extravaganzas have always been self-correcting. Fanatical devotees to an aberration generally end by destroying the doctrines they have tried to live by.

The Shakers give us our most dramatic example of this automatic corrective process. For reasons known only to the Shakers, they renounced sexual intercourse as a sinful practice, and so today there are no Shakers. Other cults are also self-limiting even though they do not, like the Shakers, lead their devotees to extinction. Mennonites and Orthodox Quakers can be cited as examples of religious folk who can exist as prosperous minorities, but who can never dominate a nation or run a country of their own. What limits their growth and power is the fact that they can exist only where they are protected by those who do not believe as they do. Such sects, however, may not injure the cultures or the societies that harbor them. Indeed, their deviant behavior may be valuable in itself. The Mennonites are excellent farmers, while the Quakers, as a whole, are valuable and substantial citizens who make money, perform good works, and let the rest of mankind know about and observe their virtues. In any society that they do not dominate and where they are tolerated, the Mennonites and the Quakers are eminently fit. In times of war especially, their pacifism gives them an additional survival value.

The behavior of these two sects raises ethical questions of major import. If we had absolute and valid standards for judging, we could settle once and for all the question whether their acts are good or evil, but we have no such standards, and we can devise none without resorting to dogma. When, however, we apply the biological criterion of survival, we can decide very easily that their behavior is good. In certain ecological niches, the Mennonites and Quakers are fit, and in these niches they prosper. But in the greater part of the world, they are definitely unfit. They are unadapted to the intellectual climate in the Communist countries and in nations like prewar Japan and Germany. Consequently, in all such regions they soon disappear. Their normal habitat, thus, is limited, and the behavior pattern that controls their distribution and keeps them endemic is their propensity to conscientiously object in times of emergencies. In a large part of the world, as we know, conscientious objecting is simply not done. But in the ecological niche that our Western civilization supplies, the Mennonites and Quakers are well adapted, and to be fit in one ecological niche is all that we should expect of any species or subspecies.

Other deviant subcultures are also checked and controlled almost automatically by natural selection—asceticism, for example. Ascetics, if they do not go to extremes, have a good chance of biological survival, but their reproductive rate is low. Other groups such as priests and nuns are also biological failures and have to be recruited each generation from those whose parents are not priests and nuns. But religious celibacy has never endangered the future numbers of our breed. Our more sensual confreres leave offspring over and beyond the call of duty. Yet sensualism carries with it its own limiting factors, and complete sensualists tend to lead short—if happy and interesting—lives. While sensualism *as a philosophy* may appeal to but few of us, it has, at times, been elevated to an absolute code of behavior— indeed, it has been described as nature's guide to the good life.

All such philosophies, however, are based on postulates that are demonstrably false, and today they seem rather naive. Sensual gratification would be a sound biological guide for human beings only if human beings were completely and perfectly adapted to their surroundings—only if we, as a species, had reached our evolutionary goal and had ceased to evolve. Some species have practically reached this evolutionary stage. The horseshoe crab *(Limulus)* that lives in the littoral off our northern Atlantic coast is so fit that it is holding its own, although it has not changed noticeably in the last two hundred million years. The horseshoe crab is so fit that it could live as a complete Epicurean without danger and without biological sin.

Homo sapiens, however, is not so well adjusted to his cultural surroundings. Sensualism, as a code of conduct, is defective precisely to the extent that the species is unadapted. If we followed all of our ape-like impulses and discarded our inhibitions, our lives would be "nasty, brutish, and short." Indeed, our conventional moralists have drawn most edifying lessons from the fate of some philosophical sensualists. A sensualist, however, like Denis Diderot, who believed that self-gratification was the end and aim of life, but who exercised a reasonable caution in his indulgence, may avoid disaster even though his merry and prosperous life may seem wrong to many virtuous men. But the fate of others, like that of the Epicurean, Lucretius, can be used as horrible examples when, as in his case, we do not know what really happened to them.

As some justification for the pious misgivings and moralistic fictions, however, we may cite a natural hazard for sensualists. Consider the sad fate of Julien Offroy de la Mettrie (1709-1751). La Mettrie was a sensualist who believed that sensual enjoyment was the highest good and that our greatest virtue consists of following our natural impulses. On one occasion, at the age of forty-two, he stuffed himself with a truffle pastry and died in great discomfort. His place in the history of biology is secure, not so much because of his mechanistic philosophy and the famous essay he published in 1748 *(L'homme machine)*, but because he stands out clearly from the usual run of biologists. Few biologists have ever died from eating too many truffles.

Other cultural variants and ideals that come within the range of our Western complex, have, as a rule, less drastic effects, primarily because they are rarely, if ever, practiced to excess. Many of these, incidentally, are ethically absolutistic, but intellectually simplistic. Nonresistance to aggression, for example, is held by many to be a truly virtuous ideal, but it is an ideal that is generally kept in dead storage.

Returning good for evil—refusing to seek personal revenge for injuries—is also an ideal that is even more rarely practiced. Our failure to follow any such directive is, of course, fortunate for our species. Any organism with such a "moral" motivation is headed for extinction. Reasonable men, however, generally seek revenge only within limits. While perhaps they never really love their enemies, as a rule and for reasons of caution they generally avoid the dangers of implementing their dislike personally and turn over to society as a whole the task of punishing those who injure them. (Still some eight thousand murders are committed annually in the United States.) This works very well, although its efficiency is limited. Those who destroy or injure their fellow citizens are labeled criminals in all civilized societies, and, when apprehended, are punished by the state, except when they belong to a self-conscious group of voters who are aware of their political power. Then, as in many of our large cities today, they are apt to be paroled. Even so, the damage they do is generally within reasonable limits. Sometimes those on parole eliminate each other.

IV

It might be well here to explore the evolutionary effects of some of the other deviations that come within the range of tolerance of our civilized cultures and to examine their possible effects on our survival. Most of these, of course, are merely simplistic and can be expressed in some simple adage or slogan. The famous Marxian objective of "From each according to his ability, to each according to his needs" is an excellent example of these appealing aphorisms. As an absolutistic ideal, however, which it really is, it is moronic. Literally it holds that the chief end of the able is to cherish and support the ineffective. While some support of those who are in temporary need or who have suffered disaster is an essential feature of all successful societies, the ideal of subordinating the interests of the competent to those of the defective is incompatible with what we know of organic evolution. If, in the Pliocene, our own ancestors had followed this practice as an absolute standard of virtue, inherent in a moral universe, their progeny could never have evolved into human beings. Our line of descent, if freed from the corrective results of "reactionary" natural selection, would have been swamped by a flood of congenital defectives. Marxism would indeed have been "premature" in the Pliocene.

When we view the whole picture, we find that support of the

needy is both necessary and dangerous. Children, adolescents, and those aged beyond the reproductive period can be supported without harm to the breed. But when misfits and dim-wits are cherished, rescued from the trouble they habitually get into, and then allowed to run free, the biological hazard should be obvious. Under these conditions misfits and the dim-witted, who would be culled out and discarded in a state of nature, join the fit. Biological fitness, we should remember, is not absolute. It is relative and is never more than a measure of the adaptation to the conditions that exist at the time. Those who reproduce most copiously under any set of conditions are the fittest. But sometimes the conditions that determine fitness lead the species into a blind alley. If and when these conditions change, and a new norm of fitness is established, the species may, if it has evolved too far under the earlier conditions, be faced with extinction.

We may cite, as an illustration, the evolutionary effects of a situation that has recently been causing some concern in the welfare agencies of Pennsylvania. A number of discussions have appeared in the daily press, and the social workers are at odds about what should be done. In Philadelphia, a growing number of unmarried mothers have learned an effective technique for increasing their subsidy from the state. Their pay goes up with each little bastard they drop. And they have discovered that they need take few risks. They are protected through their gestation period by the welfare agencies, who also rescue them from the messes they routinely get themselves into. Now we have a group of females who make spawning their profession. It seems to be more congenial to them than working for a living. From the standpoint of the future well-being of our species, however, the uncontrolled exercise of these newly discovered techniques can hardly be considered a virtue, although even in this extreme case the biological damage that the spawners do is not great. A large proportion of their offspring become juvenile delinquents, and juvenile delinquents, unless female, rarely breed to excess.

We shall examine but one more variant in the cluster of our Western subcultures. This one is the ethical and philosophical

system known as "humanism." It is in humanism, perhaps, that
the postulates on which relativism and absolutism are based
deviate farthest from each other. It is here also that many who
think of themselves as relativists show most clearly that, despite
the label, their convictions are absolute. In fact, with many of our
contemporaries, humanism has achieved the status of a religion.
It has become a powerful *mystique,* one that is now expanding
into the vacuum left by the retreat from supernaturalism. But
even as a religion, humanism is not without its virtues. It promotes ideals that we have to respect—ideals that make a civilized
society possible. It appeals to our better nature and is, all in all,
a definite asset to our culture. It doubtless fills an emotional need
in the minds of many who are convinced that the Creator of the
universe, as the universe is understood today, is too distant and
indifferent to our aspirations to be of any real comfort in an
emergency. Humanism is definitely a religion for those relativists
who are emotionally absolutists and who have a psychological
need to anchor their ideals and aspirations to something firm,
even if that something is only their own kind.

Humanism, as a religion, also gives its adherents an opportunity
that is perhaps unique in the organic world—that of worshipping
their own species, of loving and revering their own breed. Evolution has produced a number of human beings who aspire beyond
their own local and personal affairs and who are happier when
they are concentrating their attention on the universe at large.
Some of these who are no longer attracted to the traditional
religions may still have an emotional need for a religion and
have, in consequence, developed their humanism into a religion.
*(There is no God but Homo, and Abou-ben-Adhem is his
prophet.)*

This in itself need not be too bad. True, humanists find it easy
to exaggerate their own importance and the importance of their
fellows, but this need not be harmful. It actually directs our
attention toward advancing our own interests and, from the standpoint of survival, this is "good." But humanism as a religion also
has some deleterious aspects. It keeps us from examining our

fellow men realistically; it gives us some illusion of grandeur and tends to hide our cosmic unimportance. It pushes the "truth" a little further away from our grasp. It fosters a belief in the "sacredness" of human life, and this belief affects our attitudes both to capital punishment and to euthanasia. A relativist, of course, should value human life and should have a logical basis for his humanitarianism, but at the same time he should be immune to the simplistic slogans that serve the humanists as intellectual guides—such a slogan, for example, as "the greatest good for the greatest number," an adage that, supposedly, furnishes the humanists with the final justification of an act or of a code of conduct.

While this slogan now enjoys the very greatest prestige among those who endorse relativism, it is itself an absolute conclusion, even though, when analyzed, it turns out to be ambiguous. Those who rely on it as an axiomatic ideal have never defined its meaning properly. Does "the greatest number" refer to those in this present generation or to those who will be born in all future generations? We know enough of human evolution now to know that the two greatest numbers are not the same. This question is far too technical and much too long to be discussed here, but it is worth pointing out that those who use the slogan as a guide cite no confirmatory data to support it, that they use it as they would a dogma, and that when we analyze scientifically the problem which the slogan is supposed to settle, we can reach answers that are only tentative and provisional.

As scientists, we have to admit that the absolute evades us, and that we have been forced by circumstances to distrust the effects of the absolute application of even our best-loved virtues. Today we are forced to concede that much of our current altruism is unintelligently directed and biologically dangerous. Medical charity, for example, while it alleviates suffering and is even a necessary ingredient of any decent social order, has some unhappy consequences and tends to increase the load of deleterious mutations that we carry and that we pass on to our children. At present about three per cent of our infants are born with major hereditary defects. In spite of our best efforts, most of them die, and our physicians are learning at last that it is a dubious kindness to keep alive those who would live in pain, be unable to care for themselves, or be a burden on their relatives. The early death of defectives, including those who die before birth, seems a most humane method of checking the accumulation of those "spontaneous" mutations that would, if left unchecked, extinguish our species.

The realization of these unfortunate sequelae of our remedial skill is spreading and stimulating some debate and a great deal of intellectual confusion. There is little agreement about which course of action is "right." The discussions illustrate, however, the inadequacy of any absolute rule of procedure. In all our charities, for example, absolutistic standards are self-defeating; and a relativistic compromise, when we indulge in virtue, seems to be the only sane and intelligent course of action. Absolutism needs to be simplified only a little before it becomes fanaticism, and the damage that has been wrought by virtuous fanatics is, literally, beyond measure. To illustrate: Any absolute simplicistic philosophy that defines *all* human life as sacred and demands that it be preserved at all cost will, when followed, lead to unadulterated suffering, as when the relief of euthanasia is denied to those who are dying in torment. But even if we fall into one form or other of absolutism, we shall probably recover. We have an adequate margin of safety, and our species is, in this instance, well buffered. The effects of any excessive altruism will backfire on the altruists, and they will be forced to check themselves before they harm us fatally. If too many defectives are kept alive by our efforts and multiplied by their own, the burden on altruism grows, and our altruists will be coerced by events into becoming more reasonable.

V

Thus far, in our survey of the impact of relativism and absolutism on our current cultures and ethical systems, we have been concerned primarily with their effects on our mere biological survival. This is so because the least that we can expect of any approved behavior pattern or ethical system is that in some way it promote our survival. But, as we have stated, this in itself is not enough, and all our successful systems have promised, and some have performed, a great deal more. Sometimes, however, the attempt to attain more than survival is dangerous, for it leads us into paths—into cults—where survival itself becomes precarious. Sometimes our ambitions lead us into attempts to secure not only absolute survival, that is, eternal life, but also eternal bliss, and to implement our attempts by means that are neither intelligent nor well planned. Not all our Western subcultures—not all our cults—have served even the minimum function of aiding survival, and many of them have been discarded. Anchorites no longer decorate our deserts, Shakers are no longer born, and, every now and then, the child of Christian Science parents dies because of some easily curable disease. But we still belong to the same old human race, and we still produce new cults and strike moral attitudes that have to be seen to be believed. One of the best thought of and most recent of these is now in its early growing stage. It is a well-advertised and freely admitted "sense of guilt." Indeed, this "sense of guilt," as of 1959, is held to motivate much of our individual and even our national conduct.

Those who take this up-to-date stance postulate tacitly that there is something basically wrong, if not immoral, in achieving any mundane success that all our comrades do not share or that anyone cannot achieve for himself. This "sense of guilt" supposedly is triggered and comes into play whenever a successful person makes contact with or even observes those who are failures or who are, in our modern patois, "underprivileged." How prevalent this sense of guilt is we do not know, but it is probably not as common as it appears to be, because many of those who suffer from it vocalize to even slight stimuli. With some, of course, the feeling of guilt is only a pose, a popular affectation that is now more timely than boasting about a "social conscience," which was rather the thing to do in the nineteen-thirties. Some of

the sufferers, however, perhaps most of those who have an un-
digested excess of Freud, are sincere in their protestations. They
do feel guilty. Odd as this reaction may be, it seems to be growing
in popularity and importance, and now it is worth more than a
cursory examination. Somewhere in the background thinking that
justifies the sense of guilt there must be some absolute, categorical
imperative, felt but not identified. *(It is easier for a camel to go
through the eye of a needle, than for a rich man to enter the
Kingdom of God.)* It would be difficult, if not impossible, for a
relativist to devise any set of standards that would make success
a sin in itself.

The philosophical background of our admitted sinners is vague
and almost certainly irrational. Nevertheless, in some of our
more progressive circles there are some conscientious folk who
seem to have an intuitive notion that, somehow or other, earthly
felicity is reprehensible and that those members of our species
who prosper and who enjoy a material abundance suffer—or
should suffer—the pangs of conscience. It would be hard to conceive of a viewpoint more inimical to biological survival. Certainly such an attitude is rare in the organic world, and it seems
to occur nowhere but in a small fraction of our own species. None
of our fellow vertebrates gives any evidence of having it. But our
guilt-ridden comrades seem to have reached a point of no return
in their evolution. Our species itself has evolved so far and so
well that the guilt of its success is universally distributed and is
now inherited by all its members, and, for those whose consciences
are aching, no relief is possible. Their very existence is due to the
success of their progenitors, and, as long as they live, they must
continue to enjoy the unearned spoils of ancient victories. Now
it is too late to make amends to those their ancestors wronged.
Those who live in the United States cannot give the country back
to the Indians whom their ancestors robbed and slaughtered. No
matter how sincerely human beings may repent and try to compensate the victims of their more fundamental evolutionary
success, they can never compensate their victims properly; they
can never make amends to the dinosaurs for the injuries and

injustices that the primitive mammals—including doubtless their own primitive mammalian ancestors—committed against the whole order of reptiles. At most, they can only take what comfort they can by realizing that they are not the actual thieves and murderers who violently despoiled their fellow vertebrates. They are only the receivers and inheritors of the stolen goods.

Life, of course, is complex, and successful species have long and variegated histories. Even the fittest species are almost never adapted perfectly to the conditions that exist at any one time, and the individuals who compose a species differ greatly in the extent of their individual adaptation. It would be interesting, of course, to correlate the human sense of guilt with some sort of biological maladaptation, but this is a major task in itself. Here we may note simply that some perfectly sincere men, often those who are well protected by inherited wealth, do feel a sense of guilt and have tried to escape it by any means that their fertile and active imaginations could suggest—everything from ritualistic baptism to uplifting and cherishing that fraction of mankind that is too virtuous in itself ever to succeed in anything *(. . . sell all that thou hast, and distribute unto the poor, and thou shalt have treasure in heaven).*

This widely advertised sense of guilt has actually affected our foreign policy. The United States is wealthy, and her citizens are generally healthy and live comfortably and securely while much of the world is ignorant, impoverished, underfed, and dissatisfied. In ways that are not specified and not very clear, this can be held to be the fault of the United States. Our nation, it is true, is exceptional in that our citizens have increased their material goods, including their supply of food, faster than they have increased their numbers. In the "underdeveloped" regions, however, where the inhabitants breed *ad lib.*, there is actual hunger, and the United States obviously (but for reasons that escape this sinful writer) owes assistance to these unfortunate people. The "underdeveloped" nations seem to hold this idea firmly and accept aid from the United States as if it were their natural right —the aid that the United States would be immoral to withhold.

They can, however, resent the fact of their "underdevelopment," and they can and often do—as their riots demonstrate—dislike those who come to their assistance, but who enjoy a more comfortable way of life.

It is here, in this dilemma presented by our foreign-aid program, that we have perhaps the sharpest contrast between absolute and relative ethical systems, although, from the practical necessity of devising a wise course of national policy, the systems may not conflict at all. An absolutist, firmly anchored to his assumed certainties, might favor foreign aid as a Christian duty, while a relativist might favor it merely as a means of strengthening our international position. But no honest relativist, basing his postulates on the assumed desirability of human progress in a world where the human race has evolved, could include the ability to succeed as one of the vices or the inability to prosper through one's own efforts as a virtue. (The good who, proverbially, die young, cannot be the good by any evolutionary standard.)

As we have stated, relativism has been forced on our scientists by the realization that they are only human and that the scope of their science is finite. At present the indications are that scientists will always be human and that their knowledge will always be limited. In the physical and biological sciences, this is a healthy realization. It makes for modesty and it tempts no one to rely on his ignorance as a means of evading results that may be distasteful. In the social sciences, however, where the logical implications may point to unwelcome conclusions, our lack of absolute knowledge has often served as a refuge for the emotionally committed. It is really amusing to observe how easily an intellectual avoidance reaction can be justified by an unannounced slipping backward into the soothing comfort of an absolute standard. It is by this intellectual gambit that many so-called relativists bring relativism into disrepute.

An excellent illustration of this behavior pattern came to the attention of the writer as he was writing this paper. A biography of an anthropologist, written by another anthropologist, was reviewed by a third member of the sodality. The following quotation is from the review, and it is presented here merely to call attention to the fact that a scientist can be "comforted" and that an "absolute sense" may bring a thought to a close.

As a scholarly profession, anthropology has drawn more than its share of nonconformists who are comforted by its findings that each culture has its own values and standards of behavior and that the demands of our own society are no more right in an absolute sense than those of any other. (*Science,* 129:322, 1959)

We need only point out that, if the test of survival is applied to the different human cultures, they can easily be recognized as being either fit or unfit. Some are tough and experience no difficulty in competing with the European cultures. Others, when contacted by Europeans, wither and vanish with great promptness. To conclude that all cultures are equal or equally "right" in an absolute sense is not the act of a relativist.

At present the greatest liability of relativism is to be found in its camp followers—in those who label themselves relativists, but who relapse into absolutism and demand absolute proof for any proposition that challenges their convictions. Modestly disguised as provisional and relative, their convictions are often impervious to any evidence of their dubiosities. Often, what passes for relativism is merely the rationalization of those who have rebelled against the *ad hoc* precepts that they accepted unthinkingly as adolescents, but who now have progressed to more modern and more popular views. Such camouflaged absolutism, however, cannot survive a rigid logical analysis. In anthropology particularly it is very amusing to run across instances where absolute negatives are used to refute absolutism. (*All generalizations are wrong, including this one.*) Perhaps the most easily exposed misuse of relativism in anthropology can be found when it is employed as a defense mechanism to protect the current and popular equalitarianism, because equalitarianism, by its very nature, must have absolutistic overtones.

The relativism of our greatest scientists is naturally not absolute. They recognize that their scientific knowledge is limited and that they have little chance of ever reaching the infinite and practically no chance of understanding infinity. They must, as we have stated earlier, base their work on assumptions that they cannot prove. They must assume that somewhere and somehow there exists something that can be called the "truth." Otherwise, there would be no important difference between scientists and charlatans, and this possibility is one that no scientist likes to contemplate.

3

Reiterations and Second Thoughts on Cultural Relativism[1]

Eliseo Vivas

I

Cultural relativism is not the discovery of modern or even of contemporary social scientists. It is as old as Protagoras, if not as Herodotus.[2] And the heart of the doctrine, the thesis, at any rate, that I shall discuss in this essay, consists of the fallacious inference from the fact of cultural pluralism to the axiological doctrine that we cannot discriminate in respect to worth among the value patterns described by the ethnographer. In this paper, when I speak of relativism, I refer to cultural relativism.

The plan of this essay is the following: I first examine the argument as such, without reference to any of the authors who defend it. Next I examine a number of issues posed by the doctrine as advanced by my colleague, the renowned anthropologist, Professor Melville Herskovits. Next I point out why the ideological component of the doctrine is retardatarian. And I close with a sketchy account of the reason, as I view it, that enables cultural relativism to crop up again and again, in spite of the fact that the doctrine has been demolished as thoroughly as it is possible to demolish a doctrine.

Although the fact of cultural pluralism is no contemporary

45

discovery, it must be owned that the industry of our ethnographers has made us much more aware of it than were the ancients, with their limited knowledge of the world and its peoples. The Greeks did not know, I dare say, that Malinowski's savages begin their love-making by tenderly delousing each other; neither did they know that the first wife of a Dahomey, shortly after marriage, nags her husband until he gets a second; whereas in another country the wife nags, not for a minx, but for a mink. A number of speculative doctrines have attempted to explain these facts and to ground them theoretically. I refer to the experiments of psychologists, philosophical doctrines, particularly in epistemology, the hypotheses of the ethnolinguists, and the work of the sociologists of science.[3]

If all that cultural relativism referred to were the fact of cultural pluralism, we could do nothing but accept it. As regards the speculative explanations of these facts, I find these interesting and some of them acceptable. But we can here ignore them, for the doctrine that demands examination asserts, *tout court*, that the values of a culture are determined by the culture, and, as a corollary, it asserts that the criteria of value judgments are drawn from the culture. From this it follows that it is not possible to judge the values of one culture in terms of any criteria except its own, and, therefore, that objective indices of cultural inferiority and superiority cannot be established. An American cannot feel superior to Malinowski's savages because they are lousy and dirty. It's just a matter of cultural differences—although I do not see how we can deny that they are lousy. So deeply committed is the relativist to his views that sometimes he becomes absurd. If I may fall back on my own experience, let me offer this bit of evidence: I once heard a relativist say that the bridge that we take to be held up by the laws of physics is held up, for the African, by magic. I was unable to believe my ears, but the "scientist" repeated the silly statement seriously. At this point I am forced to agree with the relativist. Only a man thoroughly "enculturated" into the values of his subgroup, those of the academic fraternity, a group that values consistency above truth and common sense, would insist on a statement he cannot seriously believe rather than admit that he has pushed his doctrine too far.

The relativist's argument, skeletally formulated, can be expressed in the following enthymeme:

> A culture determines the values acknowledged by its members.
>
> Therefore a culture determines the values its members ought to acknowledge.
>
> The implicit premise can be formulated as follows:
>
> The values determined by a culture are the values that the members of that culture ought to acknowledge.

The advantage of this skeletal formulation lies in the fact that it enables us to examine the doctrine critically by examining its essential premises.

Let us ask first whether a culture determines all the values acknowledged by its members—those the members recognize and those they espouse.[4] One consideration forces us to qualify the statement, and two others to declare it inadmissible. The statement should at least be qualified, for we do not yet know enough how and to what extent a culture determines values. *Prima facie,* it would seem that different communities exercise different degrees of determination on the values acknowledged by their members, and that within a given community different values are more strongly determined than others. These are empirical questions that call for examination. And before we can share the relativist's assurance about his doctrine, the answers to these questions will have to be subjected to analysis.

But does it not seem as if in complex societies in the midst of rapid change, the culture does not determine the values of its members in the way in which primitive cultures do? Even in a primitive community, it is not the case that a culture determines the values of its members *tout court.* The doctrine overlooks the fact that some of our values are related to biological aspects of the human being *qua* animal, aspects that are subjacent to all cultures. I say "related," perfectly aware that it is a vague manner of speaking, because to define more precisely the connection between biological factors and values would force us to take up a problem as regards which philosophers are, and have long been, violently at odds with one another. But it is not a problem that must be resolved here. Ultimately the question I refer to, social scientists need not be told, is that posed by Kroeber, the question whether or not culture is superorganic. This is a problem that, within the range of my information, is still open and does not admit of dogmatism.[5]

The second consideration that makes the theory inadmissible is more important. The premise assumes that human beings are incapable of exercising spontaneity (or creativity or freedom) in the discovery and the actualization of values. But the hypothesis that there is a modicum of creativity exercised by the members of almost all human societies has not been shown to be false by the relativist. Nor has the rigid determinism he assumes been adequately demonstrated; nor could it be, since it is a cultural lag from nineteenth-century mechanism, now discredited. I said, "almost all human societies," for I do not wish to prejudge to what extent very small, isolated, highly custom-bound, primitive societies lacking history have been the result, not of uncontrolled factors, but of the intelligent exercise of the creative power of their members. Malinowski emphasizes that his savages are not custombound and seems to intend his thesis universally.[6] But I doubt whether we can generalize from the Trobrianders. We are here confronted with a difficult problem, a crucial one, and one which until it is properly elucidated deprives the relativist of the major premise of his syllogism.

I hasten to admit, however, that the problem of freedom (or of spontaneity or creativity) is a difficult one that I cannot discuss in this paper. Suffice it to acknowledge that cultures do in fact seek to determine in some respects some of the values of their members. But the determination is never rigid, and there is reason to believe that all cultures encourage areas of freedom in which the individual is given the opportunity to exercise discretionary and creative power. This is true for our society in vast areas of its activity and for all its members. It is most easily seen in science and in art, in which creativity is encouraged, no canons are enforced, and no strictures imposed. In American universities of quality, freedom of thought is an operative reality, even though it is often used to inculcate erroneous and pernicious doctrines. And it is a reality in all the disciplines, even in theology. Whether scholars make use of the freedom given them or whether they remain in bondage to the dominant intellectual fashions is an empirical question on which I have no accurate information. But my observations lead me to believe that too large a number of scholars in the fields with which I am acquainted are inhibited by fear of what their colleagues consider disreputable.

The statement about freedom in American universities calls for an important qualification. In principle there is freedom of thought in all areas. But in certain fields freedom is covertly discouraged. For instance, in universities of my acquaintance a scholar is free to be a social-political liberal. But he is not equally free to be a conservative, and in order to profess his conservative convictions he must be prepared to stand up to the disapproval of the majority, his "liberal" fellows. But the statement must be further qualified, for if a man is willing to pay the price—and if he is not, he is not a man—he is free to espouse what social or political opinions he may wish to espouse.

Thus the categorical assertion of the relativist is hardly justified. What he ought to do is to ask in the spirit of inquiry in what respect and to what extent culture determines values.

We turn next to the implicit premise of the enthymeme: "The values that a culture determines are the values its members ought to acknowledge." This is Sumner's old thesis and is inadmissible for a number of reasons. The first is that it overlooks the important distinction between the actual mores and the not altogether operative ideals and norms of conduct of a community; it ignores the difference between the way men act and the way they are expected by themselves and others to act. If the mores were in fact exactly congruous with the norms of a group, the way to teach a teen-ager to drive in Chicago would be to take him to the Outer Drive and ask him to observe carefully how people actually drive—an excellent way to increase the accident rate and the cost of automobile insurance. The second reason the premise is inadmissible is that even in societies in which the mores are almost altogether congruous with the morals (they never are altogether, of course) *the authority* of the operative moral code cannot be said without qualification to derive from the mores, although the members of societies in which such a congruity exists may trace the source of authority solely to custom. Here we are confronted with a difficult problem, calling for what delicate handling we can give it. It arises from the fact that mores, when they do not impose intolerable hardship on a group, do finally end by obtaining authority by a process that seems similar, apparently, to that by which squatters' rights are obtained. But even then it cannot be held *tout court* that it is from the *is* of actual conduct that the *ought* arises. Therefore, wherever the relativist obtained his implicit premise, he never obtained it solely from the observations of the actual conduct of a group. Philosophers, as is to be expected, do not agree with one another concerning the source of the authority of the norms governing a group. But even naturalists, who perform the miracle of obtaining the *ought* from the *is*—from interests, desires, bodily needs, and other such sources—must grant that one of the components of some of the interests that are acknowledged in a society are not culturally determined. And the reason for this is, in the last analysis, that a rigid, unqualified determinism could offer one explanation and one only of the changes that take place in the mores of a group, namely, accident.

That the authority of the norms of conduct cannot, without extensive qualifications, be traced to the mores, we shall see below. Here it is only necessary to consider cases in which men are confronted with perplexities that cannot be by-passed, whatever the condition of the mores of the society. Such perplexities are constituted by conflicting courses of conduct both of which, for any reason whatever, appeal for espousal. The conflict may be between desire and our sense of what is right, or between two courses of action each of which is *prima facie* right. In such cases only one can be chosen. However one chooses on such occasions, or however one ought to choose—and for my purposes, at the moment, it does not matter which we take—the maxim governing the decision cannot be selected on the grounds that it is culturally determined, for on the cultural relativist's doctrine both are culturally determined.

Let me shift the standpoint in order to reinforce the argument. If it were true that the authority of a moral maxim is grounded on the culture, as the relativist holds, men would be much worse off than they are now, for they would not be able to find answers to questions they now desperately seek and to which they sometimes do find answers. Overlook the fact that the term "culture" is hopelessly polysemic. The notion "Dobu culture" or "Pueblo culture" is, no matter what meaning we choose for the term "culture," relatively clear, as compared with the expression "American culture," or "French culture." If Dobuans can go to their culture for answers to their moral perplexities, Americans and French cannot. In Rome do as the Romans do. Let us grant it. But how do *the Romans* do? For in Rome we find Roman Catholics, Anglo-Catholics, Protestants, Jews, Muslims, Mormons, and, for all I know, a few Shintoists. We also find royalists, republicans, fascists, communists, and nonpolitical men. We find "respectable" people—which is to say, people without police records —and pimps, whores, pickpockets and people addicted to practices Krafft-Ebing describes in Latin. As of my last information, one Roman was the distinguished former guest of our Federal Government, the Honorable Lucky Luciano. There are Italianates including Americans—and, I almost forgot, Texans. There are scholars and nonscholars. There are Bohemians from Bohemia and bohemians from Greenwich Village and Sausalito. And there are in Rome even some relativists who do as the Romans do— although how they do, remains a mystery. Clearly, with the exception of the relativists, a reference to the way the Romans do is of no help in resolving moral perplexities.

A philosophy that overlooks this problem is intellectually and morally irresponsible. Morally, because it provides the Dobuans and the Pueblo Indians with means of resolving moral perplexities and leaves us and the French without any. Now I say that's downright mean of the relativist. And what is more, it's a clear case of cultural discrimination: aren't we and the French as good as the Dobuans? Besides, everybody but the relativist knows that the French could do with a little more morality and a little less *vin ordinaire*. It is intellectually irresponsible because it overlooks the fact that the categories it applies to primitive cultures cannot apply, or at least cannot apply in the same way, to complex cultures in process of rapid change. A primitive man can go with his problems to the old men of the tribe, and they can answer his questions without hesitation because their traditions and customs are relatively well defined and more or less fixed— which is to say that their morals and their mores *seem* to be congruous. But, of course, the force of this argument is to show that their congruity is irrelevant to the moral problem.

Essentially the same criticism, formulated in different terms, has frequently been made against cultural relativism by moral philosophers. Cultural relativism leads to individual relativism, which is to say, moral nihilism. Let us see how. The relativist asserts that it is the culture that defines the values and the criteria of a society. But this could only be true so long as the members of a society, for whatever reasons, accept its values as operative realities. When, for whatever reason, any member of a society ceases to accept its values, the conception that culture determines values becomes pernicious and refers to nothing whatever. What we then have is a collection of individuals who seem to constitute a society, but who in the moral sense do not constitute it, for their society fails to provide them patterns of behavior that are viable and operatively real. This happens the moment a member of a given society decides on grounds of his own to reject some or all of the values approved of by his society. What can the relativist say to him? He can say, "These are the values that are approved of by the society to which you belong." But a rebel, unless he is an utter fool or a craven coward—and rebels seldom are either fools or cowards—simply answers: "The values in question are approved by the others, but not by me." What can the relativist reply? He can say, "Society will see to it that you behave according to its norms." But a genuine rebel will reply, "Let it try and we shall see what happens." A genuine rebel is willing to submit the difference to the arbitration of force. Now this may be the truth of moral relations—that is another question entirely. The point here is that the relativist ought to acknowledge that, on his conception of morality, when a society loses its power to enforce its values, the upshot is individual rather than cultural relativism, and he also ought to acknowledge that the term "individual relativism" is but a pretty synonym for moral chaos. This is one of the reasons that responsible moral philosophers consider cultural relativism pernicious.

That men, particularly members of folk societies, have respect for custom, no one doubts. That that respect helps give the moral maxims of a community an authoritative weight and permanence that without it they would probably lack, seems to be true. But that the authority of the norms arises solely from the fact that they are culturally determined is nonsense and, as I have shown, pernicious nonsense at that.

From a logical point of view, cultural relativism suffers from a defect that condemns it and that has been noticed by a number of writers. But since relativists do not seem to have reckoned with this objection (I do not know of a single relativist who has seriously attempted to meet the many weighty objections advanced against this doctrine, although they are irrefragable and devastating ones), it seems advisable to state it again: Relativism is an incoherent philosophy, because it falls into Epimenides' trap. Could the relativist assert that all judgments are relative except this one? This would be of no help to him, for if the statement is true, he would have to show that the method by which he arrived at this truth cannot be employed in the discovery of other truths, and this statement is, of all horrible things, another truth. And now we are shackled by at least two truths. Would it help to call on the theory of types? The relativist fares no better, for on this theory the statement that all judgments are relative is a statement of the second order, but it is itself true, and falls outside the incapacitating relativity that condemns all statements of the first order. There are truths, therefore, that are not culturally determined in the vicious sense, although they are truths of the second, not the first order. But we have exactly the same situation at this level that we encountered at the lower level. We have one truth and a method. As regards the latter we know that it can or cannot be employed in the discovery of other truths, and this knowledge constitutes a second truth. Pity the relativist, for he must acknowledge that there are at least two truths that hold irrespective of cultural determinants, or he must acknowledge that he is still caught in Epimenides' trap. I am afraid we have caught the relativist with the goods—and what shameful goods to catch a scientist with, too, some truths, no less. Oh, Epimenides, you old Cretan, you should be ashamed of spoiling our relativist's nice absolutistic game.

Still another error of cultural relativism needs to be examined: The doctrine asserts that because the values of a group are culturally determined, they are not objectively valid. And on this ground it denies the validity of a judgment made across cultures. Subjectivity is confused with relativity.[7]

It must be admitted that it is extremely difficult, in practice perhaps impossible, to draw up an order of rank for high cultures. Anyone asserting that American culture is superior to English or vice versa, or to German or Italian, is making a statement that seems to express his predilections and little else. Its objectivity is suspect. And the reason is obvious: the objects compared are too complex and the values embodied in them too elusive for comparative judgments to carry much weight. This may also be true of primitive cultures. But this does not hold if you take a society that has achieved high civilization and compare it with one that has not. At any rate, the difficulties are practical, not theoretical, and it is not difficult to see that some cultures must be adjudged inferior to cultures that have achieved the status of civilization. This is true of the primitives of central Australia as compared with the great African kingdoms before imperialism destroyed the latter, although I would not classify the latter as civilized societies. Since the principle is most easily revealed in extreme situations, consider the group of human beings recently discovered in Paraná, Southeastern Brazil, the Xetás. This pitiful group is said to be a remnant of the Stone Age. We are told that they have no agriculture, know no metal or pottery. What their life span is we are not told, but we know it cannot compare with ours. If conditions are somewhat similar to those that obtain in the Sierra Parima, as they probably are, we know they starve for several months of the year. In times of plenty their diet is inadequate from a biological, which is to say, from a noncultural, nonrelativistic point of view. Their moral, intellectual, aesthetic development must be abysmally low, compared to ours. Their religion, demon-ridden, is an index of their harsh life. Their culture lacks the richness of value ours has. They have a false picture of their place in the world and in the universe. They are considerably more in bondage to nature than we are. They bring to mind Hobbes' description of man in the state of nature, ending with the often quoted: "And the life of man, . . . poor, nasty, brutish and short." *Qua* human beings, I owe each and every one of these unfortunate people unqualified respect. But my acknowledgment of my debt to them is the result of the good luck that we have superior ethical knowledge. One wonders what makes men espouse a doctrine, come hell or high water, when it is self-evident that our lives are better than those of the Xetás in almost every conceivable respect. If a scientist or a philosopher tells me that I cannot judge them, culturally speaking, to be inferior (*qua* human beings, let me reiterate, they are not), I repeat that for reasons I do not pretend to know they have failed to develop capacities we members of Western civilization can and do develop. And if he reiterates that his doctrine shows my judgment to be invalid, I reply, *tant pis* for *your* doctrine; it seems to filter out all common sense.

It will not do, however, to deny that truth is relative to the techniques and the categorial schemes employed in obtaining it. And this is the reason we must distinguish between subjectivity and relativity. That truth is relative means that a change in method or in categorial scheme or in both alters the results. This does not hold only for truth, but for all other values. Anglo-Saxon justice is relative to Anglo-Saxon jurisprudence and Roman justice to Roman jurisprudence. But the matter is not hopelessly subjective or arbitrary, and we can present the reasons that justify our preference for our own judicial system to the system of trial by water or fire once employed by our ancestors. But to infer that from the relativity of value, in the sense under consideration, the subjectivity of value follows, and therefore that it follows that value judgments cannot be objectively validated, is a *non sequitur* resulting from the failure to distinguish between a value and the means of ascertaining its presence. So long as there are means of correcting it, a judgment of value is not relative in the vicious sense. As regards scientific truth, such means are available and the universality of science establishes the fact beyond doubt. But, of course, neither universality nor truth is obtained by vote. If science were culturally determined in the vicious sense, anthropology would be impossible—or would be valid only for the culture from which the anthropologist stems. I do not believe that it is necessary to show in detail that the primitive who disposes of science and technology with the dictum, "White man's magic differs from black man's magic," is sufficiently answered with the reply, "What you call 'white man's magic' is not magic; it is science and technology." And if the unfortunate does not agree, his failure to agree does not alter the truth of the statement. Let me say once more that truth is not determined by counting heads —and least of all the heads of nonliterates who are illiterate.

II

When we come to science in the broader, the European, sense of this term, the problem in practice is more difficult, but still it is not hopeless. In the less rigorous sciences, such as the social sciences, in disciplines like that of psychoanalysis and the purely speculative discipline of philosophy, objectivity is possible even though it may not be encountered frequently. A philosopher can read another and acknowledge that what he has read is decisive and that he is in error. I shall give only one instance; and if it were the case that this is the only time in the history of philosophy when such acknowledgment has occurred, it would be sufficient to establish the argument that it can happen. Bertrand Russell has put it on record that he changed his mind in regard to value theory after reading Santayana's criticism of his views.[8] In my opinion Russell was closer to the truth before reading Santayana's arguments than afterwards. But the pertinent question is not the right or wrong of the issue, but the fact that on rational grounds a philosophical doctrine can be abandoned. In cases in which a doctrine is held as a hypothesis, rational argument can achieve a modicum of objectivity. Lest my example of a philosopher changing his mind be misinterpreted, because both Santayana and Russell belong to the same culture, let me offer another example: of recent years, Americans have shown a great deal of interest in Indian thought. Those who do so respond to what they take to be the depths and subtlety of classical Indian thinkers. If the approach of some of these men to the philosophical heritage of India has traces of the religious attitude (and I would not doubt it for a minute, were it to be asserted), it is simply gratuitous to say that such is the case with all of them.

The fact, then, that a modicum of objectivity can be achieved in philosophical dialogue cannot be denied. How is it achieved? The technique of philosophy is the technique of dialogue. As Plato put it in the Seventh Epistle, it is the technique of giving and receiving answers in friendly intercourse.[9] And this is just as possible between an Indian and an American as it is between an American and a fellow citizen. Truth is objective. What existentialists call "subjective truth" is a value of high worth, but one not to be confused with what traditional philosophers and scientists call "truth."

Objectivity in moral judgments is more difficult to achieve and less frequently encountered. A full discussion concerning how it can be obtained is not possible here, and in any case all I have to say on the subject is already in print. Here I shall only sketch the grounds on which I hold it to be possible, not only within a culture, but across cultures.

Let me first note that anthropologists and philosophers have long tried to define "cultural universals." These are abstractions from all human groups; we find no human societies that fail to provide the means of rearing the young, obtaining food, preserving themselves against men and nature, managing their internal affairs, and the like. But for the purposes of the moral philosopher *whose main objective is to discover means of resolving value conflicts morally,* these cultural universals do not help. He needs other means, and I suggest that these are to be found in what F. C. Sharp called "the unity of the moral consciousness of the race." [10] Outside of Sharp and the Gifford Lecturer for 1948-49, Professor A. Macbeath, I know of no other contemporary philosopher who has sought to resolve the conflict of value judgments at this level. Sharp found the unity he sought in universalistic utilitarianism. I cannot agree with his findings. But for me what is significant about his inquiry is that he sought for the unity in *the form,* and not *in the matter,* of the moral judgment. Macbeath, too, if I read him correctly, looks for the unity in the form of the judgment, although he does not put it in these terms. But I think he comes closer to the truth than Sharp did. Macbeath writes that, with one possible exception, ordinary moral rules regarded as right are empirical generalizations "based on the experience of mankind as to the conditions necessary for realizing the form of life which is worthwhile." The exception,

the one rule which seems to be not an empirical generalization but a rational principle, which like the categories is true universally and admits of no exception which is not morally wrong, is the principle of justice or equity, which seems to be implied in one form or another in every moral code and in the ideal, if not always the practice, of every society.[11]

Macbeath goes on to point out that justice does not mean equality. And he continues:

Now the real basis of this principle—a basis which comes to light especially in its more developed forms—is the nature of personality and the recognition by the individual that others are personalities, manifestations of the moral consciousness, like himself.[12]

And in a later chapter, coming close to the conclusion of his lectures, he writes:

In my treatment . . . I have assumed, and I have tried to defend the assumption, that the main structure of the moral life, the nature of the moral ideal and the grounds of moral obligations are in principle the same everywhere and for all men.[13]

This is not the place to air my serious disagreements with Macbeath's important contribution to moral philosophy. What is here relevant, as it seems to me, is to note that for Macbeath the ground of the moral life is the recognition by one individual of the personality of those he comes into practical relations with. There is no question that nonliterate groups live in what Bergson called "a closed society," ruled by "closed morality"; and there is no question that Christians, who profess to live in an open society, according to an open moral code, seldom live up to their professions.[14] And to me, at least, it is equally clear that, as Bergson held, the difference between an open and a closed society and morality is not one of degree, but of kind. When these matters are properly considered, I think we have grounds for arriving at the doctrine of the unity of the moral consciousness of mankind—not the unity of the matter of the moral judgments, but the unity of their form. But this is sufficient to achieve objectivity in value judgments—in principle at least. The cultural relativist is right about the facts on which he bases his doctrine—facts that no one has ever dreamt of denying. He is wrong about the inferences he bases on those facts. For rare as in actuality it may be, it is in principle possible to utter objectively valid value judgments across cultures.[14a]

III

In this section I turn to the examination of certain aspects of cultural relativism as formulated by my colleague, Professor Melville Herskovits. I single out his treatment of the doctrine, not only because I am better acquainted with it than with other formulations but for three more weighty reasons: (1) Other formulations of relativism have been examined by other members of this Symposium. (2) Herskovits has been a persistent defender of the doctrine and in the last decade has published at least four discussions of it.[15] An examination of these discussions leads one to admire Herskovits' loyalty to his doctrine. But it must be pointed out that in spite of the many radical criticisms to which relativism in general, and his formulation in particular, have been subjected, it has not been withdrawn or seriously modified, although slight *ad hoc* modifications of an unacknowledged nature will be found in his publications on the subject. (3) Herskovits calls the doctrine of cultural relativism "a philosophy," and it is indeed a doctrine that demands technical philosophical competence to present. But while I find that his formulation of it is backed by the scientific prestige of the writer, it does not seem to me to meet, as I hope to show in this section, the philosophical demands that one has the right to make of it.

I turn to those aspects of Herskovits' presentation of the doctrine that are of special interest to me. I emphasize the limitations of my examination of Herskovits' formulation because he has criticized me, among others, on the ground that I do not share his interests, Alas, I am no ethnographer. But I must insist on my right to my own interests. Herskovits writes:

This tendency to restrict relativism to morals, ethics, and values has the unfortunate result of throwing the problem at issue out of focus, since it undercuts the enculturative factor in cultural learning in general.[16]

Herskovits would stress "perception and cognition," rather than the problem of morals and truth. How one can examine *cognition,* in any of its several legitimate meanings, and by-pass the problem of truth, we are not told. But I am more interested in pointing out that the assumption that a complex and broad area of investigation, made up of distinct disciplines, each of which is recognized as having relative independence, contains, nevertheless, a single focus, whose locus is decided by the interest of anthropologists or the members of any other profession, is false absolutism. The focus of a problem is defined by each student in terms of his own interests in an area of investigation which can be relatively isolated and which is recognized as worthy of attention. Since cultural relativism extends its doctrine, called by Herskovits "a philosophy," into the fields of cognition and of morality, the epistemologist and the moral philosopher, each from his own point of view, is fully entitled to investigate the claims of relativism. A doctrine applicable, as the relativist claims his to be, to so many disciplines, has as many foci as there are disciplines to which it is applicable.

Consider next Herskovits' paper entitled "Tender and Tough-minded Anthropology and the Study of Culture." We are told that the "paper represents an attempt to analyze some of the reactions" that the presentation of the doctrine of relativism has called forth. After stating that William James' terms "are particularly applicable . . . in considering cultural relativism," the writer adds: "for make no mistake, cultural relativism is a 'tough-minded' philosophy. It requires those who hold it to alter responses that arise out of some of the strongest enculturative conditioning to which they have been exposed . . ." [17] It requires, in other words, some sort of conversion, which puts it beyond the pale of rational argument. It is not difficult to see that whatever the writer intended, the result is the old, pre-Freudian *ad hominem* technique of psychoanalyzing the opposition—a game two can play, but that a scholar should scrupulously avoid playing since it is not conducive to dialogue.[18]

There is a good reason why scholars are seriously interested in the implications of relativism for morality and truth, and that is that the doctrine is not only false but pernicious. As regards knowledge, cultural relativism leads to a facile skepticism, which ill becomes a man seriously in search of the truth. In morality the effect is to bruise, if not to destroy, the moral fibre of students. That it in fact has this effect can be shown by an illustration. I was once told by one of my students in Wisconsin that on occasions when girls resisted the sexual advances of boys, the boys would reply: "You ought to take a course with X." X was a very popular teacher who, under the mask of teaching philosophy—a thin diet at best was what he preached—employed great vehemence and persuasive powers to destroy the student's values and to substitute for them relativism and a second-hand version of Dewey's good-will humanism. From the preaching the students drew a conclusion Herodotus would have rejected: since morality is relative, there is no point in hanging on to prudish, restrictive morals when the sexual mores of the Polynesians are much more pleasant.

Herskovits tells us that the doctrine of cultural relativism has three aspects, a methodological, a philosophical, and a practical one.[19] I shall examine the first two of these, for the third is of no interest to me.

In respect to the methodological aspect we are told that:

As method, relativism encompasses the principle of our science that, in studying a culture, one seeks to attain as great a degree of objectivity as possible; that one does not judge the modes of behavior one is describing, or seek to change them. Rather, one seeks to understand the sanctions of behavior in terms of the established relationships within the culture itself, and refrains from making interpretations that arise from a preconceived frame of reference.[20]

The first comment this statement calls for is that, although it sounds odd to call the methodological prescription of objectivity "cultural relativism," the counsel itself is sound. It is imperative that the anthropologist achieve as great a degree of objectivity as possible. An Evangelical missionary is not likely to understand the sexually uninhibited culture of the Polynesians. But without qualification the statement is not true. Thus, a streak of paranoia may enable a man to discover traits in those he imagines are persecuting him that an irenic, objective observer may altogether miss.

The next comment refers to the lack of methodological sophistication entailed by the statement's empiricism. The writer would have the anthropologist refrain from making interpretations that arise from a preconceived frame of reference. But how can anyone perform such a logical feat? Surely a man who refers with approval to Sherif's experiments as regards the manner in which judgment depends on experience, as Herskovits does, knows better than to assume it can be performed.[21] But we do not need psychologists at this late date to tell us that the questions we ask and the acts we observe are deemed worthy of attention in terms of criteria of relevance that are a priori to our observations and queries and that these criteria are in fact frames of reference. Judgments about what is trivial and what is important, what typical and what not, in the behavior of the nonliterates studied are possible only if the field worker is provided with some notions of what he is looking for. The frame of reference is unavoidable. But it is not vicious so long as the observer is prepared to modify it as his knowledge of his nonliterates progresses.

The next comment is that the statement is unacceptable for another reason. While counseling the anthropologist not to judge the behavior he is describing, Herskovits tells us that cultural relativism is a "philosophy that recognizes the values set up by every society to guide its own life and that understands their worth to those who live by them." [22] How we can recognize the values of a society and how we can understand their worth— which is to say, how we can recognize them to be valuable for those who live by them, but not judge them valuable for the society—how to perform this feat we are not told. In any case, if the anthropologist passes no value judgments on the society that he is studying, those who break this methodological rule must be considered poor anthropologists, and this would force on us the absurd conclusion that Miss Benedict and Malinowski, to mention only two anthropologists whose stature cannot be challenged, are poor anthropologists, for they have judged the cultures they have studied in the very manner interdicted by our cultural relativist. Let me cite one passage, picked almost at random, from Miss Benedict's account of the Dobuans (which account is based, as we know, on Fortune's field work):

The jealousy, the suspicion, the fierce exclusiveness of ownership that are characteristic of Dobu are all in the foreground of Dobuan marriage, but it is impossible to give them full weight until we have considered also their manner of life in other respects. The motivations that run through all Dobuan existence are singularly limited. They are remarkable because of the consistency with which the institutions of the culture embody them and the lengths to which they are carried.[23]

Or take this other passage from a classic in anthropological literature, *The Sexual Life of Savages in North-Western Melanesia*. In his discussion of "Yausa—Orgiastic Assaults by Women,"Malinowski writes:

We now turn to the extreme south of the main island, and the adjoining island of Vakuta. We have already mentioned these districts, not very honourably, several times. They are in general distinguished ethnologically by a certain coarseness of character and habit which is displayed in many aspects of their life. In sexual matters they are undoubtedly much more crude than the northerners, and have practices which would offend the finer feeling for etiquette and decorum, if not for morals, of the latter.[24]

But we are not done with the incoherence of cultural relativism. For note that the methodological prescription advises the student to seek as great a degree of objectivity as possible. And this means that in respect to the study of other cultures the anthropologist can transcend the ethnocentric limitations of his own culture—something which, let us not forget, cannot be done, for all values are determined by cultural factors, and the truth that the anthropologist seeks is a value. But if he can transcend the limitations of his own culture, why can't anyone else? The virtues of objectivity, tolerance, and accuracy of observation he practices are common virtues possessed by many men in varying degrees in all walks of life. Even if we grant—as I do—that the training of the anthropologist refines these virtues and tends to make them more efficiently operative than they otherwise would be, we know that they have been used by others in the observation of alien cultures. The Father of History was not trained by Boas, but he recorded the fact of cultural pluralism with a cool, objective eye. Again, Livingston, who was trained as a missionary, we have been told by a recent biographer, was fairly objective in his attitude towards Africans. And so was Fr. Sahagún towards the Mexicans.[25]

Consider another point: Herskovits grants that the technology of the West is superior to that of the primitives. But technology did not grow *in vacuo*—which is to say, that it depended for its development on the effectively operative espousal of certain virtues. What virtues? Technology presupposes science, and science presupposes the pursuit of truth, and that in turn presupposes a number of virtues: the suppression of the self, the control of the passions, particularly vanity and egoism, at least during and in the pursuit of truth, the willingness to apply intelligence in a disciplined fashion, and something that, as regards science in the narrow sense, may not occur to an American, the abrogation of the belief that a gentleman does not get his hands dirty. He who grants the superiority of Western technology should either grant the superiority of these values or give us a fully reasoned argument as to why he does not need to recognize these virtues as superior to other virtues the nonliterates possess.

IV

It is well known, in some circles at least, that one of the functions of cultural relativism is to defend nonliterates from the well-meaning, but often catastrophic, meddling of missionaries and the ruthless exploitation of the imperialists. But note, before I proceed, that I am speaking of the intention of the doctrine, and not the intention of those who forge it and defend it. The assertion regarding the intention of the doctrine, I own, is difficult to prove, since it cannot be shown in the manner that a patch of color can be shown, but can be shown only in the way that meaning is shown. In any case, I take it that it is generally conceded that cultural relativism contains an ideological component—in the sense that the term "ideology" has acquired of recent years.

Faced with the results of missionary meddling with the mores of a people, or with imperialistic exploitation, the anthropologist

reacts, and his reaction is not only justified, but is indicative of
the goodness of his heart. Here are peoples who, at whatever risk
to their souls, have learned the hard way how to master nature
for their own ends and are at least living a life of relative happiness and dignity in terms of their mores. A few years of meddling
or of exploitation, and they become a pathetic lot. They lose their
skills. Disorganization sets in. Their nakedness is covered—with
ugly garments. They lose the urge to toil and they become beg-
gars. In some cases they are destroyed not by somatic illnesses
imported from the white world, but by something more insidious,
moral illness, for somehow they lose their morale and their will
to live. They become cultural beachcombers, ethnographic Bow-
ery bums. True, in some cases cannibalism is abolished by their
exploiting masters, and in many cases modern medicine helps
them. But what their "benefactors" do not, cannot, see is that in
spite of their own cultural superiority, they themselves are just
as cannibalistic as their primitive charges, although what they
devour are healthy, living cultures rather than dead bodies. Nor
can they see that when primitive people lose their identity and
their dignity, there is nothing you can say in their favor except
that they are seldom to blame. To the missionary the anthropologist, as is to be expected, objects as much as he objects to the
imperialist, or perhaps even more, for he does not usually share
the religious convictions of the missionary. Cultural relativism,
by preaching that the nonliterates have as much right to their
ways as we to ours, seeks to protect the primitives from the ra-
pacity of their exploiters and the ravages of those who would save
their souls at the cost of their identity and dignity.

Thus viewed, cultural relativism cannot be condemned outright. But thus viewed, relativism is an ideology, and if it is
valid, it is valid only during the period that the conditions that
gave rise to it are operative. It is not valid in the sense that the
most abstract maxims of morality are valid, but valid only cir-
cumstantially, for a period of time, and at specific places. But
circumstances have changed recently, and as an ideology relativism has become hopelessly retardatarian. Primitive peoples hardly
require today the protection of the cultural relativist. What they

seem to require at the moment is protection from their own blind and fanatical nationalism. In a world and at a time when the pressing political need is to find means of mediating the differences among peoples, emphasis on the radical differences among them and denial of any possibility of reaching across their cultural frontiers is, to put it in the most generous way that occurs to me, hardly prudent. By insisting on the gestalt and monadic quality of each culture, on its autarchy, the doctrine of relativism sanctions separatism. Were nationalism on the wane, emphasis on the irreducibility of each culture, although theoretically erroneous, would not threaten practical harm. But circumstances are rapidly changing. Here we have another sense in which cultural relativism is pernicious: it is today politically pernicious. Any doctrine that, however indirectly and however subtly, prevents the peoples of the world from coming together, from mediating their differences—which is to say, from reaching beyond their boundaries in terms of moral judgments—is today an obviously pernicious doctrine.

V

The preceding criticism of cultural relativism should have made it clear that the confusions, the fallacies, and the lack of adequate comprehension of the problems that lead relativism to its pernicious conclusions in respect to truth and morality are not difficult to detect. Its logic is inadmissible, but it is obviously so. Its approach to epistemological and ethical problems is lamentable, because it fails to make important distinctions, but the errors and deficiencies it displays in these disciplines are easily descried. Why, then, does this obviously erroneous and pernicious doctrine keep on cropping up again and again, in spite of the devastating criticisms to which it has been subjected? A full answer to this question would call for several essays of the length of this one. But one of these answers deserves attention here, for it points to a problem of profound interest and great importance, and one that, so far as I know, awaits as yet a satisfactory solution.

I have in mind the problem of our conception of man's nature.

It is no secret that never in our culture have we had the amount of factual knowledge we have today about man. It pours in from armies of researchers in tremendous quantities: political scientists, economists, sociologists, anthropologists, psychologists, not to mention theologians, literary scholars, and philosophers. There is no system of government among the multitudinous ways men have devised to make a mess of their political life on which we lack a monograph, and on many of these systems we possess veritable libraries. There is no social institution that has not been studied: we know about the berdaches and the sacred prostitutes, the Fong's hundred wives and Hollywood seriatim polygamy, English drug addicts and New York call girls, voodoo and Buddhism. We are fairly certain that no human group is six-toed, although we must expect sports among men who have more or less than five toes per foot. We know about the Duk Duks, the Dobuans, the Hopi and the Patagonians, the Sumerians and the ancient Egyptians. We know what men eat and the ways in which they make love. If there is a human group about which we have no knowledge, we can feel confident that an expedition is, or soon will be, on the way to study it and that a monograph will be available to scholars a year or two after the expedition's return.

But what do we *know* about man? We have facts and when we ask for more knowledge we get more facts. We professors have a ravenous appetite for facts and on short call can produce overwhelming quantities of them. We are a busy and diligent army, and like endless columns of parasol ants, we labor to bring facts to the heap in serried and tireless rows. But while we suffer from an *embarrass de richesse* in terms of the facts we have on hand, if the truth be acknowledged, we are a poverty-stricken lot, because the ingenious hypotheses we so busily build on the facts are not coherent with one another and have as yet resisted all effort to synthesize them. Whether they will continue to do so in the future we must leave to those who can see into it. In any case, at the moment there is no agreement among the scientific students of man—in the narrow sense of the term "science." The unity of science is at present a pretty dream, so far given the lie by its reigning disunity. And it does not take the knowledge of Macaulay's schoolboy to know that among philosophers any professor who can catch a graduate student or two can found a school. In fact, I have been thinking seriously of founding one of my own. But facts and mutually incompatible scientific hypotheses do not add up to knowledge. *Knowledge is systemic; it is coherent.* Consider the depth psychologists—not that I have anything against them, for some of my best friends are among them. We shall have knowledge of man in this respect when Freudians and Adlerians, Jungians, Sullivanians, Rankians, Frommians, Rogerians, and the thousand other tribes that work in this area compose their differences and, instead of the mutually incompatible insights they offer us today, put forth a coherent hypothesis about the human psyche and the manner in which it develops its illnesses. But exactly the same can be said of academic psychologists and of sociologists and the rest. Within each discipline, the bewildering chaos of Babel reigns. But even if we could claim coherence within a discipline, it would not be enough, for we shall have no knowledge of man until sociologists and psychologists, political scientists and anthropologists of whatever school or persuasion, and the rest of the busy army of scientific professors, compose their differences and arrive at some agreement.

But I have been speaking of *scientific* knowledge of man in the narrow, or American, sense of the term "science." Shall we ignore the historians? Don't they also contribute to our knowledge of man? And what are we going to do with the philosophers and the theologians? Are we going to wait until they resolve their differences? Or are we going to disregard their prattle, since they have been carrying on for over two and a half millenia and seem no closer to intellectual harmony today than when they started? Whatever will be decided, until all differences are composed and the lamb lies at peace with the lion, the knowledge we can claim about man must be acknowledged to be sadly defective. But until that future Golden Age, it looks as if we shall have to continue to live with our difficulties, and these constitute a breeding ground for all kinds of erroneous and pernicious doctrines.

For some reason this obvious fact—for such it seems to me—seems to offend many scientists and philosophers who study man

and his ways. Every time I have had occasion to call attention to
it, it has elicited a reaction that is the opposite of the irenic
response one expects of those who profess to seek the truth. Yet
it is, as I see it, necessary to call attention to it; for the truth is
not served by avoiding giving offense to dogmatists. Had Galileo,
Darwin, and Freud been afraid of offending the established
orthodoxies of their day, other men might have made their contributions, but not they.

But how is this fact, if it is one, relevant to the problem of
cultural relativism? The answer is that without adequate knowledge of man, we can expose the fallacies and incoherences of cultural relativism, but we cannot offer the relativist a clearly defined
set of criteria by means of which we can order in a hierarchy the
cultural pluralism that confronts us. There are some things we
can do: we can be reasonably certain that high civilizations allow
for more and fuller expressions of many of the possible modalities
of the human spirit than do primitive cultures such as those of
the Navahos, the Hopi, the Duk Duk, and the Xetás. On this
ground we can say that civilization is superior to the primitive
condition of man. It enables men to find themselves more easily
and to realize themselves more fully. We also know that a society
in which such institutions as the extermination factories of Belsen
and Buchenwald flourish and in which human monsters such as
Ilse Koch were given the opportunity to commit their pathological crimes, is a society that must be condemned by a man who is
not a moral imbecile.

But these criteria and others of a similar nature that could
easily be put forth, good as they are as far as they go, are not good
enough. And until we arrive at an adequate set of criteria that
can cut through the plurality of human cultures and in view of
such plurality order hierarchically the cultural modalities in
which the human spirit finds expression, judgments about human
cultures that stand the test of objectivity are defended only in an
ad hoc, hand-to-mouth, manner that fails to satisfy the exigencies
of the philosophic mind. Until that day the incoherences and
fallacies of the relativist will crop up again and again. For one
of the factors fostering the growth and dissemination of relativism

is what European thinkers refer to as "the crisis of man." It is the fact that in the last hundred years man has become a problem to himself as he never was before and that that problem is in part a consequence of the abundance of facts and hypotheses and the lack of integrated and reliable knowledge that enables the radically incoherent and pernicious doctrine of cultural relativism to claim for itself the honorific title of being "a philosophy" supported by science. Where so many pseudo sciences and quasi sciences and so many philosophies, involving partial insights, thrive, why not accept the "philosophy" of cultural relativism? The answer is that, while the facts on which relativism is founded are irrefragable, the conclusions drawn by the relativist from them are inadmissible.

NOTES

1. The reason for the title is that some years ago I examined the doctrine of cultural relativism in my *The Moral Life and the Ethical Life* (Chicago, 1950), pp. 25 ff.
2. I refer, of course, to the well-known story in which Darius asks some Greeks how much he would have to pay them for eating their fathers and some Callatians for burning them. Whether or not we can infer from this passage that Herodotus was a relativist, in the sense in which the term is employed in this paper, is a point that requires more careful consideration than it has received from those who cite it to prove the age of the doctrine. The point of Herodotus' story seems to be that a people holds its values in reverence and is outraged when it is asked to depart from them, not that one people's values are as good as another's.
3. One piece of psychological evidence is mentioned by Melville J. Herskovits in *Man and His Works* (New York, 1948), p. 66. For relativistic philosophical doctrines, *see* Arthur Lovejoy, *The Revolt Against Dualism* (New York, 1930), chaps. III, IV, V, where references to the works of philosophers defending relativism will be found. *See also* Evander Bradley McGilvary, *Towards a Perspective Realism* (LaSalle, Ill., 1956) and Arthur E. Murphy, "McGilvary's Perspective Realism," *The Journal of Philosophy*, LVI (1959), 149-165. Consult also the work of Ernst Cassirer, *An Essay on Man* (New Haven, 1944) and *The Philosophy of Symbolic Forms* (New Haven, 1953, 1955, 1957); Thomas Robischen, "What is Objective Relativism?" in *The Journal of Philosophy*, LV (1958), 1117-1132. For an able exposition of a doctrine seldom defended today, *see* Judith Jarvis, same journal, XV (1958), 1043-1053. For the work of the ethnolinguists, *see* Benjamin Whorf, *Language,*

Thought, and Reality, ed. by John Carroll (New York, 1956) and *Language and Culture,* ed. by Harry Hoijer, The American Anthropological Association, LVI (1954). For speculations concerning the relation between science and technology, see the work of the late sociologist of science, Edgard Zilzel, "Copernicus and Mechanics," *Journal of the History of Ideas,* I (1940), 113-118; "The Origin of William Gilbert's Scientific Method," same journal, II (1941), 1-32, and "The Genesis of the Concept of Physical Law," *The Philosophical Review,* LI (1942), 245-279.

In Herskovits' "Some Further Comments on Cultural Relativism," *American Anthropologist,* LX (1958), 266-273, the reader will find a bibliography on the subject of relativism. To it add the following later publications: Charles D. Bolton, "Sociological Relativism and The New Freedom," *Ethics,* LXVIII (1957), 11-27; Raymond Firth, "The Study of Values by Social Anthropologists," *Man, A Monthly Record of Anthropological Science,* LIII (1953), 230-260; Clyde Kluckhohn, "Values and Value Orientation," *Towards a Theory of Action,* ed. by Talcott Parsons and Edward A. Shils (Cambridge, Mass.), pp. 388-433; "Universal Categories in Culture," in *Anthropology Today,* prepared under the chairmanship of A. L. Kroeber (Chicago, 1953), pp. 524-553; Robert Redfield, *The Primitive World and Its Transformations* (Ithaca, 1953), p. 165; "Social Scientist, Man Between," *Chicago Review,* VIII (1954), 35-43; "Anthropological Understanding of Man," *Anthropological Quarterly,* XXXII (1959), 3-21. This is not an exhaustive bibliography.

4. For the way I use the terms "acknowledged," "recognized," and "espoused" values, see my *The Moral Life and the Ethical Life,* pp. 71, 190, 217-218.

5. A. L. Kroeber, *The Nature of Culture* (Chicago, 1954), Part I, particularly "The Superorganic," pp. 22-51. Also David Bidney, *Theoretical Anthropology* (New York, 1953), especially chaps. II and III.

6. Bronislaw Malinowski, *Crime and Custom in Savage Society* (New York, 1953). A valuable study of this problem, including a very perspicuous analysis of Malinowski's views on morality, has been contributed by A. Macbeath in his Gifford Lectures, *Experiments in Living* (London, 1952).

7. I employ the term "valid" advisedly, because I wish to by-pass a problem, at the moment under lively discussion among Anglo-American philosophers, which cannot be taken up here, namely, that of determining how value judgments, other than judgments of truth, are established (or justified or substantiated). Value judgments cannot be *demonstrated,* in the mathematical sense of this term, for in this sense the demonstration depends on postulates that, in respect to the values demonstrated, are arbitrary. My own view on this question, stated as succinctly as I can put it, is that we cannot succeed in establishing the validity of a value judgment, or a constellation of judgments, in conflict with others. The result of such an attempt is an eristic encounter in which each party strengthens the conviction that he is right and leaves the others unconvinced of the rightness of his position. The problem is to find means of

resolving value conflicts, not by demonstration, but by other rational means. And the human mind employs other rational means of validating its judgments than demonstration. How conflicts can be resolved, I have discussed as regards aesthetic and moral judgments, elsewhere.

8. Bertrand Russell, *Philosophy* (New York, 1927), p. 230.
9. *Thirteen Epistles of Plato,* Introduction, translation and notes by L. A. Post (Oxford, 1925), p. 99.
10. F. C. Sharp, *Ethics* (New York, 1928). See especially chaps. I, II, III, XII, XIV, XV.
11. Macbeath, *op. cit.,* p. 52.
12. *Ibid.,* p. 53.
13. *Ibid.,* p. 429.
14. Henri Bergson, *The Two Sources of Morality and Religion,* translated by R. Ashley Audra and Claudesley Brereton, with the assistance of W. Horsfall Carter (New York, 1935), chap. I, especially pp. 22 ff.
14a. Whether objectivity does not demand the positing of some sort of absolute, as some philosophers hold, or does, as I would maintain, and if it does, how we are to understand it, is an important philosophical question. But it need not be explored to show that the cultural relativist is in error.
15. To the two works of Herskovits already cited add "Tender- and Tough-minded Anthropology and the Study of Values in Culture," *Southwestern Journal of Anthropology,* VII (1951), 22-31 and *Cultural Anthropology, An Abridged Revision of Man and His Works* (New York, 1955), pp. 348-366.
16. Herskovits, "Some Further Comments," p. 267. By "cognition" Herskovits probably means "perception," and not what philosophers mean by it. But even if he does, the problem of truth turns up in the form of the question of veridical as against false perception, which philosophers deal with under the terms "reality" and "appearance."
17. Herskovits, "Tender- and Tough-minded," p. 23.
18. This is not the only time that Herskovits has psychoanalyzed the opposition. In "Some Further Comments" he also does it. See p. 266.
19. "Tender- and Tough-minded," p. 24.
20. *Loc. cit.*
21. *Man and His Works,* p. 65.
22. *Cultural Anthropology,* p. 364.
23. Ruth Benedict, *Patterns of Culture* (Boston and New York, 1934), p. 141.
24. Bronislaw Malinowski, *The Sexual Life of the Savages in North-Western Melanesia* (New York, 1929), p. 273.
25. George Seaver, *David Livingstone* (New York, 1957). Among many references to Livingstone's objectivity and freedom from the prejudices of his training and commitments, see pp. 284, 318, 319, 320-321, 374, 386. Fr. Bernardino de Sahagún, *Historia general de las cosas de Nueva España* (Mexico, D. F., 1938), I, xiv-xvi.

4

Relativistic Absolutists and Public Policies

HELMUT SCHOECK

I

Today's sociologist and cultural anthropologist finds it comfortable to pose in the role of a relativist. He does this, however, mostly as a man influenced by fads and trends in our contemporary intellectual world. Many of the fads were examined elsewhere in this Symposium. When pressed to argue precisely on the ground of his discipline, our modern social scientist often turns out to be something less than a consistent relativist. In regard to specific issues, problems, and possibilities he is even a determined absolutist capable of bending his empirical discipline to serve "what ought to be." For this reason certain contributions of modern social scientists to our public life are hard to understand unless we realize that they switch basic assumptions—turn relativist or absolutist—depending on their focus at the time. This "flexibility" is apparent especially when we compare positions taken in regard to the past, the present, and the future of our society and culture.

But first, let us dispose of the "angry young men," the plain relativists. Suppose we can show to a relativist that his studied nonconformity, his doubt for doubt's sake, is harmful to the continuation of his society. He may then retort, "So what? I don't care what the results will be. I am not my society's keeper."

Are we left without an argument to deal with the anarchist and nihilist who does not concede that his utterances may be valued in reference to his audience, holding the survival of his audience constant and as an absolute point of reference? Perhaps not. At least we can reply, "Why do you speak at all?" Of course, some relativists are said to have chosen silence, not wishing to commit themselves even to the recognition of the existence of a meaningful audience. But today's relativists are quite vociferous. And if our question could silence them, we would not be worse off. So let us ask of them: Does not your urge to tell people what you think is relative suggest that you are living by an audience? Who else but your surrounding society or societies can be your audience? And does your urge to be heard, esteemed, and presumably remembered for some time, not also suggest that your act of communicating, indeed, your faculty of speech, is inevitably part of a multigenerational society?

Well, you may feel free to say, "The past be damned"; but what about the future of your audience? Can you really convince us that your utterances were meant for a momentary flash only? Are we to believe that your act of grasping the tail of a thought, of formulating one of your brilliant phrases, was not derived from your anticipation of a future audience that would listen and act upon your idea? And if you cannot deny this, are we not justified in doubting the relevancy of ideas that negate, even so remotely, the continuation of society as a meaningful value?

It is a remarkable fact that all adversaries today, as well as most mutual enemies of former times, always agree on one goal: the show must go on. Why is it that we cannot even conceive of a dictator, of some charismatic leader, who will whip his followers into blind fanaticism by addressing himself only to the present generation? Why is it impossible for him to promise a totally parasitic, yet politically "ideal," short-term society, without any professed regard for future generations? Is that not proof of the compelling presence of the family in the human situation?

So much for the future. What about the past? The relativist, in his role as social critic or plain sociologist, viewing the past for clues to the present, is likely to say: No intrinsic value can be established for any structure, any custom, form, or content of the present social scene because of its extension through time, for "it could have been otherwise." [1] Indeed, to look upon any present structure as having a substantial function, carried over from the past, as is done in the functional analysis of societies, is likely to be attacked as a "defense of conservatism," about the worst sin of which a social scientist can be accused. Thus, proponents of that approach, such as Robert K. Merton, feel obliged to defend themselves against an attack the premises of which they apparently concede for prescientific reasons. [2]

I need not add here that the mere presence of a trait in the fabric of social life surely does not grant axiological standing. But neither should mere age be an a priori justification for disdain. The relativist's refusal to acknowledge meaningful longitudinal structures extending from the past into the present is in curious contrast to his knowledge of the future. The moment he turns toward things to come, he divines a limited number of firm structures and pressures. He knows exactly what is going to happen and why it cannot be otherwise. Socialism and communism, growing labor unions, nationalism, and perhaps even Fidel Castro, "are here to stay." They represent the absolute structures and processes of our century and the next. Indeed, the phrase "are here to stay" has almost become a fetish. We can detect relativists by the use of that slogan.

Actually, in some relativists today the sense of relativity toward the past is matched by a fierce insistence on absolutism for the future. If this attitude is combined with lip service to empiricism, the contrast becomes even stronger. For our relativist turns absolutist precisely where all is built on faith and wish, nothing on facts; whereas he disdains even a token of meaningful nexus between past and present although this is the only source of sequential empirical study.

There is a weak spot in the usual argument used by the spokesmen of our existing free and open society. We say our culture is preferable to one in which individuals have less freedom of choice, both in relevant and in routine matters of life. We assume pluralism to be a self-evident value and we are disturbed when the man from the Soviet Union says: "Why should I want freedom of choice? It is much more comfortable to let the state worry about what I should do and what my children should grow up to be." The unsophisticated proponent of western ideals in such "cultural contact" becomes confused and meek. How can he convince the captive of a positive program of the absolute superiority of another social system when this superiority is precisely claimed to rest on the relativity of choices? Do we not say: *Relativism* is *absolutely* better than a society dedicated to absolutism interpreted by leaders in accordance with a one-track doctrine?

How can we convince a member of another society of the preferability of our own by telling him that in America, England or France he can be Buddhist, Shintoist, Catholic, Protestant, agnostic, even communist? He might say: "I prefer a society where all those bewildering creatures are not officially recognized."

We are still left with the problem of how to make a firm case for the free society that seems to enjoy relativity for its own sake. I am aware of a theological escape hatch. "Our Christian culture," some people believe, should be "shown" at fairs inside the Soviet empire. But again, we cannot make ourselves understood by a man to whom faith and state are identical. What are we to say to him when he asks, "Why is your Christian heritage superior to what I have if you yourself say that you let anybody choose whether he wants to be a Christian, a Jew, a Shintoist, or an agnostic? If all are relative to you, why should I adopt any faith absolutely in preference to what I think I have at home now?"

Some will say: "Let us simply convince him of the superior value of a plain humanism, the essence of which is tolerance." This may make fine rhetoric, but it does not help us much, because that tolerance, an eighteenth-century achievement, stems typically from an extreme sense of relativism in spiritual and cultural things. One solution might be to say: It is not relativism at all that we are talking about. We merely meant that each individual has freedom to choose what he wants to believe in absolutely.

Significantly, our relativistic and pluralistic society will not recognize the exemption claimed by the conscientious objector unless he can show that his religious commitment is genuine and absolute. Thus, in a sense, our western societies keep going reasonably well, for the time being at least, precisely because, relativism in general notwithstanding, they are always oriented toward an absolute commitment of their members, even though its nature may change from man to man. We do not hold that there is any relativity involved for him. On the contrary: we insist that each individual may claim his own absolute, no matter where he takes it from. But, and this is most important, the norms of our society also expect that no man shall coerce others on the basis of his own private commitment. Existential oddity is legal only on the premise of reciprocal tolerance. And, by contrast, our visitor from the Soviet camp, while priding himself on a share in an absolute venture and doctrine, is not talking about absolutism from the individual point of view. In his society everyone, regardless of his individual inclinations, is, at least in theory, relative to the state. Individual wishes, needs, and hopes—even science and scholarship—are relative to the demand and doctrine of a central state.

II

I now come to what may be the worst consequence of modern relativism. Others can use it as a lever with which to coerce us into harmful bilateral agreements and then proceed to force us to continue to deliver the goods because they can expect us *also* to live up to our previous absolute standards of conduct.

The profession of relativism in the realm of ideas, at least the type of profession now in vogue in the West, therefore, leads to a peculiar weakness and vulnerability. Non-Western political figures, the Soviet Union as well as the leaders of gangs in the streets of New York, accept at face value our professed commitment—if there can be such an absolute act—to relativism. They often succeed in coaxing us into positions, laws, treaties or agreements—such as the cultural exchange agreements between the USA and the USSR—along lines of ideological relativity, which we concede, and then insist that we deliver, or continue against our interests, from that position—construed by reference to relativism—for reasons of absolute principles to which we once said we would adhere.[3]

To me, one of the most disturbing developments is that the adversaries of the West and our domestic underworld can play simultaneously upon our commitment to relativism as well as on the preceding commitment to absolute principles. Prominent legal thinkers are capable of inviting a theoretical consideration of the overthrow of government—"because a free society requires experimentation with all kinds of social ideas affecting social arrangements"—yet at the same time derive the specific protection of the intruder by insisting that the society against which he works is absolutely bound by a number of constitutional principles. No exception is allowed, not even for convicted Soviet spies. Between 1957 and 1960, the Federal Bureau of Investigation, for instance, had not been able to proceed with a widening investigation and prosecution of a Soviet spy ring because the United States Supreme Court had not yet ruled whether evidence seized in a hollow pencil, at a time when the agents had only a warrant for the search of a room in general, can be used in court. The defense attorney for the Soviet spy can argue on behalf of his client by an absolute and literal insistence on a constitutional requirement. The pragmatic and experimental approach is denied to those who would try to keep intact a society with its supporting norms that made possible the absolute principles used by the attacker for shielding himself.[4]

This paradox should not be glibly defended as a virtue. Rather, it seems to result from a confusion of relativism and segmentally selective constitutional absolutism. In other words, the paradox does not emerge from any compelling logical-legal reasoning, but from political-emotional junctures in historical time.

An especially telling formulation of this judicial habit of

employing sociological relativism for absolute ends is found in a concurring opinion of Associate Justice Felix Frankfurter. On June 17, 1957, in the contempt case of Paul M. Sweezy versus the New Hampshire Supreme Court, Frankfurter wrote:

Progress in the natural sciences [note the scientistic fallacy: what is true of the realm of nature must also be true and applicable to the realm of human affairs!] is not remotely confined to findings made in the laboratory. Insights into the mysteries of nature are born of hypothesis and speculation. The more so is this true [Why "the more so"?] in the pursuit of understanding in the groping endeavors of what is called the social sciences, the concern of which is man and society. . . . Political power must abstain from intrusion into this activity of freedom, pursued in the interests of wise government aims and the people's well being.

Frankfurter goes on to state explicitly that this certainly must include social experimentation even with ideas such as socialism or communism for the possible benefit of our society.

Whenever I hear this argument, and it is the usual one in academic circles today, I simply ask whether the speaker would wish a practicing, or at least convinced, polygamist to teach one section of the sociology course in marriage and family since, after all, that system is even more a happily "going concern" in many parts of the world than communism or socialism. I have yet to get an answer to that question. The really crucial point probably is this. Justice Frankfurter, and many others, confuse "idea" with "idea." Anything anyone says is an idea is an idea and thus protected to the ultimate. But we have only the word of Mr. Sweezy that his advocacy of socialism for America is guided by his concern for the well-being of the people. It may have any number of covert reasons. And why should the polygamist or polyandrist not also profess the same concern? After 1945, when Berlin had about three or four females for every male, some women asked the city magistrate to legalize, temporarily at least, polygamy. Certainly there was a compelling social need for it, and I wonder how the present United States Supreme Court could have refused to hear those women favorably? More decisive, perhaps, is this question: Can any idea claim the same protection and status as is claimed by the idea of a new model of molecules, for instance, or a new idea about genes, when it is a germinal idea leading to a social system that no longer recognizes the premises on which societies developed that released the human mind to pursue knowledge freely? But we have not yet reached the end of the confusion created by the Court's *metabasis eis allo genos.*

This concept of a mandate for unlimited, even perhaps potentially suicidal, experimentation with a therapeutic goal leads to puzzling questions. If a society is told by its ultimate arbiter of its own initial compact that it may not, on the premises on which it based its social contract, keep anyone from experimenting with its structures and trends, no matter how contrary they obviously are to its initial intent, where can we draw a line, if any line can still be drawn? If no limits can be placed on experimentation with the whole structure of society, or large institutions and subdivisions of it, how can we still insist on limits in personal (interpersonal) and individual experimentation, for instance, in medical and psychiatric practice and research?

Can we any longer hold the physician to his oath of Hippocrates? In the age of the "Freudian ethic" (Richard La Piere) and post-Kinseyan "ethics by panel," we can conceive of a physician who wants to find out whether the seduction of female patients works better than tranquilizers to ease the lot of our allegedly frustrated, status-seeking, suburban housewives. For instance, a psychotherapist, practicing in California, published a book in his field in 1949 in which he renounced the Hippocratic oath and said he would not refrain from making love to any patient if he deemed it best in the interests of therapy.[5]

And, in October of 1955, Dr. James Milton Parker, school pediatrist, before the Superior Court in Litchfield, accused of encouraging homosexuality among emotionally disturbed boys in his care, pleaded in his defense that he was trying out a new psychotherapeutic technique. The old-fashioned judge did not agree, but key figures of public opinion in New England chided him for sentencing the doctor.[6]

I could go even further. Many authors fail to see any good

reason for making homosexual acts punishable when the same society does not prosecute adultery (unless, perhaps, charges are pressed by an injured party). But why stop after including homosexuality as one possible activity in our pluralistic society? What would then enable us to be harsh on bestiality? After all, H. D. Lasswell, apparently in all seriousness, proposed to extend universal human rights to subhuman primates.[7]

Could we not rely on human nature and a concomitant notion of natural law that permits us to distinguish normatively between adultery and homosexuality? After all, the former may lead to procreation, the latter never; whereas the former may lead to another marriage and family formation, though at a grave cost, the latter cannot lead to a new family unit.

Lasswell's plea for the chimpanzees (perhaps provoked by the British zoologist who suggested breeding apes to take over the deserted role of domestic servant) shows clearly the perversion of a principle, coined to grant absolutes, into a tool of absurd relativism. The idea of, the wish for, absolute human rights stems from an era that knew that man must set norms, taken from his *humanness,* and then stick to them. But now we are asked to use that very principle to force men, eventually perhaps, to abdicate before apes, in case they could outbreed and outvote us.

There is good reason to think that a specific human nature has contributed through time to certain social forms that are better than others. Monogamy, for instance, seems better suited to lead to a surveyable kind of society to live in than unlimited polygamy. And by "surveyable" society I mean exactly what the word implies. Provided we really want most of the blessings of a modern and rational society, as professed by most social scientists, we can probably show that the legal framework for such a society and its economy can best be secured when families are formed on monogamous principles. If our cultural relativist insists that people who have chosen polygamy have a right to as high a standard of living or to as much legal protection of individuals as some monogamous societies attained, he is inconsistent.

The fact of such different social arrangements as monogamy

and polygamy cannot be used as proof that there is no general human nature that would permit us to decide on the merit of alternatives. The dilemma of our relativist stems from his desire to grant cultural relativism on issues where he feels relativistic in his own society (e.g., marital affairs, crime) while insisting on rigid goals and norms regarding need-fulfilment on the material level.

Moreover, there is the curious willingness with which non-Western peoples submit to the absolutes of our fashion and styles in wearing apparel. The same man or woman from the Congo, the Ganges, or the Tigris who tells us that our society is out of line with what the majority of the world expects or does is impeccably clad in the latest, and often most expensive, style from Fifth Avenue or Paris. He hardly ever tries to underline his argument by wearing what the majority of the world wears, i.e., little, nothing, or, at any rate, non-Western gear. Why this extreme generosity and tolerance toward the whims of our fashion combined with an equally charming contempt for all the other mores and standards of our Western tradition? If Western dress is so suitable to winning arguments in the United Nations and conducting business that Nasser outlaws the traditional Egyptian long shirt for men, can we not ask whether perhaps a capitalistic orientation toward private property and reward of individual effort by a free market might be as essential a requisite to economic growth as the wristwatch and pen? Curiously, Ghana outlawed bare bosoms, but the Boston city censor let bare-bosomed dancers from Africa perform, rationalizing the exemption from the code by cultural relativism. It is not simply that the man or woman from Ghana, if only half clad, would get arrested in New York, no matter how suitable his outfit might be for the climate. *He* would also have *us* arrested in Accra if we wore what his brethren there are wearing.[8]

Perhaps the clash between cultural relativists and their opponents would be less loud if we distinguished "recognition of superiority" (of trait or culture X) from "signs of preference for X." We do not have to taunt anyone by saying our way of life is superior. Let us simply say: More people, freely and individually choosing, seem to prefer it. If our critic wishes, he can console himself by believing that the majority prefers trash to his promise of a golden future in Utopia.

Monogamy and polygamy would seem to be a pair of very different marital patterns, indicating a wide divergence, thus relativity, in how humans arrange for basic needs. But is this really so? Are the human problems, the decisions to be made in order to assure a minimum of conflict, really so different in either situation? If we find that murderous jealousy has little survival value for any group, and if we also find that provocation of jealousy must be avoided both in the monogamous and in the polygamous household, it would seem that the human necessity leading to specific patterns is so close in kind that what appears to be different in approach is really much more similar in a universal way.

III

But how does the relativist arrive at a position from which the axiological link between present and past can be cut exactly where it suits his whim or politics? And just how relativistic is a present-day sociologist or anthropologist supposed to be? As revered and moderate a sociologist as Everett C. Hughes, of the University of Chicago, answered this question as follows:

Some teachers of English literature or classics are, in my experience, inclined to nineteenth-century liberalism . . . as contrasted with the quasi-professional and more modern liberalism of, say, the anthropologist or sociologist. I refer not to professional support of causes, but to the more subtle, implied "liberalism" that inheres in our very objects of study. . . . For we play with the notion that the underdog race might, under certain conditions, have been on top. Our very study implies always the attitude about everything that made Robert Musil's *Der Mann ohne Eigenschaften* so intriguing. . . . "It could have been otherwise." This is an intolerable and dangerous idea, in a world of conflicting social ideologies.

The peculiarity of the social scientist is not that there is a realm toward which he has this attitude, for all true academic people have this attitude toward social arrangements and sentiments. Our particular objective attitude demands an apparent neutrality toward those very problems where neutrality makes one appear a potential ally of the enemy. The social scientist, to the extent that he claims and acts upon a mandate to think that any social arrangement might be otherwise, is the ultimate equalitarian in that he can conceive the underdog being on top. . . .[9]

While doubting the assumption "it could have been otherwise," that the underdog might have been on top, I suspect strongly that on the level of imputation of individual satisfaction and covert power a great deal might be very different from what the sociologist deduces from the overt structure. It might be possible to discover solid reasons for showing why some people remained in a subordinate position. But the most important point to keep in mind is this: no matter how seemingly hopeless a social situation may be, we can always find categories of people, or individuals, who succeeded in turning the social structure to their advantage. We might mention the Jews and Chinese who, as discriminated and excluded minorities, have usually succeeded in offering to the host culture those skills and services in which the members of the host culture could ill afford to engage. Thus, the fact of exclusion became not infrequently an advantage. And even Simone de Beauvoir's lament about "the second sex" may be superfluous. Those females who really know how to rule men often win ascendancy regardless of the social system, a fact strikingly shown in some cultures.[10]

Perhaps the "what-might-have-been" sociologist might better reflect on what some people could have made of their given social structure rather than on what other kind of social structure might have put them on top.

Moreover, Hughes fails to see that his "ultimate equalitarian" is not a true equalitarian at all, because, as Hughes continues, "he can conceive the underdog being on top." This "liberal" social scientist is not really for a society of equals (though some are), but merely wants a turnover of elites because he happens to dislike the specific persons in the elite position at the moment. But we should also ask of the contemporary social scientist why he has to be that way. What would happen to his discipline if he also "were otherwise"? I doubt that it would suffer. Indeed, he might come closer to his great ideal, the natural scientist.

Does the social scientist adopt this attitude for genuinely methodological reasons? Is it as essential to him as a comparable approach might be to the researcher in other fields of study? And to what degree do we find this approach in the natural sciences at all? It would seem to me that outside the field of sociology the researcher focuses and sharpens his thrust into the unknown by precisely ruling out a fair number of situations, connections, or sequences that he is sure could not have been. The physical anthropologist, as we know at least since the Tuscany skull, should be open-minded about the possibility that apes derived from some sort of man long after man had appeared on this planet, but it is doubtful whether he should consider seriously the possibility that man might have been the domestic animal of dinosaur households. The essential difference, however, is this: no matter what the scientist assumes to have been possibly otherwise, beyond his experiment at least, this will not affect the present and future behavior of his subject-matter units, nor will it incite those subject-matter units to begin reinterpreting their own history in the vein of his hypothetical suggestion.

Albert Einstein alluded to this advantage for the natural scientist when he wrote that the Creator of the universe put into it many elusive mysteries which stall the physicist, but, as far as he saw, the Creator was not given to mischief. (Einstein wrote in German: *"aber raffiniert ist er nicht"; raffiniert,* not exactly a high-style German word, can best be translated into English as "studied malice, artful, crafty, wily, cunning"). The implication is that the physicist would be confounded if his subject matter, on learning how much he has learned about it, were to begin intelligently evading him. The exchange between researcher and subject matter in the field of social relations, however, more closely resembles the game between a detective and a suspect. The more the latter senses what the former has found out, the more he can adjust his subsequent moves toward maximum evasiveness.

If the studied attitude of the social scientist, announcing his relativism, reaches the intended target for study, the subject may start behaving very differently. In recent discussions of the criminal behavior of youths, there is a faint awareness that their conduct and self-image may already reflect the progressive theory of crime causation. Up to a certain point, this is the lot of nearly all approaches in the social sciences. It is very difficult to keep the subject from responding to the fact, or suspicion, that he is being studied for a purpose. Much has been written about this troublesome aspect of our work. Yet, why make things worse than they have to be?

Social scientists are eager to tell their subjects how relative everything is. Just a few trends might have gone differently, and the people of Philadelphia would be receiving aid for economic growth from Ghana. Contemporary textbooks in criminology are likely to show to any prospective criminal that in the final analysis there is really no absolute difference between criminal and "normal" action. True, it would be difficult to keep such notions from the general public. But it is obvious that few social scientists would keep their doubts to themselves even if they could. In other words, the relativism of the investigator becomes a constituent part of the self-conception of his subject. And if our search for a reasonable amount of truth hinges on the subject's constant response through time to our initial contact with him, it is possible that with a relativistic approach we shall learn what we ourselves have produced, in part at least. It may be, for instance, that we can discover a curious inhibition to enterprise in some culture. Instead of realizing that some of our proffered theories about the relativity of the factors in human achievement may have intensified latent barriers in that culture, our social scientists will turn back to their own economic history and try to reconstruct it, to treat as relative the principles upon which we have succeeded. In such ways there may be created a facile case supporting that other culture's need to achieve economic growth by means which run counter to both economic theory and common sense.

Some social scientists and some administrators trained by them,

I fear, cater in the undeveloped areas to erroneous, yet culture-congruent, notions about the origins and factors of economic and technological accomplishment, not, unhappily, aware that they thus contribute to the very blockages that in turn call for the application of certain social sciences. Joseph Schumpeter, in his chapter on "Marx the Sociologist," showed that Marx never found a full answer to the question "how capitalists came to be capitalists in the first instance or how they acquired that stock of goods which, according to Marxian doctrine, was necessary in order to enable them to start exploiting." [11] Marx, of course, rejected, as do many authors today, what he called the "bourgeois nursery tale" that "some people rather than others became, and are still becoming every day, capitalists by superior intelligence and energy in working and saving." Schumpeter agrees that Marx had no reason to concede that "the best man wins," that "the good boys come out on top"; but, after all, what does "best" or "good" mean until a standard for comparison has been achieved?

Schumpeter continues:

Nobody who looks at historical and contemporaneous fact with anything like an unbiased mind can fail to observe that this children's tale, while far from telling the whole truth, yet tells a good deal of it. Supernormal intelligence and energy account for industrial success and in particular for the founding of industrial positions in nine cases out of ten.[12]

But how did Marx explain the origin of inequality in productive possessions?

Force-robbery-subjugation of the masses facilitating their spoliation and the results of the pillage in turn facilitating subjugation—this was all right, of course, and admirably tallied with ideas common among intellectuals of all types, in our day still more than in the day of Marx. But evidently it does not solve the problem, which is to explain how some people acquired the power to subjugate and to rob.[13]

Schumpeter sums up the problem as follows:

The only frank way of expressing the situation is that from a Marxian standpoint there is no satisfactory explanation, that is to say, no explanation without resorting to non-Marxian elements suggestive of non-Marxian conclusions. This holds true even if we admit robbery to the utmost extent to which it is possible to do so without trespassing upon the sphere of the intellectual's folklore. Robbery actually entered into the building up of commercial capital at many times and places. Phoenician as well as English wealth offers familiar examples. But even then the Marxian explanation is inadequate because in the last resort successful robbery must rest on the personal superiority of the robbers. And as soon as this is admitted, a very different theory of social stratification suggests itself.[14]

And it is probably in the area of social and economic stratification where the scientifically unwarranted, but emotionally compelling, relativism of the social scientist plays him the worst tricks. A social scientist will often go on the most imaginative and longest detour if it helps him to avoid a fact that might make it more difficult for him to view stratification as a wholly relative and accidental phenomenon. Quite recently Wolfram Eberhard reviewed the lifework of the great anthropologist Richard Thurnwald (1869-1954) and wondered why that scholar, compared with his contemporary Boas, for instance, had remained relatively unknown in American scholarship. Eberhard attributed this gap in the diffusion of ideas to Thurnwald's matter-of-fact approach and assessment of social stratification. The all-pervading commitment to "ultimate egalitarianism," as Hughes calls it, precluded consideration and assimilation of a body of data and theories that might have endangered the doctrine.[15]

But can we call such timidity for a doctrine's sake a "scientific approach," "scholarship"? Is this a relativism for the sake of science any longer?

Everett C. Hughes spoke of the (self-imposed) "mandate" of the social scientist "to think that any social arrangement might be otherwise." This attitude, it would seem to me, implies a relativism entirely different from the methodological relativism of the scholar and scientist in other fields. There, the learned mind is always trying to establish additional segments of truth which then no longer need to be worried about. Perhaps we might even suspect that the progress of the nonsocial sciences, in part, came from this different approach to the object of study. The natural sciences, and a few other disciplines not yet wholly corrupted by the "philosophy" of the modern social scientist, can rely fully on the principle of the least effort. Every day almost, for the past hundred years and more, the exploration of at least one segment of reality could be declared settled. Of course, a major break-through in the future might conceivably call for a complete reconsideration; but generally this has to wait for a genius and his lucky star. The daily routine work of thousands of researchers is not consumed with feverish speculations and attempts trying to show that everything "might be otherwise." This is in healthy contrast to the social sciences where only too many writers are anxious to show, for dozens of social and economic arrangements, that they might have been (and therefore perhaps ought to be made) otherwise. Once certain valences of chemical elements were discovered, we cannot easily imagine a chemist occupying himself to find out that element X really would like to be attractive to element Y and that it is just too bad that the universe has not provided for that sympathy.

Of course, some scholarly and scientific procedures require a degree of relativity. For the most fruitful study of their possible relatedness most variables under investigation require mental insulation from absolutes outside. This we could call *methodological relativism;* it is a process, sometimes a mere procedure. It has its place in many fields. But it does not follow that this limited and temporary relativism of the scientific method ought to become the basis for public philosophy. It has no place in ethics. And yet, for all practical purposes, it is this methodological relativism that has spread in many areas outside of its original domain of operation. In this way it has affected the standards in our society.

This methodological relativism sometimes makes its first impact on the young college student who is overwhelmed by the import-ance—and seeming all-inclusiveness—of scientific relativity.

A British historian, H. Butterfield, summed it up very well when he wrote:

More serious still, it happens that the historian has to try to see Christian and Mohammedan . . . , conservative and socialist all somewhat from their own point of view . . . And some people have complained that by such a policy they have found themselves doomed to a perpetual relativism, as though between Christianity and Islam it were a matter of indifference—they have been trapped into a habit of mind that sees no values as absolute in themselves. This last point is particularly important and it equally affects the students of the natural sciences; because it is true that we fall into certain habits of mind and easily become the slaves of them, when in reality we only adopted them for the purpose of a particular technique.[16]

It seems possible that the relativistic attitude in some fields (education, law, politics, for instance) is still capitalizing on the prestige of disciplines in which the role of relativism has recently diminished.[17]

NOTES

1. Everett C. Hughes, "The Academic Mind: Two Views," *American Sociological Review,* XXIV (August, 1959), 570 f.
2. Robert K. Merton, *Social Theory and Social Structure* (Glencoe, 1957), p. 37: "In many quarters and with rising insistence, it has been charged that, whatever the intellectual worth of functional analysis, it is inevitably committed to a 'conservative' (even a 'reactionary') perspective. For some of these critics, functional analysis is little more than a latter-day version of the eighteenth-century doctrine of a basic and invariable identity of public and private interests. It is viewed as a secularized version of the doctrine set forth by Adam Smith, for example, when in his *Theory of Moral Sentiments,* he wrote of the 'harmonious order of nature, under divine guidance, which promotes the welfare of man through the operation of his individual propensities.' Thus, say these critics, functional theory is merely the orientation of the conservative social scientist who would defend the present order of things just as it is, and who would attack the advisability of change, however moderate. On this view, the functional analyst systematically ignores Tocqueville's warning not to confound the familiar with the necessary: '. . . what we call necessary institutions are often no more than institutions to which we have grown accustomed . . .' It remains yet to be shown that

functional analysis inevitably falls prey to this engaging fallacy, but, having reviewed the postulate of indispensability, we can well appreciate that *this* postulate, if adopted, might easily give rise to this ideological charge. Myrdal is one of the most recent and not the least typical among the critics who argue the inevitability of a conservative bias in functional analysis."

3. See, for instance, the reports on the one-sidedness of the U. S.-Soviet cultural exchange program, bluntly defined by the Soviet government as a one-way street to their benefit only, in the *New York Times* on September 9, 1959 ("Soviet Warned by U. S. Colleges"); November 1, 1959 ("West Denounced on Culture Issue"); December 25, 1959 ("U. S. Students Get Rebuffs in Soviet").

4. "Abel Suit Calls Evidence Illegal," *The New York Times,* November 10, 1959. In the Abel case the evidence was eventually allowed by a split 5-4 decision of the Supreme Court. See also *The New York Times,* February 26, 1960.

5. A. W. Kneucker, *Richtlinien einer Philosophie der Medizin* (Vienna: Verlag Wilhelm Maudrich, 1949), p. 89.

6. *National Review,* December 7, 1955, pp. 9-15. In June, 1959, ruling on New York's ban on the "Lady Chatterley" movie, Justice Potter Stewart wrote the prevailing opinion of the U.S. Supreme Court, which, as I read it, probably would now also protect the academic freedom of the hypothetical polygamist mentioned in the text. Justice Stewart wrote (*The New York Times,* June 30, 1959, p. 22 C):

   Yet the First Amendment's basic guarantee is of freedom to advocate ideas. The state, quite simply, has thus struck at the very heart of constitutionally protected liberty.

   It is contended that the state's action was justified because the motion picture attractively portrays a relationship which is contrary to the moral standards, the religious precepts, and the legal code of its citizenry.

   This argument misconceives what it is that the Constitution protects. Its guarantee is not confined to the expression of ideas that are conventional or shared by a majority. It protects advocacy of the opinion that adultery may sometimes be proper, no less than advocacy of socialism or the single tax. And in the realm of ideas it protects expression which is eloquent no less than that which is unconvincing.

7. H. D. Lasswell, speaking as President of the American Political Science Association, declared: "Apparently we are closer than most of us like to think to the production of species that occupy an intermediate position between man and the lower animals (or even plants) . . . A garrison police regime fully cognizant of science and technology can, in all probability, eventually aspire to biologize the class and caste system by selective breeding and training. Such beings can, in effect, be sown and harvested for specialized garrison-police services or for other chosen operations.

   "Great strides have been taken in brain design. Experimental models of robots have been built that solve problems of a rather complex order in a given environment. Some of these machines look after themselves to a degree, obtaining and using the raw materials required for energy and repairs. Already it is claimed that the function of reproducing its kind, and of interacting with others, can be in-built.

"The question then arises: Given our concern for human dignity, when do we wisely extend all or part of the Universal Declaration of Human Rights to these forms? When do we accept the humanoids—the species intermediate between lower species and man, and which may resemble us in physique as well as in the possession of an approximately equivalent central nervous and cortical system—as at least participants in the body politic? And at what point do we accept the incorporation of relatively self-perpetuating and mutually influencing 'supermachines' or 'exrobots' as entitled to the policies expressed in the Universal Declaration?

"It is obvious that we are not very well-equipped by cultural tradition to cope with these problems. A trait of our civilization is the intense sentimentalization of superficial differences in the visible format of the groupings to be found even within the human species. Recall the theologians, ethicists, and jurists who have devoted themselves to the elaboration of symbols to show that the white race alone is genuinely human and hence solely entitled to the dignity of freedom. Recall, too, the counterassertions, nourished in the soil of humiliation, that have arisen among ethnic groups who seek to overcome their contempt for themselves by dragging down the pretentions of the white imperialist.

"Let us recognize that the traditions of certain non-Western European civilizations are in some ways better adapted to the problem than the Greco-Roman and Judeo-Christian perspectives. They possess a relatively broad basis for identifying the primary ego of the individual with a self that includes more than strictly human species in the congregation of living forms. A world view that includes the possibility of reincarnation in lower animal shapes, for example, may prepare its devotees to empathize more readily with other than strictly human species and varieties. (Even they, however, may have their troubles with a mobile power plant in nearly human form.)" The *Scientific Monthly*, LXXXIV (January, 1957), 41 ff. The speech was also printed in the *American Political Science Review*, December, 1956.

8. Actually, on September 25, 1959 *The New York Times* reported a protest by African leaders against Europeans who played golf wearing shorts! AFRICANS BAR NUDISM—Uganda School Cracks Down on Half-Naked Europeans—Kampala, Uganda (UPI)—The African Technical Institute near Kampala has protested against the presence of "half-naked Europeans" on its sports fields.

    In a letter circulated to all householders in the area, the principal said: "It does not add to the tone of the institute to have Europeans, stripped to the waist, practicing golf on our playing fields."

9. Everett C. Hughes, "The Academic Mind: Two Views," American Sociological Review, XXIV (August, 1959), 570 f.

10. George P. Murdock, *Africa: Its Peoples and Their Culture History* (New York, 1959), pp. 388 f., writes: "The Lovedu, incidentally, demonstrate how unsafe it is to infer the functioning of a social system from its structure. With polygyny, patrilocal residence, patrilineal descent, local exogamy, and patriclans, the Lovedu structure brings together in a settlement a group of closely related men who have known one another since childhood and a disparate collection of adult women assembled from other localities and often initially strangers to each other. It might seem reasonable to infer from this a low and depressed status for the female sex. The exact reverse is true. By capitalizing upon certain possibilities inherent in the system, women have gained for themselves an enviable position.

"First of all, they have turned polygyny to their own advantage. Most African societies require a polygynous husband to treat his wives impartially. The Lovedu women insist on this with unusual strictness, so that if a man exhibits the slightest act of favoritism toward one wife, all of them 'gang up on him' and render his life miserable until he makes amends. Since a single wife lacks such a punitive weapon and can perhaps even be dominated with relative impunity, the first objective of a woman, when she marries, is to plan and scheme to obtain a second wife for her husband. Small wonder that the Lovedu women, when they observed the deterioration in status of the wives of the first monogamous converts to Christianity, presented a solid front against further missionary enterprise."

11. Joseph A. Schumpeter, *Capitalism, Socialism, and Democracy* (New York), pp. 16 ff.

12. *Ibid.*

13. *Ibid.*

14. *Ibid.*

15. Wolfram Eberhard, "In Memoriam Richard Thurnwald," *Revista do Museu Paulista,* Nova Série, IX (São Paulo, 1955), 298: "Thurnwald started out from the point from which many theories started, the obvious connections between the economic system of a society and its societal structure. But keeping away from the one-sidedness of economic determinism, he tried by careful field work, or by painstaking study of the reported data, to uncover the exact type of economic-social inter-relations. As one of the many studies of details, his article on the economic system of Buin is typical. Here, as in many other similar studies, he came to results which deviate widely from those of ideological speculations. Carefully he tried to gain general rules from his material. This led him to his theory of 'superstratification' (*Überlagerung*) as a factor of decisive importance. Although he makes it perfectly clear that stratified societies can originate by different processes of internal character, for example, specialization of some occupations in the hands of a family or a clan, such as iron-smelting, he attributes more importance to the conquest of one society by another, after which the conquering society becomes the upper, the conquered the lower, class in a basically

two-class society. Historical materialists naturally could not accept such a theory, because it largely disregarded economic factors and stressed the importance of leadership and of individuals. Resistance against this theory in the United States seems to stem basically from a feeling that to accept as 'normal' a hierarchical order of people in all higher organized societies would go against a belief in democracy."

16. H. Butterfield, *Christianity and History* (1949), pp. 20 f.

17. If a reader should think that I have drawn on several occasions a too extreme picture of the relativistic position, he might find the following paper illuminating:
H. J. McCloskey, "Practical Implications of the State's Right to Promote the Good," *Ethics,* LXXI (January, 1961). One sample may suffice (p. 111):

It would seem that there is no knockdown moral case for any one code; men of high intelligence, sincerity and good will assent to vastly different codes. To take monogamy for example: the present prevailing morality of monogamy in the Western world would seem to be partly merely conventional, partly a summary of the practical wisdom of men as to the most satisfactory institution, rather than a conclusion entailed by objective morality. Exponents of the natural law find it notoriously difficult to deduce monogamy from the natural law. All sorts of different, ingenious deductions are offered only to be rejected by others who despair and claim that monogamy is a dictate of divine and not of natural law. And if we look to moral theories other than the natural law theory, it is difficult to see how monogamy could be thought to be intrinsically morally preferable to any other system. Again it is clear that other family units are possible and that they work out well in other countries. Consider the polygamous system of the Chinese, the less successful but still impressively stable polygamous system of Mohammedan countries, the curious type of successive polygamy that is becoming most apparent in the U.S.A., and then the closer approximation to true monogamy in the U.K. and the U.S.S.R. On what grounds, in the light of such diversity of beliefs and practices, can a state claim to have sufficient knowledge and certainty to impose a rigid code in this general area? To consider a more specific case: it is difficult to see how there could be any justification at all for denying Mormons the right to polygamy if this were again to be commanded by their religion, if both sexes accepted their religion's ruling in this matter, and if serious social evils did not result.

5

Relativism from a Theological Standpoint

J. V. LANGMEAD CASSERLEY

The aim of this paper is neither to demonstrate a conclusion nor to verify a hypothesis, but merely to expound a point of view. If there is any argument at all that would constrain us to adopt the point of view expounded here and accept the panorama that it lays open to our gaze as the only, or at all events the most adequate, one available, it is the consideration that this point of view would permit, indeed compel us, to assert the covalidity and coreality of ideas that otherwise considered and approached might appear to be incompatible. The reconciliation of the truth that underlies ethical absolutism and the more obvious truth expressed in ethical relativism is, in my view, one of the most important tasks of contemporary theological thought.

The more profound and, to some, obscure case for ethical absolutism has been built up by the classical moral philosophers; the more obvious, conceivably superficial, and certainly empirical case for ethical relativism has emerged from the researches of the social anthropologists and the comparative sociologists. Ethical absolutism interprets ethical norms in terms of the will or commandment of God or in terms of natural law or in terms of a demonstrative rational morality like that of Immanuel Kant. There has been some argument among these three languages, but to the theologian it makes very little difference which we use. The rationalistic language indicates the form of the ethical absolute; the Stoic natural-law language, the breadth of its range; while reference to the Biblical will or commandment of God points to its source. Ethical relativism, on the other hand, tends to reduce ethics to comparative and descriptive sociology and regards the social order or culture pattern as that which creates rather than merely that which to some extent receives and transmits, while to some extent ignoring, the ethical norm.

As I have suggested, the case for some sort of ethical absolutism seems quite overwhelming to many philosophers, whereas the case for ethical relativism seems equally overwhelming to most social anthropologists. It is important to notice, however, that not all philosophers would necessarily subscribe to ethical absolutism, and that not all comparative sociologists are convinced by the case for ethical relativism. In neither discipline, in other words, is the case for the favorite hypothesis quite so overwhelming as it sometimes appears. There have, after all, been some philosophers, and some students of philosophical jurisprudence—not perhaps very good ones, but nevertheless by no means insignificant—who have rejected any kind of ethical absolutism for a more empirical and tentative approach. The Benthamite utilitarians are perhaps the best example, but this kind of approach goes back to some of the Greek sophists—sometimes attacked and sometimes satirized in the Platonic Dialogues. If man really is the measure of all things, there would appear to be no measure of man, and, oddly enough, no man either, only a large number of very different men.

Conversely, a more careful analysis of the kind of ethical data provided by social anthropology would indicate a greater degree of ethical convergence among the various culture patterns than at first sight appears. Most peoples, for example, appear to have a strong prejudice against offenses like murder and theft, at all events when crimes of this kind are committed by one member of the social group against another; the objection, of course, may not be so strong if these offenses are committed against a member of another social group. Again, the areas of life regulated by ethical norms and laws tend to be the same even where the regulations themselves differ. Life, property, sex, mating and marriage are almost never, perhaps never at all, entirely unpatterned by custom and law. The actual disciplines imposed may differ widely, but the perception that these things call for some kind of ethical regulation seems to be the perception of a universal human necessity.

In other words, we seek everywhere a genuine convergence and agreement underneath and within the extraordinary variety of moral customs, and to some comparative sociologists this fact of convergence is even more striking and evident than the more obvious fact of the variety and disagreement. The relativities that we can find in the morality of the more ancient and simpler peoples cloak and often disguise their absolutes, but the absolutes are nevertheless present, and often even visible to the eyes of the more careful investigator. It is certainly possible within the limits of comparative sociology to argue a case along these lines—indeed, I argued precisely this case in my own book, *Morals and Man in the Social Sciences,* but I do not propose to argue it again here. I merely mention it in this place in order to indicate that although the general tendency of social anthropology is in the direction of some sort of ethical and cultural relativism, this is nevertheless not an inevitable tendency; it is one that we choose rather than one to which we are forced by empirical facts that stubbornly refuse to tolerate any other interpretation.

We may sum up by saying that although the general tendency of moral philosophy and philosophical jurisprudence is toward some kind of absolutism, and the general tendency of social anthropology is toward some species of relativism, yet the actual situation within both specialized spheres is a little more fluid than we sometimes suppose, so that some combination of the two views will perhaps prove to be nearer the truth than any dogmatic assertion of either to the total exclusion of the other.

Perhaps two other important qualifications may be briefly noted before concluding this introductory section of my paper.

It is sometimes supposed that a doctrine of ethical relativity is peculiarly appropriate in an age of relativity physics. We may, I think, decisively set aside any impression of this kind as a merely accidental consequence of the choice of the same word to express very different ideas. There is no possible inference from relativity in physics to relativity in ethics. Relativity in physics does not in the least mean that there is no absolute point of view; it simply means that there is no hope that the physicist will ever command it. Relativity in ethics, on the other hand, does appear to imply that there is no absolute point of view where human morals are concerned. It could, of course, be argued that there are indeed ethical absolutes, but no prospect of our ever knowing what they are. (In fact, I have never seen such a point of view argued, but I suppose it is conceivable. Possibly a complete theological agnosticism would result in the acceptance of such a position.) But there is no reason to suppose that the ascertainable limits on the range of our thought in physics in any way imply or necessitate similar or parallel limitations of ethical vision.

Here, we come to a more important consideration. The case for some kind of absolutism in ethics and philosophical jurisprudence depends in part on our sense of what is needed in a world in which the people of the human race are pressed by circumstances into higher and higher degrees of unity. It is by no means insignificant that it was the experience of a new imperialism, the necessity of superintending a new universalism, pressed upon their attention by Hellenistic and Roman types of empire, that gradually led the Stoic lawyers to formulate their theory of natural law. Behind, above, and below the *ius gentium* loomed the impressive heights and depths of the *lex naturalis,* and it was only upon this latter that the laws of a polyglot cosmopolitan empire could be based. In these days, faced as we are with the same problem of the unity of the widely differentiated human race, on an even larger scale, the rejection of any kind of absolutism at all by some of our thinkers is, to say the least, extremely untimely and unhelpful. It is urgently necessary that we find our way back to some kind of absolutism, yet we shall do this best, not by dogmatically affirming absolutism and totally rejecting relativism, but rather by reaffirming absolutism in a context that understands and comprehends the validity of a wide degree of relativism, and even appreciates its humanizing contribution to the total synthesis.

I. *The Language of Morality*

In the discussion, definition, and description of moral questions, customs, and laws, we employ a variety of words, to each of which is attached a rather different shade of meaning, implying a different degree of ethical development and maturity. We speak of "custom," "convention"—with its opposite, "unconventional"—"moral" and "immoral," "legal" and "illegal" or "criminal," "ethical" and "unethical." Of these, "conventional" and "unconventional" are the most frankly relativistic pair of words. The convention is always a characteristic of some group pattern of life and behavior, and there is little or no suggestion that the conventional has any connection with any absolute ethical code. In this respect, morals are an advance upon conventions or customs. Morals, we may say, are conventions to some extent fused with, to some extent supplemented by, ethical considerations. Morality still contains many relative elements, but it also acknowledges in its own confused way some absolute elements; the danger is that in the confusion of ordinary morality so many relative elements will be mistaken for absolute ones. Morality is thus a kind of halfway house between the merely conventional and the purely ethical, to some extent an elevation of the conventional to the status of ethics, but to an almost equal extent a lowering of the ethical to the status of the conventional.

In recent years there has grown up a new habit of using the word "morals" in a merely descriptive sense, so that the morals of a people become a catalogue of what they actually do. But, in fact, the word "morals" is better considered as a description of what rightly or wrongly a people believe they ought to do, so that they experience some sense of shame and some fear of blame and censure when, as so frequently happens, they fail to live up to the standards of their own moral system. Morals, in other words, always retain a certain normative force, which is a sign of the influence of ethics on the morals of any mature society. Nevertheless, it is important to add that no living moral system ever is or can be purely ethical. Why this is so we shall examine a little later on. For the moment we shall content ourselves with noting that any living moral system must contain relative elements that affiliate ethics to the actual condition and locality of a people's life. The point for us to seize upon at the moment is that moral systems as we now know them contain so many relative elements that it is always plausible, although never quite convincing, to interpret them in purely relativistic terms.

In actual ethical development, however, there is always an appeal away from the moral, from what the people in their own conscious life regard as right, wholesome, and familiar, to the sterner demands of some more nearly absolute standard. This is very clear in the case of the Hebrew prophets in the Old Testament. Here we find a stern denunciation of merely revelant elements in the culture, and a strong appeal to absolute standards interpreted in this case in terms of the will and commandment of God. If the children of Israel would follow in the way of the prophets, the whole popular and familiar life of the people must be revolutionized. Even before the age of the prophets, we find Abraham ashamed of not having sacrificed his eldest son—an act hitherto accepted as part of ordinary morality—and substituting an animal for a human sacrifice. In such an example we must not let the fact that one relativity replaces another blind us to the genuine sense of an ethical imperative that causes this substitution. In the prophets themselves the conflict between mere mores, hardening into morals, and the ethical is too obvious for us to spend any time on it here.

But if the Hebrew prophets in the Old Testament are one of the best examples of the conflict between the ethical and the moral, they are very far from being the only ones. We can trace the same sort of confrontation in the Socrates of the Platonic Dialogues, and again in the building up by the Stoics of the theory of natural law, the idea of a morality that befits man as such and binds men universally, as distinct from the codes of custom and convention that have only local and temporary sway and bind groups of men only in their isolation from one another. Reinterpreted by the Christian theologian, the same doctrine of natural law was employed in the Middle Ages to evolve a genuine, ethically integrated Europe out of the tribal life and conventions that the Gothic peoples built up on the ashes and ruins of the Roman Empire. Most of the European peoples ended by accepting the Roman law, or some variant thereof, as the basis of their public and social life, but even those of Anglo-Saxon stock, tradition, and influence who built up the idea of the common law were greatly influenced by the notion of natural law, as we can see, for example, in the pages of the medieval lawyer, Bracton. At a later stage still, for example, in the French Revolution, the appeal is to some principle of rational law and morality against important customary elements that had still contrived to survive from the earlier Middle Ages.

I have already suggested that, from the point of view of ethics itself, it makes very little difference whether the prophetic consciousness employs language involving reference to the will and commandment of God or to the natural law or to some kind of principles of rational morality. Philosophically, of course, there may be some argument among these systems. Language referring to the will and commandment of God can easily absorb, use, and interpret the other two systems. But natural-law language may acquire a rather different shade of meaning when it is used by lawyers rather than theologians, and language involving reference to principles of rational morality, if and when it becomes utilitarian and empirical rather than genuinely rationalistic, may easily produce a new kind of relativism suited to the new kind of society evolving in a primarily scientific and technological age. The important thing, as it seems to me, is to keep the three types of language as close to and interchangeable with each other as possible, and this is primarily a task for the theological thinker, a task which contemporary Protestant theology, with its distaste for natural law and rationalism, tends most irresponsibly to ignore.

In suggesting that we understand and define morality as an

inevitable halfway house between convention or custom, on the one hand, and ethics on the other, as something that is not purely ethical in its nature, but sensitive and responsive to the government and lure of the ethical, I would not wish to depreciate in any way the role of morality in social life. Morality is always in part the adjustment of the people to its situation in time and space, to the degree of its technological equipment and cultural maturity. On the other hand, a people whose morality is to some, and to an increasing, extent dominated by a more universal ethic is essentially a people who acknowledge that the human situation is not merely a situation in time and space, but also a situation that relates time and space to some kind of universal will, purpose, law, and destiny. In this sense we may say that the role of all religion and all morality is to make man's life three- instead of two-dimensional. Three-dimensional life is certainly more stressful than two-dimensional life, but its drama is deeper and more enthralling, its purpose more stimulating to the intellect, its sense of destiny more evocative of the life of the spirit. Psychologically, three-dimensional life is more dangerous than two-dimensional life, but aesthetically, intellectually, and spiritually it is far more invigorating and satisfying; it is certainly one of the strains that press men on from the lower and simpler to the higher and more complex modes of civilization.

An example of this is the role of shame or guilt in a society with an elaborate moral code to some extent responsive to the demands of ethics. There is much talk nowadays of the dangers of a guilt complex, but the dangers of an innocence complex are far greater and yet hardly ever mentioned. Of course, we all recognize there is such a thing as a pathological sense of guilt, semihysterical guilt feelings which a man can experience and be appalled by, but which yet he is intellectually incapable of tracing to any particular cause or locating at any appropriate point in his life. There is nothing new about this. Moral theology has discussed and deplored the so-called "scrupulous conscience" for centuries. Normally, to feel guilty healthily is to know and acknowledge oneself guilty of this or that. There is, of course, a more generalized sense of unworthiness, a consciousness that life is unsatisfactory and fallen well below the level of its potentialities, which again can be understood and rationally accepted in terms of original sin. Always it is the intellectual act that is capable of interpreting guilt feelings by relating them to positive realities that preserves sanity in the midst of the sense of guilt.

The innocence complex, as it seems to me, is far more dangerous, and in modern life it tends to be rather more common. In the first place, it reduces man to a kind of animalism, for innocence, so far as we know, is the characteristic of animals rather than men; whereas guilt feelings have some sort of connection with profound realities, and hence at their best a deep sanity, innocence convictions estrange us from the reality about ourselves and immerse us in a realm of fantasy. The assertion of our innocence is a kind of unrationalized, indeed positively irrational dogma, which can only take possession of us through frequent repetition and exercises over us a kind of tranquilizing hypnotic power. Certainly the illusion of innocence is an enervating, unstimulating condition. I sometimes think it would be helpful to examine carefully the connection between some of the bad psychology and bad social anthropology so popular in contemporary intellectual circles and eighteenth-century utilitarianism, which is perhaps the weakest and most unconvincing type of ethical philosophy our culture has ever produced. The Polynesians are happier than we are, but the Polynesians have stayed Polynesians for a suspiciously long time! Anyhow, who under heaven wants to be a Polynesian? Far better to be Kierkegaard or Dostoevski, or, as another writer put it, better Socrates unhappy than a pig happy.

Perhaps we might conveniently conclude this section with a brief note on the terms "legal" and "illegal." Just as the ethical cannot entirely dominate or altogether exclude morality, so the moral cannot altogether dominate or exclude the legal. Medieval life tended to restrict the term "law" to the mere application and enforcement of natural law. St. Thomas Aquinas once went so far as to suggest that a positive law not based on natural law is really no law at all, but a species of tyranny. Hence, medieval parliamentary institutions were characteristically not legislatures.

Their business was to keep a watch on policy, particularly fiscal policy. Only occasionally did they enact new laws. Since the eighteenth century, however, parliamentary assemblies have become legislatures, and the consequence may well be that most modern societies have far too many laws for the health of law. Even declarations of policy and fiscal enactments are often given a statutory form that give them the appearance of law, and, of course, the purely relative elements of law (e.g., laws regulating the speed of automobiles) have grown to such mountainous proportions that the ethical elements are almost lost sight of, so that there are many transgressions of law of which it is now almost psychologically impossible for the ordinary citizen to feel guilty. This state of affairs is breeding a widespread disrespect for law, and many thinkers have suggested that law has nothing to do with ethics or morality at all. Now we should all agree that there are many things in ethics and morals that cannot be usefully or successfully legislated. For example, laws repressing and penalizing homosexual conduct are felt by people by no means tolerant of, or blind to, the homosexual problem to be rather pointless and unjustifiable in states that have long ceased, or perhaps never begun, to repress or penalize adultery by legal means. But the fact that the spheres of law and morality by no means coincide does not imply that they need not overlap, just as the spheres of morality and ethics, while never coincident, come to overlap more and more as peoples move toward a profounder ethical and moral maturity.

II. *The Nature of Absolutes*

The absolute is not only far more difficult to comprehend than the relative; it is also more difficult to define. Relativity is an inevitable consequence of our location in space and time. Our relation to local and temporary needs and structures begets ideas and customs that may well be unintelligible in other cultures. The relative is the relevant. Of course, we are all aware that this truth extends far beyond the context of ethics. Ethical relativism, after all, is only one particular aspect of a general cultural relativity.

It is inevitable in human existence that there should be many things—deeds done, thoughts thought, and passions deeply experienced—which cannot be understood or interpreted without some reference to the particular social and historical climate in which they were brought forth. *Relativism is not simply the observation of the many relativities, but the dogma that life is such that it can contain nothing else but relativities.* This reduces to the dogma that man is nothing but a spatiotemporal creature, and that his whole being is entirely contained within a network of spatiotemporal relations.

This is a doctrine, however, that we have every reason, right, and duty to call into question. There is in human consciousness an element of what we can only describe as a kind of self-transcendence. Within the unity of the human personality we certainly find or discover a *me* that is entirely involved in spatio-temporal relationships, but there is also an *I* that knows that *me* and marks its limitations, and, in knowing it, in some sense transcends it. Of course there is a sense in which the *I* that knows must be identified, and indeed identifies itself, with the *me* that is known. That is what makes self-consciousness unique among all forms of consciousness and transforms it into a peculiar, indeed unique, philosophical problem, the problem of the subject that identifies itself as the object, but the *I* is not identical with *me* in every conceivable sense. Freud uses the terms *superego* and *id,* but I prefer the more familiar terms *I* and *me* in order to place my observations within the systems of common speech and the traditions of Western philosophy and perhaps also in order to avoid the inevitable overtones of Freudian psychology. It is possible for the *I* to be scandalized by the mere temporality of the *me,* to be ashamed of its worldliness, to reproach the *me* for passively acquiescing in conditioning processes that from the standpoint of pure historical relativism seem not merely actual, but also inevitable.

Thus, in prophetic religion it is always ethnic religion and ethnic morality, the kind of religion and the kind of morality that may rightly be interpreted as mere aspects of the prevailing culture pattern, that are so bitterly attacked. The prophets really want their religion to be a genuine religion of the folk, but they do not want it to be a mere folk religion. The general tendency of the mass of mankind, caught up in the tension between ethnic and absolutist forces, is to interpret many of their relativities as absolutes. From the standpoint of the prophetic consciousness this constitutes idolatry. All this is still as true today as in Old Testament times. There is still a tendency, for example, for many groups of local Christians to twist their Bible or their theology ideologically in such a way as to suggest that the characteristic details of their own local culture patterns are, in fact, the revealed will of God, and it is still true that the prophetic consciousness within Christianity must be largely taken up with the ruthless exposure and repudiation of such illusions. But to observe that there is a tension in history and society between the absolute and the relative, and that indeed this tension is the source of the most dynamic elements of the historical and social process, is not necessarily to tell us what this absolute is.

Perhaps we may begin by observing that there is a distinction between the absolute, which is certainly never absolutely known, and that which is absolutely known, for the absolutely known is nearly always not merely a relativity, but even a triviality. For example, I know with an approximation to absolute certainty so close as to be in practice indistinguishable from it, whom I had the pleasure of dining with last night. It is true that I am aware of cases in which people have suffered delusions about matters like this, who have felt absolutely certain that they dined last night with, shall we say, the President, when, in fact, they had done nothing of the kind. I suppose I cannot entirely exclude the possibility that I am suffering from a delusion of this kind, and this consideration may prompt me to say that although I know that I know whom I dined with last night with absolute certainty, yet I must admit that there remains a slight doubt about the truth of what I know that I know. However, most of the time in matters of this kind my expression of some lingering doubt is little more than a formal and conventional doffing of the hat to a respected rule of the intellectual game, and the fact of the matter is that I do not really feel the slightest doubt whatsoever. In this case, doubt is a ritual rather than an existential matter. Professions of ritual doubt are part of the good manners of intellectual procedure. The trouble is that it is usually so difficult to give them any underlying reality.

We speak rightly of "relativities," in the plural, because there are so many of them and the phenomena described by this comprehensive term dictate this plural usage. The word "absolutes," however, is rather more questionable. Properly speaking, at all events so far as any kind of theistic philosophy is concerned, there are no absolutes, only *the Absolute,* in the singular, God, and a plurality of relationships to the absolute inevitably enjoyed by creatures inhabiting space and time that we may entitle with the paradoxical phrase *relative absolutes*—relative, that is, because they occur and recur in many different ways in space and time, and yet absolute because what they relate us to is *the Absolute.* Those who would cling to some kind of belief in absolutes apart from the philosophical context of a theism of this kind are usually reduced to what we may call a doctrine of propositional absolutes. This means that absolutes are ethical rules possessing the quality of self-evidence, claims upon men which we can perceive on simple inspection to be absolute and universal. No doubt for earlier believers in a doctrine of propositional absolutes, the analogy was with the axioms and definitions that gave a mathematician like Euclid his point of departure. Nowadays, however, we find a doctrine of this kind a more difficult one to accept, and perhaps one reason for the widespread skepticism about absolutes is the failure of various brands of nontheistic moral idealism to state a clear and convincing doctrine and definition of absolutes apart from its proper and appropriate philosophical background, theism.

If relativities are relationships with, and adjustments to, local and temporal realities, absolutes are the product of relationships with, and adjustments to, the absolute reality. The difficulty is, as we have seen, that the temporal realities are sometimes absolutely known, whereas the Absolute Reality cannot be absolutely known. My thesis is that while it is true that man as we know him is always man in the context of the local and the temporal, it is also true that man as he knows himself is always man face to face with the Absolute. The result is a tension that gives to the drama of human existence its peculiar aesthetic flavor and quality and releases in human society and history the characteristic energies that give history its dynamism and man his meaning. As I have suggested, this kind of tension is possible in human existence because man himself, in the dimension of his self-transcendence, is a kind of absolute. It is his own qualified, but within the limits of the qualifications very real, absoluteness that responds to the reality of that Absolute in whose presence the human drama is performed.

Spatiotemporal man, man in his relativities, can be skillful, talented, and clever, but man in conscious relation to the Absolute—he is genius. That is why the vehicle through which this sort of consciousness thrusts itself upon culture, intrudes itself into the orderly context of relativities, is always some kind of inspired individual. We must never let our amply justified contemporary belief that society is best organized politically along democratic lines mislead us into supposing that history is democratic. Always in history we are confronted by the essential role of what Toynbee has called "the creative minority." Since Carlyle's time there has been considerable criticism of his cult of the hero. This is perhaps because so many of Carlyle's heroes were not really heroes at all. The true hero is not the man who helps the folk to do what they want to do, but rather the man who forbids them to do what they want to do and then persuades them to desire new things that they never thought of desiring before. The true heroes of history are neither the conquerors nor the despots, certainly not the demagogues, but the prophets, the artists, and the poets, the men who strike against the grain of the relativities and foster in lesser mortals a dawning, precarious consciousness of what manner of men they truly are.

This gives us an important criterion in terms of which we may evaluate cultures. There are cultures so placidly successful as almost completely to exclude the prophetic challenge. There are others, on the contrary, that seem by their very nature to encourage and foster it, however strongly they may at the same time resist its challenging accusations. These latter are cultures in which the energizing tensions that make men discontented and unhappy and sporadically great, the tensions between the relativities and the absolutes, are sustained over a long period of time at their highest possible point. The supreme example of cultures of this kind is the culture that produced the Bible and the later cultures that have come under its purging, disillusioning spell. In this sense, we may distinguish between relatively closed and relatively open cultures and insist strongly on the higher value of the open kind of culture.

One of the reasons for those movements of contemporary thought that gladly embrace a pure relativism and tend to idealize the placidly successful, closed culture, in which it is possible for almost all men to be happily well adjusted, is the particular phase through which our own Western culture is passing. We find it more and more difficult to contain either intellectually or spiritually the tensions that have supplied us with our historic energies, and, no longer recognizing the realities from which these opposed forces inevitably spring, we experience the consequences of this internal conflict, not as energy and creativity, but as neurosis and psychic pain. In this mood we look back wistfully at the closed cultures that seem to our eyes so successful in keeping men little and happy.

The vogue of relativism is itself a culture symptom. The cost of being ourselves has amounted to so much bloodshed and so much pain that many of us have lost any strong robust belief in the goodness of being ourselves. There were times when Freud wondered whether the psychic deprivation that is the price of civilization had really been worth it, or, to refer to another and greater than Freud, ours is an age in which the burden of St. Paul's "weight of glory" seems so heavy that we begin to question whether we really need to bear it. Ours seems to us at the moment, at all events in our more depressed moods, a culture whose energetic, creative, revolutionary work is done, so that we are entering upon our placid, conservative phase. Of course, if this seems to be the truth to a sufficient number of us, it will inevitably become the truth, but that will not make it an inevitable truth; it will simply add one more episode to the sad history of the declinings and fallings of great cultures and peoples.

To be sure, in seeming to adopt and recommend a position of this kind, the relativist, in fact, sins against his own logic. We hear stories of students so mesmerized by the enthusiasm with which the professor of sociology lectures on the merits of the Polynesians and the kind of wisdom enshrined in their cultural institutions that they go out and try to live like Polynesians in the midst of our Western culture. But surely the consistent relativist should warn them that this is impossible. The cultural leopard cannot change his historic spots, at least not according to relativism. The burden of his message should be that just as the Polynesians must remain Polynesians, so we cannot choose but to be ourselves. Whatever excellence their kind of culture produces, it is an excellence that can never be ours.

Indeed, perhaps the true refutation of thoroughgoing relativism consists in the very possibility of history and comparative sociology. If relativism is true, we can never really know or understand other cultures in the present or in the history of other peoples in the past. All we can know, if relativism is true, is what the shape of our own culture compels us to think about these other cultures when we contemplate them.

It was this consideration that made Croce declare in his downright fashion—and, with greater qualification, Collingwood took much the same line—that all history is contemporary. We think we are understanding other ages and cultures better, whereas, in fact, all we are doing is understanding our own age and culture better. Yet Collingwood himself in his own historical work (especially the delightfully condensed and lucid historical sketches in his philosophical books) displayed an extraordinary aptitude for getting under the skin of dead philosophers and interpreting what they said as a series of answers to the questions that they themselves had asked. Compare, for example, Collingwood as a historian of philosophy with Bertrand Russell (*The History of Western Philosophy*). For all his pretentious talk about using the historical method, Russell persistently falls into the fallacy of treating the formulae of dead philosophers as a series of answers to the questions that Bertrand Russell asks himself whenever he philosophizes. Yet Collingwood, the professed relativist, never makes these mistakes.

I feel inclined, at this point, to quote something I wrote in my book, *The Christian in Philosophy* (p. 205), some years ago that seems to me to express very clearly the criticism I am pressing at this point.

The paradox of historical relativism may be expressed schematically as follows: Let X be a contemporary historian working under the influence of contemporary historical pressures X_1. Let Y be an historical character who lived and worked under the influence of historical conditions Y_1. X is engaged on the composition of Y's biography. In so far as X accepts the assumptions of historical relativism, he will endeavor to give us $Y - Y_1$, but if historical relativism is true, he can succeed only in giving us $Y - X_1$. It follows that to the extent to which he succeeds in carrying out his aim he refutes his own assumption. The doctrine of historical relativism can thus be regarded either as truth or as a useful and convenient methodological assumption, but it cannot be regarded as both. If it is true, it is useless; if it is useful, it is untrue.

But the fundamental difficulty about the hypothesis of relativism is even more profound than this. It is, indeed, an aspect of that perennial quarrel between science and philosophy which is even more acute in the case of the newer social sciences than in that of the older natural sciences. A hypothesis is adopted and affirmed if and when, to use the medieval phrase, it appears to us "to save the phenomena" better than any alternative hypothesis known to us. Now it is certainly true that the hypothesis of ethical and cultural relativism appears to us to save the phenomena revealed by the researches of ethnology and social anthropology better than any other with which we are acquainted. The difficulty is that the intellect rebels against regarding human phenomena of this kind as mere phenomena, mere appearances. In the natural sciences we are certainly confronted with mere phenomena. We are incapable of even imagining what a physical thing could be in itself apart from the fact of its appearance; but in the social sciences human events do not merely appear, and the intellect cannot grasp them merely by describing them. Human events not only appear, but mean, portend, imply, symbolize, and betray. For the intellect to grasp human events, it must diagnose and dramatically interpret as well as describe. It is when the phenomena of the social sciences are grasped by the intellect in this more profoundly appropriate way that the hypothesis that appeared to save the phenomena so long as we contented ourselves with a superficial and merely phenomenological survey is seen, in fact, no longer to save the phenomena at all. In other and briefer words, a merely and purely phenomenological attitude toward society and culture is rather like treating a poem printed in a book as a series of marks on blank paper and trying to interpret it by embarking on a chemical analysis of the ink.

Yet, to say all this is not to deny the reality of the relative and the inevitability of purely relative elements in social life. It is a mistake to depict man as though he were a merely spatiotemporal being. The concepts of space and time and history and culture are achievements of the human mind, not prison houses for the human spirit. We are in error if we mistake the products of human thought for self-existent realities that at the same time condition the thought process that gave them birth. This is to mistake our concepts for factual percepts. Yet, at the same time, man really is in space and time, and thus some part of his life, at least, is very largely concerned with the making of some sort of adjustment with his spatiotemporal situation.

Traditional Christian thought, despite its general and inevitable tendency toward absolutism, has usually shown itself well aware of the inevitability of relativism. Thus, the early Church Fathers distinguished carefully between absolute natural law— that which God wills for His creation in all circumstances—and relative natural law—that which God wills for His creation in these particular circumstances. At a later date St. Thomas Aquinas was well aware of the importance of custom and relativity in social life and insisted that the reign of custom should not be interfered with except where manifestly necessary. Of course, this

point of view can easily become a sanction for an overly conservative attitude, but totally to ignore the truth it contains may produce a ruthless and inhuman radicalism. On the whole, it is the
people that have most of all relied on a system of ethics composed
exclusively of universal rationalistic moral principles who have
been intolerant of what they have called a customary or traditional
ethic, which they have contrasted again and again with the lu-
cidity of what they would regard as a rational ethic. In the case
of any human community actually conducting its business in
space and time, the ethics that founds itself on the universal,
rational, natural law expressing the will of God can never be the
whole of ethics. On the contrary, the task of absolute ethics is
not to destroy or supplant the relativities, but rather to guide,
shape, control, and reform.

A successful living ethical system is a mating and fusion of
absolute with relative elements. In our earlier illustration of
Abraham's ultimate refusal to sacrifice the "male that openeth the
womb," we saw that the actual consequence of this victory of the
absolute principle was the substitution of one relativity for another. And, of course, this is always true in the case of all prophetic movements. The prophets want the people to embrace the
absolute, but this always means that they desire the absolute to
acquire something of the force, familiarity and "at-homeness"
with the life of the people that is characteristic of the relative.
This is the way in which actual moral progress and development
takes place. It could not occur without the prophetic challenge
that confronts men with the absolute. But neither could it occur
without the popular response that domesticates the absolute and
gives it the outward appearance of a relativity.

So it is, to use a Christian phrase, that in the course of moral
development the absolute again and again becomes incarnate in
the relative to such an extent that superficial and indiscriminating
observers, the crass empiricists who suppose that everything is
what it looks like, will again and again be led into the error of
supposing that the absolute is the relative. Philosophically speaking, we may perhaps describe incarnation as a trick to deceive the
vulgar empiricists. In the New Testament, of course, it was the

devils that haunt human civilization who were deceived by the incarnation, but perhaps the New Testament was right not to distinguish between devils and bedeviling empiricists too carefully.

III. *The Ultimate Relativity of the Absolute*

But in this sketch of a point of view we have still left the ultimate reconciliation untouched. We have seen that the drama of human ethical development demands interpretation in terms of a conflict between absolute and relative. Nor is this a conflict that can conceivably result in the total victory of either over the other. So long as men are men in space and time, men in history, men in terrestrial society, absolute and relative elements must necessarily coexist in space and time, growing together until the harvest. But we have still to ask the question: What is the absolute itself relative to?

It might, at first sight, appear that the absolute can only be the verdict of some kind of rationalistic or religious dogmatism that is simply so because it must be so, and there is nothing more to be said. I do not believe that this is in fact the case. Those who believe in the possibility of an absolute religion, which I take to mean not an absolute human religiousness, but a religious system based upon some kind of divine revelation, will feel compelled to say that the absolute ethic must be the kind of ethic that inevitably accompanies, is implied and demanded by that religious system. So that the absolute ethic turns out to be relative to, a relevant adjustment to, the ultimate reality that is manifested by, loved and worshipped in that religious system. If a relativity is a relevant adjustment to the spatiotemporal condition of man, an absolute is a relevant adjustment to the eternal condition of man.

Now I do not wish to say anything here about the possibility of an absolute religious system. It is obviously a possibility in which some of us believe, while to others it is inconceivable and unimaginable. Certainly we must all agree that it is not *prima facie* impossible. As to whether it is actual or not, there are obviously wide varieties of opinion. I would merely say two things. First, to the genuinely religious philosopher who, like Jaspers, is apt to believe in the possibility of some kind of religious philosophy or philosophic religion that enables him to dispense with and rise superior to all positive historical religious systems, I would say, "It is a grossly unphilosophical error to suppose that the highest reality that philosophy can embrace belongs to philosophy alone and reveals itself exclusively to philosophical analysis. All realities have philosophical aspects, but there is no reality of which the philosophical aspect is the only aspect. The philosopher knows nothing that was not known before. His contribution to culture is not a new datum or a new observation. What he does is to know the things that were known before in a new way. The recognition of this truth goes back at least to Socrates. To put it in another way, philosophy indeed embraces existence, but existence is never philosophical. Indeed, how could it be?"

To the mere empiricist, who has almost become accustomed to being the least intelligent member of any discussion in which he takes part, I would say, "In a manner that you never dreamed or foresaw you are ultimately right after all! The ultimate sanction of a genuine empiricism is the positivity of revealed religion. The ultimate fact, the ultimate reality, can be analyzed and, within severely circumscribed limits, comprehended by the idea, but it can never be dissipated into ideas. In the beginning and at the end we find, not an idea, but a Fact, and a genuine moral idealism is not the ethical counterpart of a philosophical idealism; rather it is a relationship to that Ultimate Fact that was in the beginning, is now, and ever shall be."

6

Epistemological Relativism in the Sciences of Human Action

LUDWIG VON MISES

I

Up to the eighteenth century, historians paid little or no attention to the epistemological problems of their craft. In dealing with the subject of their studies, they again and again referred to some regularities that—as they themselves and their public assumed—are valid for any kind of human action irrespective of the time and the geographical scene of the action as well as of the actors' personal qualities and ideas. But they did not raise the question whether these regularities were of an extraneous character or inherent in the very nature of human action. They knew very well that man is not able to attain all that he wants to attain. But they did not ask whether the limits of a man's power are completely described by reference to the laws of nature and to the Deity's miraculous interference with them, on the one hand, and to the superior power of more puissant men, on the other hand.

Like all other people, the historians too distinguished between behavior complying with the moral law and behavior violating it. But, like all other people, they were fully aware of the fact that nonobservance of the laws of ethics did not necessarily—in this life—result in failure to attain the ends sought. Whatever may happen to the sinner in the life hereafter and on the day of the Last Judgment, the historian could not help realizing that on earth he could sometimes fare very well, much better than many pious fellow men.

Entirely new perspectives were opened when the economists discovered that there prevails a regularity in the sequence and interdependence of market phenomena. It was the first step to a general theory of human action, praxeology. For the first time people became aware of the fact that, in order to succeed, human action must comply not only with what are called the laws of nature, but also with specific laws of human action. There are things that even the most efficient constabulary of a formidable government cannot bring about, although they may not appear impossible from the point of view of the natural sciences.

It was obvious that the claims of this new science could not fail to give offense from three points of view. There were first of all the governments. Despots as well as democratic majorities are not pleased to learn that their might is not absolute. Again and again they embark upon policies that are doomed to failure and fail because they disregard the laws of economics. But they do not learn the lesson. Instead they employ hosts of pseudo economists to discredit the "abstract," i.e., in their terminology, vain teachings of sound economics.

Then there are ethical doctrines that charge economics with ethical materialism. As they see it, economics teaches that man ought to aim exclusively or first of all at satisfying the appetites of the senses. They stubbornly refuse to learn that economics is neutral with regard to the choice of ultimate ends as it deals only with the methods for the attainment of ends chosen, whatever these ends may be.

There are, finally, authors who reject economics on account of its alleged "unhistorical approach." The economists claim absolute validity for what they call the laws of economics; they assert that in the course of human affairs something is at work that remains unchanged in the flux of historical events. In the opinion of many authors this is an unwarranted thesis, the acceptance of which must hopelessly muddle the work of the historians.

In dealing with this brand of relativism, we must take into account that its popularity was not due to epistemological, but to practical considerations. Economics pointed out that many cherished policies cannot result in the effects aimed at by the governments that resorted to them, but bring about other effects that—from the point of view of those who advocated and applied those policies—were even more unsatisfactory than the conditions that they were designed to alter. No other conclusion could be inferred from these teachings than that these measures were contrary to purpose and that their repeal would benefit the rightly understood or long-run interests of all the people. This explains why all those whose short-run interests were favored by these measures bitterly criticized the "dismal science." The epistemological qualms of some philosophers and historians met with an enthusiastic response on the part of aristocrats and landowners who wanted to preserve their old privileges and on the part of small business and employees who were intent upon acquiring new privileges. The European "historical schools" and American Institutionalism won political and popular support, which is, in general, denied to theoretical doctrines.

However, the establishment of this fact must not induce us to belittle the seriousness and importance of the problems involved. Epistemological relativism as expressed in the writings of some of the historicists, e.g., Karl Knies and Max Weber, was not motivated by political zeal. These two outstanding representatives of historicism were, as far as this was humanly possible in the milieu of the German universities of their age, free from an emotional predilection in favor of interventionist policies and from chauvinistic prejudice against the foreign, i.e., British, French, and Austrian science of economics. Besides, Knies wrote a remarkable book on money and credit, and Weber gave the deathblow to the methods applied by the schools of Schmoller and Brentano by demonstrating the unscientific character of judgments of value. There were certainly in the argumentation of the champions of historical relativism points that call for an elucidation.

II

Before entering into an analysis of the objections raised against the "absolutism" of economics, it is necessary to point out that the rejection of economics by epistemological relativism has nothing to do with the positivist rejection of the methods actually used by historians.

In the opinion of positivism, the work of the historians is mere gossip or, at best, the accumulation of a vast amount of material that they do not know how to use. What is needed is a science of the laws that determine what happens in history. Such a science has to be developed by the same methods of research that made it possible to develop out of experience the science of physics.

The refutation of the positivistic doctrine concerning history is an achievement of several German philosophers, first of all of Wilhelm Windelband and of Heinrich Rickert. They pointed out in what the fundamental difference between history, the record of human action, and the natural sciences consists. Human action is purposive, it aims at the attainment of definite ends chosen, it cannot be treated without reference to these ends, and history is in this sense—we must emphasize, *only* in this sense —finalistic. But to the natural sciences the concept of ends and final causes is foreign.

Then there is a second fundamental difference. In the natural sciences man is able to observe in the laboratory experiment the effects brought about by a change in one factor only, all other factors the alteration of which could possibly produce effects remaining unchanged. This makes it possible to find what the natural sciences call experimentally established facts of experience. No such technique of research is available in the field of human action. Every experience concerning human action is historical, i.e., an experience of complex phenomena, of changes produced by the joint operation of a multitude of factors. Such an experience cannot produce "facts" in the sense in which this term is employed in the natural sciences. It can neither verify nor falsify any theorem. It would remain an inexplicable puzzle if it could not be interpreted by dint of a theory that had been derived from other sources than historical experience.

Now, of course, neither Rickert and the other authors of the group to which he belonged, the "Southwestern German philosophers," nor the historians who shared their conception went as far as this last conclusion. To them, professors of German universities at the end of the nineteenth and the beginning of the twentieth century, the very idea that there could be any science claiming for its theses universal validity for all human action irrespective of time, geography, and the racial and national charactersistics of people remained unknown. For men living in the spiritual climate of the second German Reich, it was an understood thing that the pretensions of "abstract" economic theory were vain and that German *wirtschaftliche Staatswissenschaften* (the economic aspects of political science), an entirely historical discipline, had replaced the inane generalizations of the school of Hume, Adam Smith, and Ricardo. As they saw it, human action— apart from theology, ethics and jurisprudence—could be dealt with scientifically only by history. Their radical empiricism prevented them from paying any attention to the possibility of an a priori science of human action.

The positivist dogma that Dilthey, Windelband, Rickert and their followers demolished was not relativistic. It postulated a science—sociology—that would derive from the treatment of the empirical data provided by history a body of knowledge that would render to the mind the same services with regard to human action that physics renders with regard to events in the sphere of nature. These German philosophers demonstrated that such a general science of action could not be elaborated by a posteriori reasoning. The idea that it could be the product of a priori reasoning did not occur to them.

III

The deficiency of the work of the classical economists consisted in their attempt to draw a sharp line of demarcation between "purely economic activities" and all other human concerns

and actions. Their great feat was the discovery that there prevails
in the concatenation and sequence of market phenomena a regularity that can be compared to the regularity in the concatenation
and sequence of natural events. Yet, in dealing with the market
and its exchange ratios, they were baffled by their failure to solve
the problem of valuation. In interpersonal exchange transactions
objects are not valued according to their utility, they thought,
because otherwise "iron" would be valued more highly than
"gold." They did not see that the apparent paradox was due only
to the vicious way they formulated the question. Value judgments of acting men do not refer to "iron" or to "gold" as such,
but always to definite quantities of each of these metals between
which the actor is forced to choose because he cannot have both
of them. The classical economists failed to find the law of marginal utility. This shortcoming prevented them from tracing
market phenomena back to the decisions of the consumers. They
could deal only with the actions of the businessmen, for whom
the valuations of the consumers are merely data. The famous
formula "to buy on the cheapest and to sell on the dearest
market" makes sense only for the businessman. It is meaningless
for the consumer.

Thus forced to restrict their analysis to business activities, the
classical economists constructed the concept of a science of wealth
or the production and distribution of wealth. Wealth, according
to this definition meant all that could be bought or sold. The
endeavors to get wealth were seen as a separate sphere of activities.
All other human concerns appeared from the vantage point of this
science merely as disturbing elements.

Actually, few classical economists were content with this cir-
cumscription of the scope of economics. But their search for a
more satisfactory concept could not succeed before the margin-
alists substituted the theory of subjective value for the various
abortive attempts of the classical economists and their epigones.
As long as the study of the production and distribution of wealth
was considered as the subject matter of economic analysis, one
had to distinguish between the economic and the noneconomic

actions of men. Then economics appeared as a branch of knowledge that dealt with only one segment of human action. There were, outside of this field, actions about which the economists had nothing to say. It was precisely the fact that the adepts of the new science did not deal with all those concerns of man which in their eyes were qualified as extraeconomic that appeared to many outsiders as a depreciation of these matters dictated by an insolent materialistic bias.

Things are different for modern economics, with its doctrine of the subjective interpretation of valuation. In its context the distinction between economic and allegedly noneconomic ends becomes meaningless. The value judgments of the ultimate consumers express not only the striving after more tangible material goods, but no less the striving after all other human concerns. The narrow viewpoint of a science of—material—wealth is surpassed. Out of the discipline of wealth evolves a general theory of all choices made by acting men, a general theory of every kind of human action, praxeology. In their behavior on the market people evidence not only their wishes to acquire more material goods, but no less all their other preferences. Market prices reflect not only the "materialistic side" of man, but his philosophical, ethical, and religious ideas as well. The observance of religious commandments—to build and maintain houses of worship, to cease working on holidays, to avoid certain foods either always or on specific days and weeks, to abstain from intoxicating beverages and tobacco, to assist those in need, and many others—is one of the factors that determines the supply of and the demand for consumers' goods and thereby the conduct of business. Praxeology is neutral with regard to the ultimate ends that the individuals want to attain. It does not deal with ultimate ends, but with the means chosen for their attainment. It is merely interested in the question whether or not the means resorted to are fitted to attain the ends sought.

The enormous quantity of antieconomic literature published in the last hundred and fifty years turns around one argument only. Its authors repeat again and again that man as he really is and acts strives not only after more material amenities, but also after some other—higher or loftier or ideal—aims. From this point of view the self-styled Historical School attacked what they called the absolutism of the economic doctrine and advocated a relativistic approach. It is not the theme of this paper to investigate whether the economists of the classical school and their epigones were really guilty of having neglected to pay due attention to the nonmaterialistic concerns of man. But it is to be emphasized that all the objections raised by the Historical School, e.g., by Knies in his famous book,[1] are futile and invalid with regard to the teachings of modern economics.

It is customary in German political literature to distinguish between an older and a later Historical School. As the champions of the older school, Roscher, Bruno Hildebrand, and Knies are named. The younger school consists of the followers of Schmoller who after the establishment of the Reich in 1870 held the chairs of economics at the German universities. This way of subdividing into periods the history of ideas is an outcome of the parochialism that induced German authors to slight all that was accomplished abroad. They failed to realize that the "historical" opposition against what was called the absolutism of economics was inaugurated outside of Germany. Its outstanding representative was Sismondi rather than Roscher and Hildebrand. But it is much more important to realize the fact that all those who in Germany as well as in other countries after the publication of the books of Jevons, Menger, and Walras criticized economic doctrine on account of its alleged materialism were fighting against windmills.

IV

Max Weber's concept of a general science of human action— to which he applied the name of sociology—no longer refers to the distinction between economic action and other activities. But Weber virtually endorsed the objections raised by historicism against economics by distinguishing between genuinely rational action, on the one hand, and other kinds of action. His doctrine is so closely connected with some untranslatable peculiarities of the German language that is rather difficult to expound it in English.

The distinction that Weber makes between "social action" and other action is, from the point of view of our problem, of little importance. The main thing is that Weber quite correctly distinguishes between *sinnhaftes Handeln* and the merely physiologically determined reactions of the human body. *Sinnhaftes Handeln* is directed by the *Sinn* the acting individual attaches to it; we would have to translate: by the meaning the actor attaches to it and by the end he wants to attain by it. This definition would appear as a clear distinction between human action, the striving after a definite end, on the one hand, and the physiological—quasi-automatic—reactions of the nerves and cells of the human body, on the other hand. But then Weber goes on to distinguish within the class of *sinnhaftes Handeln* four different subclasses. The first of these subclasses is called *zweckrationales Handeln* and is defined as action aiming at a definite end. The second subclass is called *wertrationales Handeln* and is defined as action determined by the belief in the unconditional intrinsic value *(unbedingter Eigenwert)* of a certain way of conduct as such, without regard to its success, from the point of view of ethics, aesthetics, religion, or other principles. What Weber failed to see is the fact that also the striving after compliance with definite ethical, aesthetical, and religious ideas is no less an end than any other end that men may try to attain. A Catholic who crosses himself, a Jew who abstains from food and drink on the Day of Atonement, a lover of music who forgoes dinner in order to listen to a Beethoven symphony, all aim at ends that from their point of view are more desirable than what they have to renounce in order to get what they want. Only a personal judgment of value can deny to their actions the qualification *zweckrational*, i.e., aiming at a definite end. And what in Weber's definition do the words "without regard to its success" mean? The Catholic crosses himself because he considers such behavior as one link in a chain of conduct that will lead him to what for him is the most important success of man's earthly pilgrimage. It is tragic that Max Weber, the eminent historian of religion, the man who tried to free German sociological thought from its naive commitment to judgments of value, failed to see the contradictions of his doctrine.[2]

Other attempts to distinguish between rational action and nonrational or irrational action were likewise based on crass misconstructions and failed. Most of them called "irrational" conduct directed by mistaken ideas and expectations concerning the effects of definite methods of procedure. Thus, magic practices are today styled as irrational. They were certainly not fitted to attain the ends sought. However, the people who resorted to them believed that they were the right technique in the same way in which physicians up to the middle of the past century believed that bleeding is a method for preventing and curing various diseases. In speaking of human action, we have in mind conduct that, in the opinion of the actor, is best fitted to attain an end he wants to attain, whether or not this opinion is also held by a better informed spectator or historian. The way in which contemporary physicians deal with cancer is not irrational, although we hope that one day more efficacious therapeutic and prophylactic methods will be discovered. A report concerning other people's actions is confusing if it applies the term irrational to the activities of people whose knowledge was less perfect than that of the reporter. As no reporter can claim for himself omniscience, he would at least have to add to his qualification of an action as irrational the proviso "from my personal point of view."

Another way in which the epithet "irrational" is often employed refers, not to the means, but to the ends of definite modes of conduct. Thus, some authors call, either approvingly or disapprovingly, "irrational" the behavior of people who prefer religious concerns, national independence, or other goals commonly called noneconomic to a more abundant supply of material satisfactions. Against this highly inexpedient and confusing terminology there is need to emphasize again and again the fact that no man is called to sit in judgment on other people's judgments of value concerning ultimate ends. When the Huguenots preferred the loss of all their earthly possessions, the most cruel punishments, and exile to the adoption of a creed that in their opinion was idolatrous, their behavior was not "irrational." Neither was Louis XIV "irrational" when he deprived his realm of many of its most worthy citizens in order to comply with the precepts of his conscience. The historian may disagree with the ultimate ends that the persecutors and their victims were aiming at. But this does not entitle him to call the means to which they resorted in order to attain their ends irrational. The terms "rational" and "irrational" are just as much out of place when applied to ends as when applied to means. With regard to ultimate ends, all that a mortal man can assert is approval or disapproval from the point of view of his own judgments of value. With regard to means there is only one question, viz., whether or not they are fitted to attain the ends sought.

Most of our contemporaries are guided by the idea that it is the worst of all crimes to force a man, by recourse to violence, to behave according to the commandments of a religious or political doctrine that he despises. But the historian has to record the fact that there were ages in which only a minority shared this conviction, and unspeakable horrors were committed by fanatical princes or majorities. He is right in pointing out that Louis XIV, in outlawing Protestantism, inflicted irreparable evils on the French nation. But he must not forget to add that the King was not aware of these consequences of his policy and that, even if he had anticipated them, he would perhaps nonetheless have considered the attainment of religious uniformity as a good for which the price paid was not too high.

The surgeons who accompanied the armies of ages past did their best to save the lives of the wounded warriors. But their therapeutic knowledge was pitifully inadequate. They bled the injured man whom only a transfusion of blood could have saved and thus virtually killed him. Because of their ignorance, their treatment was contrary to purpose. It would be misleading and inexpedient to call it irrational. Present-day doctors are not irrational, although probably better informed physicians of the future will qualify some of their therapeutical techniques as detrimental and contrary to purpose.

V

Whenever the distinction between rational and irrational is applied to ultimate ends, the meaning is that the judgments of value underlying the choice of the end in question meet with approval or disapproval on the part of the speaker or writer. Now the promulgation of judgments of value is not the business of a man in his capacity as a praxeologist, economist, or historian. It is rather the task of religion, metaphysics, or ethics. History of religion is not theology, and theology is not history of religion.

When the distinction between rational and irrational is applied to means, the meaning is that the speaker or writer asserts that the means in question are not serving their purpose, i.e., that they are not fit to attain the ends sought by the people who resort to such means. It is certainly one of the main tasks of history to deal with the serviceableness of the means people employed in their endeavors to attain the ends sought. It is also certain that the main practical goal of praxeology and its hitherto best developed part, economics, is to distinguish between means that are fit to attain the ends sought and those that are not. But it is, as has been pointed out, not expedient and rather confusing to use for this distinction the terms "rational" and "irrational." It is more appropriate to speak of means answering the intended purpose and those not answering it.

This holds true also with regard to the way in which the terms "rational" and "irrational" are employed by psychoanalysts. They "call behavior irrational that is predominantly emotional or instinctual," and furthermore "all unconscious functions" and in this sense distinguish between "irrational (instinctual or emotional) action as opposed to rational action, and irrational as opposed to rational thinking." [3] Whether this terminology is expedient for the treatment of the therapeutic problems of psychoanalysis may be left to the psychoanalysts. From the praxeological point of view, the spontaneous reactions of the human body's organs and the activity of instinctual drives are not action. On the other hand, it is manifestly the outcome of a personal judgment of value to call emotional actions—e.g., the action with which a man may react to the awareness of his fellowmen's distress—irrational. It is further obvious that no other meaning can be ascribed to the term "irrational thinking" than that it is logically invalid thinking and leads to erroneous conclusions.

VI

The philosophy of historical relativism—historicism—fails to see the fact that there is something unchanging that, on the one hand, constitutes the sphere of history or historical events as distinct from the spheres of other events and, on the other hand, enables man to deal with these events, i.e., to record their succession and to try to find out their concatenation, in other words, to understand them. This unchanging phenomenon is the fact that man is not indifferent to the state of his environment (including the conditions of his own body) and that he tries, as far as it is possible for him to do so, to substitute by purposive action a state that he likes better for a state he likes less. In a word: man acts. This alone distinguishes human history from the history of changes going on outside the field of human action, from the study of "natural history" and its various subdivisions as, e.g., geology or the evolution of various species of living beings. In human history we are dealing with the ends aimed at by the actors, that is, with final causes.[4] In natural history, as in the other branches of the natural sciences, we do not know anything about final causes.

All human wisdom, science, and knowledge deal only with the segment of the universe that can be perceived and studied by the human mind. In speaking of human action as something unchanging, we refer to the conditions of this segment only. There are authors who assume that the state of the universe—the cosmos—could change in a way about which we simply do not know anything and that all that our natural sciences say about the behavior of sodium and levers, for example, may be invalid under this new state. In this sense they deny "any kind of universality to chemical and mechanical statements" and suggest that they be treated "as historical ones." [5] With this brand of agnostic hyper-historicism that deals in its statements with visionary conditions about which—as they freely admit—we do not know and cannot know anything, reason and science have no quarrel.

Thinking man does not look upon the world with a mind that is, as it were, a Lockian paper upon which reality writes its own story. The paper of his mind is of a special quality that enables man to transform the raw material of sensation into perception and the perceptual data into an image of reality. It is precisely this specific quality or power of his intellect—the logical structure of his mind—that provides man with the faculty of seeing more in the world than nonhuman beings see. This power is instrumental in the development of the natural sciences. But it alone would not enable man to discover in the behavior of his fellow men more than he can see in the behavior of stars or of stones, in that of amoebae or in that of elephants.

In dealing with his fellow men, the individual resorts not only to the a priori of logic, but besides to the praxeological a priori. Himself an acting being, he knows what it means to strive after ends chosen. He sees more in the agitation and the stir of his fellow men than in the changes occurring in his nonhuman environment. He can search for the ends their conduct is aiming at. There is something that distinguishes in his eyes the movements of germs in a liquid as observed in the microscope from the movements of the individuals in the crowd he may observe in the rush hour at New York's Grand Central Terminal. He knows that there is some "sense" in a man's running around or sitting still. He looks upon his human environment with a mental equipment that is not required or, to say it more precisely, is downright obstructive in endeavors to explore the state of his nonhuman environment. This specific mental equipment is the praxeological a priori.

The radical empiricism of the historicists went astray in ignoring this fact. No report about any man's conduct can do without reference to the praxeological a priori. There is something that is absolutely valid for all human action irrespective of time, geography, and the racial, national, and cultural characteristics of the actors. There is no human action that can be dealt with without reference to the categorial concepts of ends and means, of success and failure, of costs, of profit or loss. What the Ricardian law of association, better known as the law of comparative cost, describes is absolutely valid for any kind of voluntary human cooperation under the division of labor. What the much derided economic laws describe is precisely what must always and everywhere happen provided the special conditions presupposed by them are present.

Willy nilly, people realize that there are things they cannot achieve because they are contrary to the laws of nature. But they are loath to admit that there are things that even the most powerful government cannot achieve because they are contrary to praxeological law.

VII

Different from the case of the historians who are loath to take cognizance of the praxeological a priori is the case of the authors who belong to the various historical, "realistic," and institutional schools of economics. If these scholars were consistent, they would limit their studies to what is called economic history; they would deal exclusively with the past and would carefully abstain from asserting anything about the future. Prediction about events to come can be made only on the ground of knowledge of a regularity in the succession of events that is valid for every action irrespective of the time and the geographical and cultural conditions of its occurrence. Whatever economists committed to historicism or institutionalism do, whether they advise their own governments or those of backward foreign countries, is self-contradictory. If there is no universal law that describes the necessary effects of definite ways of acting, nothing can be predicted and no measure to bring about any definite results can be recommended or rejected.

It is the same with those authors who, while rejecting the idea that there are economic laws valid for all times, everywhere, and for all people, assume that every period of history has its own

economic laws that have to be found a posteriori by studying the
history of the period concerned. These authors may tell us that
they have succeeded in discovering the laws governing events up
to yesterday. But—from the point of view of their own epistemological doctrine—they are not free to assume that the same
laws will also determine what will happen tomorrow. All that
they are entitled to affirm is: Experience of the past shows that
A brought about *B;* but we do not know whether tomorrow *A*
will not bring about some other effects than *B.*

Another variety of the denial of economics is the trend doctrine. Its supporters blithely assume that trends of evolution as
manifested in the past will go on. However, they cannot deny
that in the past trends did change and that there is no reason
whatever to assume that present trends will not one day change
too. Thus, this trend philosophy is useless in prognosticating the
future. This becomes especially manifest when businessmen, concerned about the continuation of prevailing trends, consult economists and statisticians. The answer they get is invariably this:
Statistics show us that the trend you are interested in was still
continuing on the day to which our most recent statistical data
refer; if no disturbing factors turn up, there is no reason why
the trend should change; however, we do not know anything
about the question whether or not such new factors will present
themselves.

VIII

Epistemological relativism, the essential doctrine of historicism, must be clearly distinguished from the ethical relativism of
other schools of thought. There are authors who combine praxeological relativism with ethical relativism. But there are also
authors who display ethical absolutism while rejecting the concept of universally valid praxeological laws. Thus, many adepts
of the Historical School of economics and of institutionalism judge
the historical past from the point of view of what they consider
as indisputable, never-changing moral precepts, e.g., equality of
wealth and incomes. In the eyes of some of them private property

is as such morally objectionable. They blame the economists for an alleged praise of material wealth and disparagement of more noble concerns. They condemn the system of private enterprise as immoral and advocate socialism on account of its presumed higher moral worth. As they see it, Soviet Russia complies better with the immutable principles of ethics than the nations of the West committed to the cult of Mammon.

As against all this emotional talk there is need to point out again: Praxeology and economics, its up to now best developed branch, are neutral with regard to any moral precepts. They deal with the striving after ends chosen by acting men without any regard whether these ends are approved or disapproved from any point of view. The fact that the immense majority of men prefer a richer supply of material goods to a less ample supply is a datum of history; it does not have any place in economic theory. Economics neither advocates capitalism nor rejects socialism. It merely tries to show what the necessary effects of each of these two systems are. He who disagrees with the teachings of economics ought to try to refute them by discursive reasoning, not by abuse, insinuations, and the appeal to arbitrary, allegedly ethical standards.

NOTES

1. The first edition was published in 1853 under the title *Die politische Oekonomie vom Standpunkte der geschichtlichen Methode.* The second edition was published in 1883 under the title *Die politische Oekonomie vom geschichtlichen Standpunkte.* It is by and large a reprint of the earlier edition enlarged by many additions.
2. There is no need to enter into an analysis of the two other subclasses enumerated by Weber. For a detailed critique of Weber's doctrine, see my essay "Sociologie und Geschichte," in *Archiv fur Sozialwissenschaft,* LXI (1929), reprinted in my book *Grundprobleme der Nationalökonomie* (Jena 1933), pp. 64-121. In the English-language translation of this book, *Epistemological Problems of Economics,* prepared by Mr. George Reisman and edited by Mr. Arthur Goddard (Princeton: D. Van Nostrand Co., Inc., 1960), this essay appears on pp. 68-129.
3. H. Hartmann, "On Rational and Irrational Action," in *Psychoanalysis and the Social Sciences,* I (1947), 371.
4. When the sciences of human action refer to ends, they always mean the ends that acting men are aiming at. This distinguishes these sciences from

the metaphysical doctrines known under the name of "philosophy of history" that pretend to know the ends toward which a superhuman entity—for instance, in the context of Marxism, the "material productive forces"—directs the course of affairs independently of the ends the acting men want to attain.

5. Otto Neurath, "Foundations of the Social Sciences," *International Encyclopedia of Unified Science*, II, No. 1 (University of Chicago Press), 9.

7

"Relativism"

Leo Strauss

"Relativism" has many meanings. In order not to become confused by the "blind scholastic pedantry" that exhausts itself and its audience in the "clarification of meanings" so that it never meets the nonverbal issues, I shall work my way into our subject by examining the recent statement of a famous contemporary about "the cardinal issue," the fundamental political problem of our time. As a fundamental problem it is theoretical; it is not the problem of particular policies, but the problem of the spirit that should inform particular policies. That problem is identified by Isaiah Berlin as the problem of freedom.[1]

Berlin distinguishes two senses of freedom, a negative and a positive sense. Used in the negative sense, in which it was used by "the classical English political philosophers" or "the fathers of liberalism," "freedom" means "freedom *from*": "Some portion of human existence must remain independent of social control"; "there ought to exist a certain minimum area of personal freedom which must on no account be violated." [2] Positive freedom, on the other hand, is "freedom *for*": the freedom of the individual "to be his own master" or to participate in the social control to which he is subject.[3] This alternative regarding freedom overlaps another alternative: freedom for the empirical self or freedom for the true self. Still, negative freedom, freedom from, is more likely to mean freedom for the empirical self; whereas positive freedom, freedom for, has to a higher degree the tendency to be understood as freedom only for the true self and therefore as compatible with the most extreme coercion of the empirical selves to become something that their true selves allegedly desire.[4]

The freedom that Berlin cherishes is the negative freedom for "our poor, desire-ridden, passionate, empirical selves": [5] "a maximum degree of noninterference compatible with the minimum demands of social life" [6] or the "freedom to live as one prefers." [7] He seems to cherish that freedom as "an end in itself" or "an ultimate value." [8] He certainly does not believe that the older reasoning in favor of negative freedom is valid. For, contrary to the older view, negative freedom is not the "necessary condition for the growth of human genius": "Integrity, love of truth and fiery individualism grow at least as often in severely disciplined communities or under military discipline, as in more tolerant or indifferent societies"; negative freedom is a peculiarly Western ideal and even a peculiarly modern Western ideal, and even in the modern Western world it is cherished by some individuals rather than by large masses; there is no necessary connection between negative freedom and democracy.[9]

Berlin finds the true justification of negative freedom in the absurdity of the alternative. The alternative is the notion that men can be free only by participating in *the* just, *the* rational or *the* perfect society in which all just or rational ends of all members of society are harmoniously satisfied or in which everyone obeys only himself, i.e., his true self. This notion presupposes that there is a hierarchy, and therefore a fundamental harmony, of human ends. But this presupposition is "demonstrably false"; it is based on a "dogmatic and a priori certainty"; it is "not compatible with empiricism," i.e., with "any doctrine founded on knowledge derived from experience of what men are and seek"; it is the root of "the metaphysical view of politics" as opposed to the "empirical" view.[10] Experience shows us that "the ends of men are many, and not all of them in principle are compatible with each other. . . . The necessity of choosing between absolute claims is then an inescapable characteristic of the human condition. This gives its value to freedom . . . as an end in itself and not as a temporary need. . . ." [11]

Experience, knowledge of the observable Is, seems to lead in a perfectly unobjectionable manner to knowledge of the Ought. The allegedly empirical premise would seem to be the equality of all human ends. "Mill, and liberals in general, at their most consistent . . . wish the frontiers between individuals and groups of men to be drawn solely with a view to preventing collisions between human purposes, all of which must be considered to be equally ultimate, uncriticizable ends in themselves. Kant and the rationalists of his type do not regard all ends as of equal value." From the context it appears that the ends that are to be regarded as equal include "the various personal aims which their individual imagination and idiosyncrasies lead men to pursue." [12]

Interference with the pursuit of ends is legitimate only to the extent to which one man's pursuit of an end collides with another man's pursuit. Yet it appears that such collisions cannot possibly be prevented: "The possibility of conflict—and of tragedy—can never be wholly eliminated from human life, either personal or social." [13] Not all collisions, but only certain kinds of collisions can and ought to be prevented by social control: "there must be *some* frontiers of freedom which nobody should ever be permitted to cross." [14] The frontiers must be of such a character as to protect a reasonably large area; it would not be sufficient to demand that every man must have the freedom to dream of the pursuit of any end he likes.

Yet the primary question concerns, not the location of the frontiers, but their status. Those frontiers must be "sacred." [15] They must be "absolute": "Genuine belief in the inviolability of a minimum extent of individual liberty entails some . . . absolute stand." [16] "Relativism," or the assertion that all ends are relative to the chooser and hence equal, seems to require some kind of "absolutism." Yet Berlin hesitates to go quite so far. "Different *names or natures* may be given to the rules" that determine those frontiers:

they may be called natural rights or the word of God, or Natural Law, or the demands of utility or of "the deepest interests of man"; I may believe them to be valid *a priori,* or assert them to be *my own subjective ends, or the ends of my society or culture.* What these rules or commandments will have in common is that they are accepted so widely, and are grounded so deeply in the actual nature of men as they have developed through history, as to be, by now, an essential part of what we mean by being a normal human being. Genuine belief in the inviolability of a minimum extent of individual liberty entails *some such absolute stand.*[17]

That is to say, the demand for the sacredness of a private sphere needs a basis, an "absolute" basis, but it has no basis; any old basis, any "such absolute stand" as reference to my own subjective will or the will of my society will do. It would be short-sighted to deny that Berlin's comprehensive formula is very helpful for a political purpose—for the purpose of an anti-Communist manifesto designed to rally all anti-Communists. But we are here concerned with a theoretical problem, and in this respect we are forced to say that Berlin contradicts himself. "Freedom from" and "freedom for" are "two profoundly divergent and irreconcilable attitudes to the ends of life . . . each of them makes absolute claims. These claims cannot both be fully satisfied. But . . . the satisfaction that each of them seeks is an ultimate value which . . . has an equal right to be classed among the deepest interests of mankind." [18] The absolute claim for a minimum private sphere cannot be fully satisfied; it must be diluted, for the opposite claim has an equal right. Liberalism, as Berlin understands it, cannot live without an absolute basis and cannot live with an absolute basis.

Let us consider more precisely the basis of liberalism as Berlin sees it. "What these rules and commandments [*sc.* that determine the frontiers of freedom that nobody should ever be permitted to cross] will have in common is that they are accepted so widely, are grounded so deeply in the actual nature of men as they have developed through history, as to be, by now, an essential part of what we mean by being a normal human being." [19] But Berlin had told us earlier that "the domination of this ideal has been the exception rather than the rule, even in the recent history of the West," [20] i.e., that the ideal of negative freedom is not natural to man as man. Let, then, the rules in question be natural to Western man as he is now. But what about the future?

It may be that the ideal of freedom to live as one wishes . . . is only the late fruit of our declining capitalist civilization: an ideal which . . . posterity will regard with . . . little comprehension. This may be so; but no sceptical conclusions seem to me to follow. Principles are no less sacred because their duration cannot be guaranteed.[21]

But it is also true that principles are not sacred merely in virtue of the fact that their duration cannot be guaranteed. We are still waiting to hear why Berlin's principles are regarded by him as sacred. If these principles are intrinsically valid, eternally valid, one could indeed say that it is a secondary question whether they will or will not be recognized as valid in the future and that if future generations despise the eternal verities of civilization, they will merely condemn themselves to barbarism. But can there be eternal principles on the basis of "empiricism," of the experience of men up to now? Does not the experience of the future have the same right to respect as the experience of the past and the present?

The situation would be entirely different if one could assume the possibility of a peak of experience, of an absolute moment in history, in which the fundamental condition of man is realized for the first time and in principle fully. But this would also mean that in the most important respect history, or progress, would have come to its end. Yet Berlin seems to take it for granted that in the most important respect history is unfinished or unfinishable. Hence, the ideal of negative freedom can only be "relatively valid" for him: it can be valid only for the time being. In entire accord with the spirit of our time, he quotes "an admirable writer of our time" who says: "To realize the relative validity of one's convictions and yet stand for them unflinchingly, is what distinguishes a civilized man from a barbarian." [22]

That is to say, not only are all our primary ends of relative validity; even the end that suggests itself as necessary by virtue of the absolute insight into the relative validity of all our primary ends is likewise only relatively valid. On the other hand, the latter end, or the right position toward any primary end, is so absolutely valid that Berlin or his authority can build on it the absolute distinction between civilized men and barbarians. For this distinction, as set forth in the quoted passage, is obviously meant to be final and not to be subject to revision in the light of future experience.

Berlin cannot escape the necessity to which every thinking being is subject: to take a final stand, an absolute stand in accordance with what he regards as the nature of man or as the nature of the human condition or as the decisive truth and hence to assert the absolute validity of his fundamental conviction. This does not mean, of course, that his fundamental conviction is sound. One reason why I doubt that it is sound is that if his authority were right, every resolute liberal hack or thug would be a civilized man, while Plato and Kant would be barbarians.

Berlin's statement seems to me to be a characteristic document of the crisis of liberalism—of a crisis due to the fact that liberalism has abandoned its absolutist basis and is trying to become entirely relativistic. Probably the majority of our academic colleagues will say that no conclusion can be drawn against relativism from the inadequacies of Berlin's statement because these inadequacies arise from his wish to find an impossible middle ground between relativism and absolutism; if he had limited himself to saying that liberalism is merely his "own subjective end," not intrinsically superior to any other subjective end, that since the belief in liberalism is based on a value judgment, no case or no conclusive case can be made for or against liberalism, in other words, if he had not rejected the nonliberal positions as "barbarian," but had admitted that there is an indefinitely large variety of notions of civilization each of which defines barbarism in its own way, in brief, if he had remained within the confines of the positivism of our time, he would never have contradicted himself. Whether withdrawal to the citadel of that positivism or of unqualified "value relativism" overcomes the crisis of liberalism or whether it merely conceals that crisis is another question.

The case for relativism has been restated recently by Arnold Brecht. He takes issue with certain arguments against relativism that I had advanced. He is not impressed by my reasoning. He deals with it chiefly under the heading of "misrepresentations." Since I know Dr. Brecht to be a polite man, I was inclined to assume that he regarded it as impolite to accuse me of mere misunderstanding: relativism is not such a deep doctrine as to be likely to be misunderstood. He blames me for having ascribed to Max Weber the view that all values are of the same rank: Weber merely asserted that " ultimate" values are "equally indemonstrable." [23] This means, however, that, as far as we know and shall ever be able to know while living on earth, or before the tribunal of human reason, the ways of life recommended by Amos or by Socrates are equal in value to the way of life of specialists without spirit or vision and voluptuaries without heart. And this assertion seems to me to be as absurd as the assertion that, as far as we know or shall ever be able to know, a man who is blind or mortally ill is as perfect regarding his body as a man free from all bodily defects.

Brecht blames me also for having seen "inconsistency in the fact that relativists cannot help using value judgments themselves."

No scientific relativist would condemn words like cruelty, civilization, prostitution, or, for that matter, crime or slums, wherever they are used within a clear frame of reference as descriptive in accordance with known standards, *as long as these standards are not themselves at issue.*[24]

But, on the basis of relativism, the standards are necessarily at issue, since all value judgments are rationally questionable; the consistent relativist ought to use "value-impregnated expressions" only in quotation marks, if at all.

In the Appendix to his book, in a subsection entitled "Misunderstandings," [25] Brecht reproaches me for having asserted that, according to relativism, "civilization is not intrinsically superior to cannibalism." He says:

Where and when has a scientific relativist ever asserted as a fact that civilization is *not* superior to cannibalism? Such apodictic negative statements would be quite contrary to the principles of Scientific Method.

I merely repeat that, according to the thesis of scientific relativism, as restated by Brecht, civilization is not, as far as we *know,* and shall ever be able to *know,* superior to cannibalism, provided that each—civilization as well as cannibalism—rests on an ultimate value of its own. This is to say nothing at all here of the fact that the use of the terms "civilizations" or "cultures" by scientific anthropology presupposes the abolition of the distinction between civilization and barbarism and therewith, in particular, the abolition of the distinction between civilization and cannibalism.

"The only question," Brecht continues, "that could be raised by some pedantic relativist or for the matter of methodological argument is, What is the scientific *evidence* for the superiority of noncannibalistic civilizations?" Since the question at issue is whether reason is completely unable to distinguish between right and wrong or noble and base, one must not be afraid of being pedantic. "How about civilizations," Brecht continues, "that abhor the eating of cattle or hogs?" Here Brecht seems to say that, according to scientific relativism, the eating of human beings has the same status as the eating of cattle or hogs.

Scientific Value Relativism . . . is at no loss to show the superiority of noncannibalism, once "superiority" is defined . . . in terms other than selfish satisfaction of personal or tribal passions and with reference to humanity . . . even if the term "superior" were used in a strictly selfish sense . . . Scientific Method would not be at the end of its resources; the long-run superiority of one pattern of behavior over another can often be demonstrated even when the question is solely that of personal satisfaction.

If scientific value relativism may be able to prove the superiority of civilization to cannibalism in terms of both selfish satisfaction and unselfish satisfaction, it would indeed seem that scientific value relativism can in principle prove the superiority of civilization to cannibalism. Or is the disjunction incomplete? Must it not be incomplete if relativism is to be maintained? Is the reference to the "definition" of superiority not tantamount to a reference to such incompleteness? Is there, then, something other than satisfaction (selfish or unselfish) that is equal in rank to satisfaction before the tribunal of human reason so that one can choose dissatisfaction (pain, suffering, anguish, failure) as one's ultimate value with the same right as satisfaction? And may not dissatisfaction justify cannibalism?[26]

Brecht concludes his argument with the remark that scientific value relativism does not deny "that there may be absolutely valid, divine standards of moral value; it merely negates that this can be shown with scientific means in a serious controversy conducted in good faith." Brecht also reproaches me for having contrasted the apparent humility with the hidden arrogance of relativism. In reply to this remark he says:

Scientific Value Relativism may indeed be too humble to offer a *scientific* decision on a question like this: whether the captain of a marooned crew ought to be condemned if he permitted his men to eat the flesh of other men killed in battle or by accident, when this was the only alternative to starving. Religious feeling and traditional education may tell us they should rather have starved, but this is no *scientific* decision.

Why did Brecht choose this example in preference to the example of men eating human flesh while they have other food in abundance? Can his science legitimate the "condemnation" of what we may call frivolous cannibalism without making assumptions regarding "ultimate values" which that very science must regard as questionable? Besides, I gladly admit that Brecht's version of relativism is humble, since it is based on the Kantian distinction between the knowable phenomena and the unknowable thing-in-itself.[27]

According to the positivistic interpretation of relativism which prevails in present-day social science and which Brecht very feebly qualifies,[28] reason is unable to show the superiority of unselfish gratification to selfish gratification and the absurdity of any attainable ends "which imagination and idiosyncrasies lead men to pursue." From this it follows that a bachelor without kith and kin who dedicates his whole life to the amassing of the largest possible amount of money, provided he goes about this pursuit in the most efficient manner, leads, in principle, as rational a life as the greatest benefactor of his country or of mankind. The choice among attainable ends may be made *en pleine connaissance de cause,* i.e., in full clarity about the likely consequences of the choice; it cannot in itself be rational. Reason can tell us which means are conducive to which ends; it cannot tell us which attainable ends are to be preferred to other attainable ends. Reason cannot even tell us that we ought to choose attainable ends; if someone "loves him who desires the impossible," reason may tell him that he acts irrationally, but it cannot tell him that he ought to act rationally or that acting irrationally is acting badly or basely. If rational conduct consists in choosing the right means for the right end, relativism teaches in effect that rational conduct is impossible. Relativistic social science may therefore be said to be one branch of the rational study of nonrational behavior.

But in what sense is the study rational? Social science proceeds by inductive reasoning or is concerned with prediction or with the discovery of causes. Yet what is the status of the principle of causality in social science relativism? The moderate Brecht is satisfied with the assertion that as regards causality, scientific method is grounded on common sense; he himself is inclined toward what he calls the Kantian view according to which "the human mind is so structured as to be unable to think [or as he also says "to imagine"] that changes have no causes." [29] According to a more widely accepted view, the principle of causality is a mere assumption. There is no rational objection to the assumption that the universe may disappear at any moment, not only into thin air, but into absolute nothingness, and that this happening may be a vanishing, not only into nothing, but through nothing as well. What is true of the possible end of the world is true also of its beginning. Since the principle of causality is not intrinsically evident, nothing prevents us from assuming that the world has come into being out of nothing and through nothing. Not only has rationality disappeared from the behavior studied by science; the rationality of that study itself has become radically problematic. All coherence has gone. We are then entitled to say that positivistic science in general, and therefore positivistic social science in particular, is characterized by the abandonment of reason or the flight from reason. The flight from scientific reason, which has been noted with regret, is the reasonable reply to the flight of science from reason.

A Marxist writer, Georg Lukács, has written a history of nineteenth- and twentieth-century German thought under the title *Die Zerstörung der Vernunft.*[30] I believe that many of us Western social scientists must plead guilty to this accusation. For obvious reasons we must be especially interested in Lukács's critique of Max Weber's conception of social science. One may summarize that critique as follows. Weber more than any other German scholar of his generation tried to save the objectivity of social science; he believed that to do so required that social science be made "value-free" because he assumed that evaluations are transrational or irrational; but the value-free study of "facts" and their causes admittedly presupposes the selection of relevant facts; that selection is necessarily guided by reference to values; the values with reference to which the facts are to be selected must themselves be selected; and that selection, which determines in the last analysis the specific conceptual framework of the social scientist, is in principle arbitrary; hence social science is fundamentally irrational or subjectivistic.[31]

According to Lukács, an objective and evaluating social science is possible provided social science does not limit itself to the study of arbitrarily selected "facts" or segments, but understands particular social phenomena in the light of the whole social situation and ultimately in the light of the whole historical process. "Historical and dialectical materialism is that comprehensive view in which the progressiveness and the rationally knowable lawfulness of history are expressed in the highest form, and in fact the only comprehensive view that can give a consistent philosophic foundation to progressivism and reasonableness." [32]

Hegel's attempt to demonstrate the progressive and rational character of the historical process was based on the premise that that process is in principle completed; for if it were not completed, one could not know, for instance, whether the future stages would not lead to the self-destruction of reason. Yet, according to Marx, the historical process is not completed, not to say that it has not even begun. Besides, Marx does not admit transhistorical or natural ends with reference to which change can be diagnosed as progress or regress. It is therefore a question whether by turning from Western relativism to Marxism one escapes relativism. "Historical materialism," Lukács had said,

can and must be applied to itself. Yet this application of materialist method to materialism does not lead to complete relativism; it does not lead to the consequence that historical materialism is not the right method. The substantive truths of Marxism are of the same quality as the truths of classical economics according to Marx's interpretation of those truths. They are truths within a certain order of society and production. As such, but only as such, they possess absolute validity. This does not exclude the emergence of societies in which other categories, other connections of truth, will be valid as a consequence of the essential structure of these societies.[33]

This would seem to mean that the substantive truths of Marxism are true until further notice; in principle we know already now that they will be replaced by different truths. Surely, the Marxist truths will be "preserved" in Hegel's sense of the term: "the 'objectivity' of the truth accessible on the lower planes is not destroyed: that truth merely receives a different meaning by being integrated into a more concrete, a more comprehensive totality." [34] That is to say, Marxism will reveal itself as a one-sided truth, a half-truth. Lukács compares the truth of Marxism also to the truth of the ideologies of the French Revolution. Marxism is as true today as those ideologies were in their time: both make or made intelligible a historical situation in such a way as to render visible for contemporaries the root of their difficulties and to show them the way out of those difficulties. But while the ideologists of the French Revolution saw clearly the rottenness of the *ancien régime* and the necessity of a revolution, they were utterly mistaken about the goodness of the new society that their revolution brought to birth.

The application to Marxism is obvious: even if Marxism were the last word regarding the ground of the rottenness of capitalist society and regarding the way in which that society can and will be destroyed, it cannot possibly be the last word regarding the new society that the revolutionary action of the proletariat brings to birth: the new society may be as rich in contradictions and oppressions as the old society, although its contradictions and oppressions will, of course, be entirely novel. For if Marxism is only the truth of our time or our society, the prospect of the classless society too is only the truth of our time and society; it may prove to be the delusion that gave the proletariat the power and the spirit to overthrow the capitalist system, whereas in fact the proletariat finds itself afterwards enslaved, no longer indeed by capital, but by an ironclad military bureaucracy.

Yet perhaps Marxism must not be applied to itself and thus made relative. Perhaps its fundamental verities are objective, scientific truths the validity of which cannot be understood in terms of their conditions or genesis. Marxism can then be regarded as a final truth of the same dignity as the theory of evolution. Yet since other truths of great importance will be discovered in the future, the "meaning" of Marxism will radically change.

But perhaps Marxism is the final truth, since it belongs to the absolute moment in history in which the realm of necessity can be surveyed in its entirety and therewith the outlines of the realm of freedom can come into view for the first time. The realm of necessity coincides with the division of labor. The realm of freedom emerges with the abolition of the division of labor. Yet the original form of the division of labor is "the division of labor," not in the generation of offspring, but "in the sexual act." [35] It would seem that the realm of freedom, if brought to its perfection, will be the realm of homunculi produced in test tubes by homunculi, if it will not be, as is more likely, the earth of "the last man," of the one herd without a shepherd. For, to quote Machiavelli, "as has been written by some moral philosophers, men's hands and tongue, two most noble instruments for ennobling him, would not have done their work perfectly nor would they have carried the works of men to the height to which they are seen to have been carried, if they had not been driven on by necessity": the jump from the realm of necessity into the realm of freedom will be the inglorious death of the very possibility of human excellence.

But let us return to that school which is externally the most powerful in the present-day West, to present-day positivism. That positivism is logical positivism. With some degree of truth it traces its origin to Hume. It deviates from Hume in two important respects. In the first place, deviating from Hume's teaching, it is a logical, i.e., not a psychological, teaching. The supplement added by logical positivism to the critique of reason is symbolic logic and the theory of probability; in Hume that supplement was natural belief and natural instinct. The sole or chief concern of logical positivism is the logical analysis of science. It has learned through Kant, the great critic of Hume, or through neo-Kantianism, that the question of the validity of science is radically different from the question of its psychological genesis.

The second important respect in which present-day positivism deviates from Hume is indicated by the fact that Hume was still a political philosopher. More particularly, he still taught that there are universally valid rules of justice and that those rules are not improperly called Laws of Nature. This means that "he thought and wrote before the rise of anthropology and allied sciences" [36] or, more precisely stated, before "the discovery of History." Hume still viewed human things in the light of man's unchangeable nature; he did not yet conceive of man as an essentially historical being. Present-day positivism believes that it can evade the problem raised by "the discovery of History" by the same device by which it frees itself from Hume's or any other psychology: through the Kantian distinction between validity and genesis. Yet Kant was enabled to transcend psychology because he recognized an a priori; and an a priori does not have a genesis, at least not an empirical genesis. Logical positivism rejects the a priori. Hence it cannot avoid becoming involved in psychology, in the question of the empirical genesis of science out of what precedes science. One cannot stop at simply trying to answer the question, What is science? One cannot avoid raising the question, Why science? or What is the meaning of science? Since positivism denies that there is a "pure reason" or a "pure mind," it can answer the question, Why science? only in terms of "the human organism." It must understand science as an activity of a certain kind of organism, as an activity fulfilling an important function in the life of that kind of organism. In brief, man is an organism that cannot live, or live well, without being able to predict, and the most efficient form of prediction is science.

This way of accounting for science has become extremely questionable. In the age of thermonuclear weapons the positive relation of science to human survival has lost all the apparent evidence that it formerly may have possessed. Furthermore, the high development of science depends on highly developed industrial societies; the predominance of such societies renders ever more difficult the survival of "underdeveloped societies." Who still dares to say that the development of those societies, i.e., their radical transformation, the destruction of their traditional way of life, is a necessary condition for those peoples' living or living well? Those peoples survived and sometimes lived happily without having an inkling of the possibility of science. While it becomes necessary to trace science to the needs of organisms of a certain kind, it is impossible to do so. For to the extent to which science could be shown to be necessary for man's living or living well, one would in fact pass a rational value judgment regarding science, and we know that, according to positivism, rational value judgments are impossible.

Some positivists avoid the difficulty indicated by finding the rationale of science in democracy, without being deterred by the fact that they thus merely appeal to the dogmatic premise or the inertia of established orders and without paying attention to the complications alluded to by Berlin, or else by conceiving of science as one of the most thrilling forms of spiritual adventure, without being able to tell us what they understand by the spiritual, how it differs in their opinion from the nonspiritual, and, in particular, how it is related to the rational. Positivism grants that science depends on conditions that science itself does not produce. They are produced by the unintended coming together of various factors that may diverge as they have converged. As long as they are together, science may progress by virtue of something that looks like an innate propensity. Yet science is not autonomous; as the saying goes, thinking does not take place in a vacuum. What renders the autonomy of science questionable is not primarily the fact that science presupposes the availability of conditions external to science. If one conceives of science as a spiritual adventure, one implies that there are other forms of spiritual adventure; one cannot exclude the possibility that, just as science influences those other forms, science itself undergoes their influence. Furthermore, one must assume that the spirit changes as a consequence of its adventures, hence that the spirit may well differ from age to age, and hence that science may depend, in the direction of its interests or of its hypotheses-forming imagination, on the spirit of the age. In other words, one cannot help raising the question of the relation between scientific progress and social progress. Given the positivistic verdict regarding value judgments, positivism can no longer speak properly, or with an easy conscience, of social progress; but it continues, even if in a more or less surreptitious manner, the older tradition that believed in the natural harmony between scientific progress and social progress.

Stated generally, by virtue of the distinction between validity and genesis, positivism tries to treat science as autonomous, but it is unable to do so; that distinction merely prevents it from giving due weight to the question of the human context out of which science arises and within which it exists. Positivism treats science in the way in which it would have to be treated if science were "the very highest power of man," the power by which man transcends the merely human; yet positivism cannot maintain this "Platonic" understanding of science. The question of the human context of science, which positivism fails and refuses to raise, is taken up by its most powerful present-day opponent in the West, radical historicism or, to use the better-known name, existentialism.

Existentialism came into being through the meeting, which first took place in Germany, of Kierkegaard's and Nietzsche's thought. While being related to these two illustrious names, existentialism is as nameless as positivism or idealism. But this is misleading. Existentialism, like many other movements, has a flabby periphery and a hard center. That hard core, or that thought to which alone existentialism owes its intellectual dignity, is the thought of Heidegger. In Heidegger's first great publication, the influence of Kierkegaard was indeed as powerful as that of Nietzsche. But with the increased clarity that Heidegger achieved afterward, it became clear that the root of existentialism must be sought in Nietzsche rather than in Kierkegaard: existentialism emerged by virtue of the "reception" of Kierkegaard on the part of a philosophic public that had begun to be molded by Nietzsche.

Nietzsche is *the* philosopher of relativism: the first thinker who faced the problem of relativism in its full extent and pointed to the way in which relativism can be overcome. Relativism came to Nietzsche's attention in the form of historicism—more precisely, in the form of a decayed Hegelianism. Hegel had reconciled "the discovery of History"—the alleged insight into the individual's being, in the most radical sense, the son or stepson of his time or into the dependence of a man's highest and purest thoughts on his time—with philosophy in the original meaning of the term by asserting that Hegel's time was the absolute moment, the end of meaningful time: the absolute religion, Christianity, had become completely reconciled with the world; it had become completely secularized, or the *saeculum* had become completely Christian in and through the postrevolutionary State; history as meaningful change had come to its end; all theoretical and practical problems had in principle been solved; hence, the historical process was demonstrably rational.

The decayed Hegelianism with which Nietzsche was confronted preserved Hegel's "optimism" after having abandoned the ground of that "optimism," i.e., the completedness of the historical process. In fact, its "optimism" was based on the expectation of infinite future progress or on the belief in the unfinishable character of history. Under this condition, as Nietzsche saw, our own principles, including the belief in progress, will become as relative as all earlier principles had shown themselves to be; not only the thought of the past but also our own thought must be understood to depend on premises which for us are inescapable, but of which we know that they are condemned to perish. History becomes a spectacle that for the superficial is exciting and for the serious is enervating. It teaches a truth that is deadly. It shows us that culture is possible only if men are fully dedicated to principles of thought and action which they do not and cannot question, which limit their horizon and thus enable them to have a character and a style. It shows us at the same time that any principles of this kind can be questioned and even rejected.

The only way out seems to be that one turn one's back on this lesson of history, that one voluntarily choose life-giving delusion instead of deadly truth, that one fabricate a myth. But this is patently impossible for men of intellectual probity. The true solution comes to sight once one realizes the essential limitation of objective history or of objective knowledge in general. Objective history suffices for destroying the delusion of the objective validity of any principles of thought and action; it does not suffice for opening up a genuine understanding of history. The objective historian cannot grasp the substance of the past because he is a mere spectator, not dedicated or committed to substantive principles of thought and action, and this is the consequence of his having realized that such principles have no objective validity. But an entirely different conclusion may and must be drawn from the realization of this objective truth. The different values respected in different epochs had no objective support, i.e., they were human creations; they owed their being to a free human project that formed the horizon within which a culture was possible. What man did in the past unconsciously and under the delusion of submitting to what is independent of his creative act, he must now do consciously. This radically new project—the revaluation of all values—entails the rejection of all earlier values, for they have become baseless by the realization of the baseless character of their claim, by which they stand or fall, to objective validity. But precisely the realization of the origin of all such principles makes possible a new creation that presupposes this realization and is in agreement with it, yet is not deducible from it; for otherwise it would not be due to a creative act performed with intellectual probity.

It is in this way that Nietzsche may be said to have transformed the deadly truth of relativism into the most life-giving truth. To state the case with all necessary vagueness, he discovered that the life-giving comprehensive truth is subjective or transtheoretical in that it cannot be grasped detachedly and that it cannot be the same for all men or for all ages. We can do no more than allude here to the difficulties in which Nietzsche became involved in trying to overcome the difficulties that afflict his solution. I have in mind his interpretation of human creativity as a special form of the universal will to power, and the question that this interpretation entails, namely, whether he did not thus again try to find a sufficient theoretical basis for a transtheoretical teaching or message. I have in mind, in other words, his hesitation as to whether the doctrine of the will to power is his subjective project to be superseded by other such projects in the future or whether it is the final truth. We limit ourselves here to saying that the movement of Nietzsche's thought can be understood as a movement from the supremacy of history towards the supremacy of nature, a movement that bypasses the supremacy of reason throughout or tries to replace the opposition between the subjective and the objective (or between the conventional and the natural) by the opposition between the superficial and the profound. Existentialism is the attempt to free Nietzsche's alleged overcoming of relativism from the consequences of his relapse into metaphysics or of his recourse to nature.

Existentialism starts where positivism leaves off. Existentialism is the reaction of serious men to their own relativism. Positivism is essentially the attempt to understand science; it acts as if it knew that science is the one thing needful or at any rate man's highest possibility. It conceives of science as essentially progressive, and hence it conceives of the future of scientific development as unpredictable *in concreto*. In fact, it conceives of science as capable of infinite progress. This character of science must, however, be traced to the character of the object of science. That object is essentially accessible to reason; otherwise there could be no science. But since it reveals itself to science only in an infinite process, one can say with at least equal right that it is radically mysterious. For he who teaches, for instance, that perpetual peace is the goal of an infinite process teaches, in fact, the perpetuity of war. Existentialism is the truth of positivism, since it teaches that being is essentially or radically mysterious and that the fundamental defect of metaphysics is the assumption upon which it is based—the assumption that being is as such intelligible.

Existentialism is, however, not merely the "pessimistic" expression of the same thing of which positivism is the "optimistic" expression. Positivism asserts that the goodness of science cannot be established by science or scientific philosophy: the choice of science, of the scientific orientation, and therewith also of the scientific "picture of the world" is not a rational choice; it is as possible and as groundless as the choice of any alternative orientation. These fundamental choices are not properly interpreted by scientific psychology, for scientific psychology explains those choices on the basis of a specific fundamental choice that is not necessary, viz., the choice of the scientific orientation. The fundamental phenomenon, the only phenomenon that is not hypothetical, is the abyss of freedom: the fact that man is compelled to choose groundlessly; the fundamental experience, i.e., an experience more fundamental than every science, is the experience of the objective groundlessness of all principles of thought and action, the experience of nothingness.

Man and ultimately everything must be understood in the light of this fundamental experience. The specific manner in which man and man alone is, is directly constituted by the fundamental nothingness. That manner of being is called *Existenz*. *Existenz* is articulated by the analysis of *Existenz*, which is the fundamental part of philosophy. *Existenz* is authentic or inauthentic: authentic when it faces the fundamental situation of man, inauthentic when it flees from it. The analytics of *Existenz* contains, then, an ethics, even if only a formal ethics: to the extent to which one understands *Existenz*, one realizes the general character of the truly human. The ethics is formal since it is based, not on the nature of man, on man's beingness, but on the human situation or, somewhat more precisely, on man's manner of being. Hence, it does not say that the good life is the life according to nature, according to the nature of man, but it does say, in effect, that the good life is the life according to the essential character of *Existenz*. It does not say this, however, according to Heidegger's own authoritative declaration. For if the analytics of *Existenz* contained an ethics, its cognitive status would be the same as that of Kant's transcendental analytics of subjectivity; it would be an objective teaching or it would supply final knowledge, infinite knowledge. Yet the analytics of *Existenz* is necessarily based on a specific ideal of *Existenz*, on a specific commitment; for only committed thought can understand commitment and hence *Existenz*. In other words, existentialist philosophy is subjective truth about the subjectivity of truth or finite knowledge of man's finiteness.

Yet how can finiteness be seen as finiteness if it is not seen in the light of the infinite? These and similar difficulties seem to have led Heidegger to a very thorough revision of his doctrine. One may doubt whether through that revision the fundamental relativism was overcome. I can allude here only to one point, to Heidegger's teaching regarding historical truth. The interpreter's understanding of a thinker is true if it understands his thought as he understood it. According to Heidegger this is altogether impossible; it is not even a reasonable goal of understanding. Nor is it possible, in his opinion, to understand a thinker better than he understood himself; true understanding of a thinker is understanding him creatively, i.e., understanding him differently from the way in which he understood himself. This understanding necessarily implies a criticism, a fundamental criticism of the thinker in question. According to Heidegger, all thinkers prior to him have been oblivious of *Sein,* i.e., of the ground of grounds. This assertion implies, in fact, the claim that Heidegger understands the great thinkers of the past in the decisive respect better than they understood themselves.

NOTES

1. Isaiah Berlin, *Two Concepts of Liberty* (Oxford: At the Clarendon Press, 1958), p. 51.
2. *Op. cit.,* pp. 9, 11, 47.
3. *Op. cit.,* pp. 15, 16.
4. *Op. cit.,* p. 19.
5. *Op. cit.,* p. 32.
6. *Op. cit.,* p. 46.
7. *Op. cit.,* p. 14 n.
8. *Op. cit.,* pp. 36, 50.
9. *Op. cit.,* pp. 13-15, 48.
10. *Op. cit.,* pp. 39 n., 54, 57 n.
11. *Op. cit.,* p. 54.
12. *Op. cit.,* p. 38 n.
13. *Op. cit.,* p. 54.
14. *Op. cit.,* p. 50; italics mine.
15. *Op. cit.,* p. 57.
16. *Op. cit.,* p. 50.
17. *Op. cit.,* p. 50; italics mine.
18. *Op. cit.,* pp. 51-52.
19. *Op. cit.,* p. 50.
20. *Op. cit.,* p. 13.
21. *Op. cit.,* p. 57.
22. *Op. cit.,* p. 57.
23. Arnold Brecht, *Political Theory* (Princeton University Press, 1959), p. 263.
24. *Op. cit.,* pp. 264-265.
25. *Op. cit.,* pp. 549-550.

26. Cf. also p. 430.
27. Cf. pp. 101, 103, 125, 158, 462 ff.
28. *Op. cit.,* pp. 124-125, 130-131.
29. *Op. cit.,* pp. 78, 81.
30. Georg Lukács, *Die Zerstörung der Vernunft* (Berlin, 1954).
31. Cf. pp. 484-489.
32. *Op. cit.,* p. 456.
33. Georg Lukács, *Geschichte und Klassenbewusstsein* (Berlin, 1923), pp. 234-235.
34. *Op. cit.,* p. 206.
35. Karl Marx and F. Engels, *Die Deutsche Ideologie* (cited from a new edition, Berlin, 1953), p. 28.
36. John Dewey, *Human Nature and Conduct,* Modern Library edition, p. vii.

8

Some Reflections on the "Relativistic" Meaning of *Wertfreiheit* in the Study of Man

BRUNO LEONI

Persönlich bin ich der Ansicht, dass kein Mittel der Welt zu "pedantisch" ist, um nicht zur Vermeidung von Konfusionen am Platze zu sein.

Max Weber

I

"Relativism" is an abused word; it may mean several things that are not necessarily similar and may remind people of different ideas that have very little connection with one another.

It is my purpose, in this paper, to take into consideration a meaning of the word "relativism" that seems to be particularly relevant for the study of man and the direction of human behavior in our age.

This meaning is probably better rendered by the German word, *Wertfreiheit,* a word that Max Weber made famous more than forty years ago in his celebrated essays relating to methodological problems in sociology and economics.[1]

A discussion about this kind of relativism involves a revision of several criticisms to which the adversaries of the Weberian doctrine have submitted it (sometimes without having properly understood it). It also implies a revision of several superficial applications on the part of some supporters of that doctrine at the present time. In their turn, these revisions require a restatement of the original Weberian meaning of *Wertfreiheit.*

As is known, Max Weber was such a serious scholar, his mastery of several fields of knowledge was so obvious, his acuteness in posing problems and in trying to solve them was so impressive, and finally, his scrupulousness in dealing with all their aspects was so indisputable that very few opponents of the Weberian doctrine of *Wertfreiheit* dared to attack it without first taking careful stock of their own resources.

Even so, it seems to me that the result of their attacks has been rather marginal so far. In fact, several, nay, almost all such strictures concern matters and arguments that Weber himself took into consideration in his time, not only to reply to his critics, but also to criticize other theories from his own point of view. Notwithstanding this, some strictures on the Weberian doctrine have been repeated recently without any reference to the previous replies of Weber, while some other critiques have been presented in disregard of the fact that Weber had consistently applied those very critiques against his adversaries. One could quote as an example of the first kind the argument that the position of the social scientist who wants to avoid value judgments would be rather contradictory, as the social scientist devotes his own work to reach one goal—truth—and actually makes value judgments whenever he prefers truth to other values or goals.[2]

Weber himself had more than one opportunity to reply to this argument in his time. In his 1917 essay on *Wertfreiheit* he made, for example, the following remarks:

The fact that science tries to reach "valid" results, that is, results correct both from the logical point of view and with reference to the facts, and that science, moreover, tries to reach results "valid," that is, *important,* from the point of view of scientific interests, and that a preliminary "evaluation" is already implied in the choice of its subject matter, these two circumstances have been seriously considered as objections, notwithstanding all we have said before in this connection.[3]

Another example of the same kind of stricture is offered by the argument, also recently presented against Weber (without any expressed reference to the fact that Weber had already refuted it), that social sciences would not be able to consider as an "object" the subjective evaluations of men and that any reference to subjective values would imply an irremediable subjectiveness also on the part of the science that deals with them.[4]

Weber could not conceal his surprise at the tendency of this misunderstanding to be revived again and again, regardless of his remark that sociology and also economics, with its doctrine of marginal utility, are based on precisely the contrary assumption.[5]

Finally, I could cite as another instance of the same kind the argument presented recently against Weber (again without any direct reference to the fact that he had already replied to it) that in the social sciences empirical research and personal evaluations are two things that are difficult to keep separate. Weber, as a matter of fact, had admitted this, but he had taken care to remark that this difficulty is not a sufficient reason to renounce altogether the attempt to keep empirical research and personal evaluations as separate as possible.[6]

As an instance of the second kind of strictures (that is, of arguments adopted against Weber without noticing that Weber himself had consistently applied those very arguments against other people), there may be cited first the assumption that while pretending to suppress every evaluation, one could try to revive, strongly and in a suggestive way, those very evaluations through the well-known device of letting "the facts speak for themselves." As a matter of fact, Weber too, in his time, criticized this procedure, which, according to him, is just the opposite of what he suggested with his *Wertfreiheit* theory.[7] Notwithstanding this, the argument has been presented very recently against Weber himself, and once again without any direct reference to Weber's position in this respect.[8]

Another and more impressive instance of this kind of argument is the assumption that the Weberian *Wertfreiheit,* as a method to be employed in the social sciences, would be more or less connected with a sort of moral relativism and subjectivism. In fact, there were few causes that Weber opposed more vigorously in his works than the cause of moral relativism or ethical subjectivism.

This circumstance has not prevented people from maintaining recently that, according to the Weberian theory of *Wertfreiheit,* a kind of "moral obtuseness" would be assumed as the necessary condition for scientific analysis. As a well-known American scholar put it: "The more serious we are as social scientists, the more completely we develop within ourselves a state of indifference to any goal, or of aimlessness and drifting, a state which may be called 'nihilism.' "[9]

In a further recent development of these strictures, the fact has been emphasized that *Wertfreiheit,* in many of its present applications, comes to act as a sort of mental paralysis on the part of the political scientist in his attitude toward vital issues of politics. An Italian scholar, Professor Giovanni Sartori, in a recent speech on *"Wertfreiheit* in Political Science," given at Heidelberg in 1959,[10] remarked that "political scientists have accepted the Weberian *platform* in a very subservient and uncritical mood."

He also pointed out a danger that (as he said) lingers in the "witch-hunting" of values: "Namely, the danger that our vocabulary [that is, the vocabulary of political scientists] is being used more and more in a flat, meaningless, misty sense. Instead of making it more precise, in the anxiety of purging it of any value *'Unterbau'* we are, in many cases, achieving the result of making it so indefinite that our mind is not acquiring, but losing control over, facts."

Sartori went so far as to say that in the *wertfrei* attitude of most contemporary political scientists the tendency emerges not only to leave values aside, but actually to subordinate values to facts, the result being that people, as Voltaire would have said, "fall back again on their four feet." According to the same scholar, on account of the kind of *Wertfreiheit* widely professed by political scientists, we are now living only off an "axiological capital," or more precisely, on an "axiological revenue," inherited from our ancestors, without realizing that we "are rapidly spending and wasting" it. In a few words, sterilizing and impoverishing language on the one side and losing sight of values and of vital political issues on the other side would be the worst results of *Wertfreiheit* as applied to political science today.

This conclusion becomes more discouraging when political scientists, bound as they presume themselves to be by *Wertfreiheit,* "permit some very ignorant and sometimes very dangerous people to instruct audiences on what they are supposed to do and what they ought to prefer." As Sartori warns us, if political scientists do not supply values, "somebody else will," and if this situation goes on too far, we could not be sure whether "the world that might grow out of [this kind of] *Wertfreiheit* would be a world hospitable to political scientists, or to anybody else."

I am prepared to admit that there is some truth in these statements. One could also point out a similar situation in economics, where so often now pseudomathematical formulae are taking the place of the old reasoning of the classics, in order to mean nothing relevant or nothing sensible, but to mean it just in a "neutral" or "value-free" way.[11]

However, unless I am wrong, even these attacks on Weberian *Wertfreiheit* do not go to the core of the argument. In fact, Max Weber himself might subscribe to them without any inconsistency with his own ideas. Nay, as we shall see, he too eventually adopted them in his own time against his adversaries. As a matter of fact, it may well be proved that today political scientists, as well as economists, are often victims of moral or political obtuseness; it may also be proved that this circumstance is to be put in relation with their own interpretation (or we might better say: misinterpretation) of what *Wertfreiheit* in a social science means and of what it implies in the actual behavior of social scientists as far as political issues are concerned.

It is not proved at all that *Wertfreiheit,* as outlined and recommended by Weber, necessarily implies this kind of obtuseness or constitutes a danger to our civilization. One could even go further and say that stubborn attempts to deny what is sound in the Weberian argument and to reject his *Wertfreiheit* in the name of the absoluteness of the values we believe in could be, at least in some cases, more dangerous for the maintenance of those values than a frank admission that the Weberian argument is not easy to attack. The more so, as it is not necessary to submit to a scientific demonstration the values we believe in and are prepared to fight for, in order to believe in them, or to convince other people to join with us in our fight, and, if possible, to win our battle against those who do not recognize our values.

To begin with, if we need to "demonstrate" the validity of our values to ourselves, this possibly means that we actually do not believe them enough to be able to dispense with that "demonstration." Moreover, if we try to "demonstrate" our values to other people, this is by no means the surest way of convincing them to accept those values. A "demonstration" is not necessarily the only means of convincing people at all: Galileo could not convince the so-called "Aristotelians" of his time that he was right in stating that Jupiter had some satellites and that everybody could observe them through his telescope. On the other hand, millions of people may be, and actually always are, persuaded to adopt faiths that would not meet the test of cold reasoning on the part of levelheaded persons. Is there anybody who could explain how it happened that millions of people suddenly changed their faith at a certain time in their history: Hinduists becoming Buddhists, Jews or Gentiles becoming Christians, or Christians becoming Moslems, and how millions of them all were prepared to die and actually did die for their new faiths, as they would have died for their old ones? [12]

It is reasonable to assume that demonstrations had little to do with all this.

II

It is not my purpose here to reconstruct the historical background on which Weber expounded his ideas on the so-called objective knowledge of social and political science and on the meaning of *Wertfreiheit* in economics and the sociological sciences. I wish only to remind my readers of the fact that he dealt with the first theme in an introductory note to the new series of the *Archiv für Sozialwissenschaft und Sozialpolitik,* XIX, 1904, pp. 22-87, and in a longer essay in the same review in the same year, while the second theme was developed more particularly in the German review *Logos* in 1917, and in another essay published in 1919 under the title "Science as a Vocation." [13]

What emerges from these essays is that Weber was reacting at that time against the tendency of some German scholars, such as Gustav Schmoller, or such celebrated historians as Treitschke and Mommsen, to take advantage of their official positions as scholars and university professors to give authority to their personal value judgments in the moral and political fields, while these value judgments were not specifically supported by any factual evidence or any objective demonstration of the kind we expect from a scientific teaching.

But what Weber reacted against above all was the tendency of some less important and less scrupulous German scholars of his own time to merge rather carelessly personal tastes and appreciations, on the one hand, and empirical research and scientific teaching, on the other, in a sort of pseudoimpersonal exposition in which the very personal predilections of the scholar or teacher were, so to say, smuggled in and presented to the public, and first of all to the students, as scientific results.

What Weber strongly objected to, therefore, was not so much the frank exposition of personal value judgments on the part of scholars and teachers (he even praised that, to a certain extent, in his old master, Schmoller, or in historians like Mommsen), but the negligent and sometimes purposeful confusion between personal predilections and scientific results that he did not hesitate to consider dishonest. He felt this the more because university professors in Germany were paid by the state, and, according to Weber's obvious interpretation of their positions and of their tasks, their fellow citizens should not be charged as taxpayers just to support that kind of crafty personal propaganda directed at the students, nor should the students be forced to listen to that propaganda in order to pass their examinations.

Weber was actually fighting against that false objectiveness made of tendentious arguments and information which he did not hesitate to characterize as a "parody" (*Mimikry*) [14] of true *Wertfreiheit,* and which he vigorously ridiculed by calling it *Professorenprophetie* [15] with reference to the tendency of German university professors of his time to play the role of a prophet instead of performing the task of a teacher. Let me add, incidentally, that if we take into account the attitudes of several intellectuals in this country, as well as in Europe at the present time, we have more than one reason to complain that Weber is not alive at this moment to renew his battle for *Wertfreiheit* in the above-mentioned sense.

To sum up, one of the main motives for Weber to preach *Wertfreiheit* was precisely a *moral one,* and this fact should always be kept in mind by those, both adversaries and purported followers, who are inclined to conceive of *Wertfreiheit* in terms of "moral obtuseness," and so on.

In fact, and strangely enough, both Weber's critics and Weber's followers often seem to have forgotten, or simply ignored, that Weber's theory of moral ideals and judgments is not relativistic at all. On the contrary, he vigorously pointed out that acting according to moral ideals always implies uncompromising decisions and choices among different and possibly contradictory values.

He also stated clearly that those choices, difficult and bitter as they could be, are inescapably due to the mutually exclusive nature of moral ideals, which are not reconcilable, in principle, with any other different ideals.

Because of these essential traits, moral life is not to be confused with the "superficial daily life" of everybody, where both the

possible irreconcilability of moral ideals and the necessity of
choosing among them are not clearly perceived, and people can
delude themselves that they are acting morally while trying to
avoid rigid choices, or "taking sides with God or the devil."

The very unpalatable, but inevitable, fruit of the Tree of Knowledge
is just this, that one has to see and to know that antithesis and that
every important action, nay, life as a whole, whenever it is not solely
a natural event but must be consciously directed, represents a chain
of final decisions through which one's soul, as with Plato, chooses its
destiny, that is, the sense of its doing and being. (My translation.)

Consistently enough, Weber rejected all kinds of "conciliatory"
moral philosophies devising a simple juxtaposition of values [16]
as well as he condemned the similar and superficial view emerging
from the daily life of common men. That juxtaposition was precisely what he considered moral relativism to consist in, while
calling "relativism" his idea that moral values could be actually
irreconcilable in human decisions and are always mutually exclusive in principle was to him "one of the greatest misunderstandings" on the part of his critics.[17]

Whatever we may think at the moment of the "relativistic"
nature of *Wertfreiheit* as a methodological and as an epistemological theory, we have, therefore, to conclude that this theory is
not based on any relativistic moral system of the conciliatory kind
we mentioned. As we shall see, we must go even further and admit
that the rejection of relativism as a moral philosophy is one of
the preliminary conditions for the establishment of a *Wertfreiheit*
as a methodological doctrine in Weber's sense. Only if we recognize that moral values are mutually exclusive in principle, and
possibly irreconcilable in fact, do we reach, according to Weber,
one of the proper criteria to found an empirical science about
human decisions and human actions whenever those actions and
decisions are dependent on the acceptance of moral values.

However, distinguishing among moral values, as well as among
any other kinds of values inspiring human action, is only a preliminary distinction. Several others are necessary to make any

empirical science effective, in Weber's view. What he actually had
in mind when he advocated *Wertfreiheit* in the empirical social
sciences was a whole series of distinctions, and what he was strug-
gling against was a whole series of confusions, in order to discard
the latter and to utilize the former in the scientific study of man.
In fact, his general program for the social sciences might be
better labeled as "freedom from confusions" than as "freedom
from values." Confusions between several kinds of values, on the
one hand, and between evaluations and ascertainments of facts,
on the other, were particularly frequent in the social sciences at
that time. Probably for that reason Weber insisted on identifying
his methodological doctrine of the social sciences with *Wertfreiheit,* that is, with what he called "freedom from value," instead of
identifying it with plain *Konfusionfreiheit* ("freedom from confusion").

"Personally," he wrote, "I retain the conviction that no means
in the world is too pedantic if it enables us to avoid confusions." [18]

The necessity of avoiding confusions was both his main tenet
and his constant preoccupation. He referred to this necessity every
time he had to argue against his critics, nay, against the confusions
made by his critics in the interpretation of the meaning of his
doctrine. One must admit that his defense was almost always
effective.

When his adversaries told him that the empirical social sciences
too must accept some values (in fact, the values of any other
sciences, that is, logical correctness and correspondence with
facts) he seemed to be impatient with such "endless misunderstanding" of his program: what he wanted (so he stated openly)
was not to renounce the value judgments of any science, but just
to try to keep separate statements relating to empirical facts and
statements relating to evaluations of those facts.[19] To adversaries
who told him that it is difficult to keep facts and evaluations
separate, he replies, "Yes, but let's try." [20]

To the people who objected to him that any reference to subjective evaluations considered as facts by the scholar would corre-
spond to an irremediable subjectivism of his science, Weber replied, once again, by invoking the necessity of keeping separate

any reference to values and any personal evaluation on the part of the scholar who makes that reference: to put it in the German terminology inaugurated by Heinrich Rickert and adopted by Weber, one should keep separate as far as possible *Wertbeziehungen* (references to values) and *Bewertungen* (evaluation).[21]

To the critics who accused him of advocating a moral relativism, he replied, once again, that we must not only avoid confusions between ascertainments of facts and evaluations, but also between the attempt to avoid these confusions and any kind of moral relativism whatsoever.

It seems to be a strange destiny for a man whose methodological program for the social sciences was to avoid confusions to have been forced so many times to struggle against these very confusions in his adversaries' criticisms of his own doctrine. His destiny seems to be even stranger if we consider that the same confusions about his doctrine are—as I said—at the base of recent strictures against it on the part of people who seem to ignore or to have forgotten his refutations.

I noted previously that, far from being founded on any relativistic moral system, Weber's *Wertfreiheit,* as a methodological and as an epistemological doctrine, is based precisely on the rejection of relativism as a moral philosophy of the "conciliatory" kind we have mentioned above. We have to realize that possibly our moral ideals, as well as any other kind of ideals, may become irreconcilable as soon as we have to decide which particular action we shall choose in the several circumstances of our lives. Only then would it be both necessary and justified to inquire about the reasons that render those ideals irreconcilable in those very circumstances, in view of the possible results of our action.

Far from acting in favor of moral relativism, such an inquiry might possibly enable people to make the decisions that are most consistent with their moral convictions. Only if one denies the possible moral tensions implied in our daily behavior and assumes that there is no possible contradiction between moral ideals with reference to the concrete actions of our lives could one then find that the methodological doctrine labeled by Weber as *Wertfreiheit* was devoid of any basis.

But Weber would reply that in such a case moral relativism is precisely the doctrine invoked to reach this conclusion.

In fact, only if we assume that moral ideals are easily reconcilable and practically interchangeable in a conciliatory system (for instance, of the kind despised by Pascal in his *Provinciales*) can we consider as useless an inquiry relating to possible contradictions between moral values in our practical life.

Of course, the inquiry proposed by Weber is not the exposition of a moral system. Are we to reproach Weber merely because he preached a methodological and epistemological doctrine instead of a moral one, and preferred to act as a methodologist rather than as a prophet? The answer should be in the negative, the more so if we consider that Weberian *Wertfreiheit* appears to be perfectly compatible, nay, complementary, with moral as well as political philosophy. On the one hand, it does not presume either to attack or to replace any moral system whatsoever,[22] while on the other hand, it may be useful, nay, precious, in the actuation of moral values on the part of people who want to keep consistently together, as far as possible, their moral values and their practical lives.

To be sure, Weberian *Wertfreiheit* cannot *create* moral or political philosophers, but only *help* them. If our time lacks moral or political philosophers, I am prepared to admit that this may be a misfortune. If some moral or political nonentities feel authorized to apply *Wertfreiheit* as a moral or political doctrine, instead of considering it merely as a methodological one, we can regret it.

But would it be fair to put the blame on Weber's *Wertfreiheit?* This would be the same as putting the blame on Petrarch for the bores who tried to imitate him for centuries.

True, Max Weber may be considered in modern times the father of a kind of relativism—the relativism that consists in submitting to a cold analysis all the implications of a constellation of values that are hypothesized, though not necessarily accepted or rejected by the scholar, in view of the analysis itself. We have already shown that this kind of relativism has *nothing to do* with moral or political relativism. We must add now that it has nothing to do with actual *indifference* toward values.

The value-free analysis proposed by Weber actually implies tremendous consequences as far as the final attitude is concerned of those who, having analyzed a given constellation of values in order to know which decisions to make in particular circumstances, try to behave according to the values they have accepted. Our analysis of possible choices is not relativistic at all. For sometimes it will indicate, with all the strength of a mathematical demonstration or of a physical test, which decisions, given some premises, are to be taken in a given circumstance. The breadth of the whole Weberian analysis seems to have been largely underestimated by those who indict the Weberian *Wertfreiheit* as a relativistic attitude toward moral and political values.

Weberian *Wertfreiheit* is not only a method to be adopted by empirical researchers. This method also implies, in a preliminary way, a process of logical analysis the purpose of which is to classify the proper meaning of the values to be taken into consideration for our analysis. That meaning cannot be taken for granted before it is examined. As Weber points out, men are often in the dark, not only as far as other people's ideals and values are concerned, but also as far as their own are concerned.[23]

The process of revealing those values through the interpretation of our daily opinions is not so easy, but its results may be such as to give us rather an unexpected picture of what we believe in. Then another kind of inquiry takes place—that of the consequences we can, nay, must derive from the basic values of our actions as revealed in the previous analysis. This inquiry, too, moves on a logical plane. Its results may again be startling, as they reveal the final picture of the implications of the values we have accepted as our own.

Finally, another kind of consideration is relevant—the analysis of the factual consequences possibly determined by our actions according to the values we accept and to their implications. This phase of the analysis moves in an empirical field, as it implies a series of statements relating to facts, without losing sight, of course, of the logical results reached in the first phase of the analysis.

One could also call this the *technical* phase of the analysis, because of the relations between ends and means that are studied in this connection. More generally, the technical aspect of the analysis lies in the connections that are studied between human actions considered as causes and all their possible results considered as effects, whether or not they are all actually desired by the author of the actions.

It is obvious that through each phase of this long and difficult process, conclusions may be reached that are to influence, possibly in a drastic manner, the final attitude of the acting man, regardless of the fact that he is also the author of the analysis or that he simply accepts its results.

To begin with, he may discover that the values he believes in are not those he had supposed he possessed. Then he may discover that some logical consequences of some of those values are logically contradictory to other consequences of other values he equally accepted as a basis for his actions.

Finally, he may discover through the factual analysis of the possible results of his actions that some of them are impossible to reach, others are scarcely probable, and also that results may emerge that are not in accordance with his ends as based on his values.

Another possible consequence of the analysis (one that perhaps Weber himself did not stress) is that several supposed ends of one's action may prove to be merely means to other ends, and possibly inadequate means to those ends.

In a few words, the impact of the whole analysis, notwithstanding its "neutral" character, may be simply enormous in the field of the values accepted or rejected by acting men.

Good evidence of this power of the *Wertfreiheit method* is presented, in my humble opinion, by those thinkers who managed to explode irremediably whole systems of values by revealing them as simple collections of inadequate means to insufficiently analyzed ends. I am reminded in this connection of the devastating critiques of socialism performed in comparatively recent times by authors who have uncompromisingly accepted and ap-

plied the *Wertfreiheit* doctrine, or, as some of them say, epistemological relativism in the sciences of human action.

III

One more observation ought to be made relating to the
historical meaning of *Wertfreiheit* as epistemological relativism.
It is obvious that the Weberian program has exercised a tremendous influence in our time, namely, in the fields of economics,
sociology, and political science. Notwithstanding this, it could
hardly be denied that the attitude advocated by this doctrine for
the scholar, and in particular for the students of the social
sciences, is by no means a new one in the history of these disciplines. Almost all the great protagonists of that history in the
West have tried to present their conclusions as the results of an
unbiased process of mind in which personal evaluations were in
some way left aside to give way to impersonal tests and demonstrations. This is particularly evident both in the classical age
of the Greeks and in the modern age in Europe since the time of
Descartes, when mathematics, and particularly Euclidean geometry, was considered an indisputable model for any kind of argument relating to the study of man.[24]

The undeniable fact that this model was often adopted in an
uncritical way and that inquiries relating to acting men were
often forced into schemes not valid for human behavior (this
is what has been rightly called "scientism" in our time) must not
prevent us from recognizing the effectiveness of epistemological
relativism whenever it was properly applied in the past.

Max Weber, therefore, is not to be considered as the brilliant
author of a new method. He is rather the brilliant author in our
time of a thorough restatement of an old method.

A restatement of his doctrine in the face of so many kinds of
strictures on the part of his adversaries may be, in its turn, unless
I am wrong, a contribution to the development of the study of
man along the lines of the Western tradition.

NOTES

1. *See* Max Weber, *Gesammelte Aufsätze zur Wissenschaftslehre* (Tübingen: Mohr, 1922), especially, "Die 'Objectivität' sozialpolitischer Erkenntnis," pp. 146 ff., "Der Sinn der 'Wertfreiheit' der soziologischen und oekonomischen Wissenschaften," pp. 475 ff., and "Wissenschaft als Beruf," pp. 566 ff. The first two essays are available, as is known, also in English translation: "The Methodology of the Social Sciences" (Glencoe, Illinois: The Free Press, 1949). I shall be quoting here the Weberian essays from the second German edition (Tübingen: Mohr, 1951).
2. *See,* e.g., L. Strauss, "Che cosa é la filosofia politica?" *Il Politico,* 1956, pp. 359 ff., and my reply to that article in the same review, "Giudizi di valore e scienza politica," 1957, p. 86.
3. See *Gesammelte Aufsätze,* p. 485. My translation. Henceforth this work will be quoted as *G.A.*
4. This argument has been developed, e.g., by W. T. Couch at the Symposium on Scientism and Values, Emory University (1958), in his essay on "Objectivity and Social Science," published in *Scientism and Values* (D. Van Nostrand Co.; New York, 1960), pp. 38 f.
5. See *G.A., loc. cit.*
6. See *G.A.,* p. 483.
7. See *G.A.,* p. 484.
8. I am referring here to a recent speech given in English by Professor G. Sartori at Heidelberg on *"Wertfreiheit* in Political Science" (1959). A corresponding essay will be published in the German *Zeitschrift für Politik* in the near future.
9. *See* L. Strauss, *loc. cit.*
10. See note 8, present paper.
11. I myself dealt with this subject in collaboration with an Italian mathematician, Professor S. Frola, of the Turin Polytechnic; see "Possibilità di applicazione delle matematiche alle discipline sociali," *Il Politico,* 1955, pp. 190 ff.
12. *See,* in this sense, Soltau, *Introduction to Politics* (1952), p. 14. A striking example in this connection is presented in the recent book by Flavia Anderson, *The Rebel Emperor* (Gollancz, 1959). A peasant born near Canton, named Hung-Hsiu Chwan, alleged that in a trance he was ordained by God to be Emperor of China. Not content with this, he claimed Christ as his elder brother. No less than twenty million lives were lost from 1851-65 as the result of his rebellion. How many million people were prepared to die for Hung's faith? And why?
13. See note 1 of this paper.
14. See *G.A.,* p. 481.
15. See *G.A.,* p. 478.
16. An example of this kind of conciliation could be offered to Weber by the *System der Philosophie* of H. Rickert. It seems that Weber was

referring to Rickert when he dealt with this subject. But he did *not* quote Rickert in this connection in *G.A.*, p. 493.

17. See *G.A.*, p. 494.
18. See *G.A.*, p. 496.
19. See *G.A.*, p. 495.
20. See *G.A.*, p. 483.
21. See *G.A.*, p. 497.
22. Weber stated clearly, e.g., that any inquiry about actual moral convictions on the part of the people could not be of any use in proving the alleged "subjective" nature of those convictions (see *G.A.*, p. 487). He also vigorously contested the assumption that a "realistic" science of ethical phenomena could contribute in any way to the creation of any ethical doctrine whatsoever (see *G.A.*, p. 488).
23. See *G.A.*, p. 496.
24. It may be sufficient to remember in this connection Hobbes' saying that geometry is the only true science that God has given to man.

9

Adventure into the Unknown: Relativist "Man-Afraid-of-His-Mind" *

JAMES C. MALIN

During the late nineteenth century, and continuing into the twentieth, Western culture exhibited a number of characteristics that suggest that it had reached about its limits of development along the lines significant to its peculiar order of magnitude. Under a conviction of sophistication, its hypercritical attitude, in its manifold manifestations, had a demoralizing effect upon almost all creativity in substance of thought. Extreme specialization tended to fragment, to isolate, and to formalize all activities. The participants in each specialty felt a compulsion to draw boundary lines and to defend them, to construct a methodology that would vindicate the new subdivision in the performance of a supposedly essential function, and justify its existence as necessary. The proliferation of specialties compelled the elimination of some. In the ruthless competition for survival, form, method, and function, rather than content, became the focus of controversy, regard-

* In order to keep this essay within the wordage limits set for publication, two sections prepared for the symposium have been omitted: "The Historical Meaning of Relativism" and "Ecological and Anthropological Perspectives."

175

less of the discipline. Each fragment proclaimed itself essential. There was classical formalism, scientific formalism, economic formalism, political formalism, administrative formalism (bureaucracy), legal formalism, philosophical formalism, art formalism, etc., with much mutual recrimination, and withal, a pretentious show of revolt, each against the other's formalism. The most pretentious was the miscellany of attitudes generally comprehended under the designation "pragmatic revolt," a sceptical, relativistic, cynical, intolerant formalism, primarily negative, and without content, except subjective emotional biases.

Perfectionism in any of its forms is, potentially at least, an ideal that may become hostile toward originality. To follow the fashion of the twentieth century and make Puritanism the scapegoat is only to exhibit ignorance and prejudice. All religions are classifiable into two groups on the basis of their treatment of the relations of God and man: likeness and difference, immanence and transcendence. The unbridgeable difference is emphasized in Zoroastrianism, Judaism, and possibly early Christianity and early Islam. The Indian type of religion, with pantheistic tendencies, emphasized likeness, the immanence of God, and man as an emanation from God, desiring purification, return and unition.[1] The mystical aspects of Greek philosophy, especially the Platonic, and mysticized Christianity and Islam (Sufi) emphasized salvation by purification—perfectionism. Even the idea of progress of Condorcet and Godwin, at the end of the eighteenth century, was only a secularized version of that major archetype.

Malthus, however, challenged this version of perfectionism and was never satisfactorily answered, when he pointed out the lack of discrimination between "a small improvement, the limit of which is undefined, and an improvement really unlimited." Among his several examples the beauty of a flower serves best. Beyond a certain point its perfection cannot be extended but becomes self-destructive.[2] Malthus did not formulate the concept of orders of magnitude, but such a point of view would reinforce his criticism. Within any particular order of magnitude development is limited. A new order of magnitude introduces novel relationships and new properties.

Perfectionism in a moderate, naive form may afford a temporary measure of inspiration, but its ultimate logical implications, in finite space-time connotations, are frustration and defeatism. In practice, among the philosophically naive, it may serve as a pretentious pose to divert attention from intellectual incompetence—a formalistic pedantry. In any case, the outcome is defeatism for independent expression in any medium. To forestall further confusion about perfectionism and the idea of progress, they are dependent upon naive space and time for meaning and can have no validity except within a given order of magnitude of the field or system.

PerfectionISM, not perfectION, is a drive that seems to stimulate men to extraordinary efforts at what is called improvement, especially self-improvement and the improvement of others. The process is a delusion that can have only one outcome—a destructive frustration that eternally falls short only of self-destruction, a Sisyphean labor. Nevertheless, it induces delusions of grandeur so compelling that men are willing to sacrifice all happiness to undertake the attainment of the delusive goal. To word it differently, victims of the delusion can attain personal "happiness" only by making themselves and others miserable, under the excuse of improvement—active and passive, "self-improvement" and being "improved" by others, whether or not the victims wish to be "bettered."

PerfectION is a state of nonbeing, which cannot be experienced first hand. If it could be attained, it would be a static condition beyond finite comprehension. Perfection, if attainable, would be fatal because, among other things, it would destroy hope, even life itself, beyond which there is nothing. Without change, there can be no hope, and without change life ceases.

The paradox of perfectionISM and perfectION lies in the fact that the goal of the dynamic (perfectionism) is to achieve the static (perfection)—a state of rest. To live is to be dynamic, to change. To be perfect is to abandon all reason for change; change from one perfection to another perfection is nonsense. Perfection is absolute, rest, death, nothing. PerfectionISM, paradoxically, is in the tradition of Sisyphean "eternal recurrence" of hope and frustration. Yet men are eternally victims of that drive, drive, drive, drive, without end.

The mystical Infinite does not necessarily impose a closed system, although that is the tradition. The immensity and the eternity of the Infinite are not static. Such terms as open and closed, or static and dynamic, as applied to philosophical systems, designate finite ideas. The Infinite cannot be defined by language because it transcends space and time. It is beyond.

Finite closed systems are always subject to abuse, and perfectionism is only one example. Fanatical versions of it occur from time to time in different cultures. Man has not yet proved his ability to outgrow such abuses, but he may profit by perspective upon the nature of the danger.

In more ways than one, language, instead of serving its supposed function of communication, has become a major barrier to both original thought and to its dissemination. Some of the philosophical difficulties have been illustrated, and in part they help to explain why such creativity in substance of thought as had been in evidence in twentieth-century Western culture has been in areas of knowledge that depend least upon the necessity of verbalization. The sciences that can employ mathematical equations are a conspicuous case in point. But in those segments of culture whose thought can be formulated only in language, the passion for so-called literary form and for popularization that relieves the reader of mental effort is fatal.

No more effective and approved method of censorship of ideas has been invented than the allegation about deficiency in literary form. If the issue of so-called literary form possessed any validity, the difficulty might be resolved, but judgments on this point being altogether subjective, and not even any two editors being able to agree, the accident of power to impose their views about both form and substance is fatal. Mutual admiration groups and conformists flourish.

Higher education should be an inspiring adventure into the unknown for all concerned. Too often the experience is otherwise, the emphasis being upon teaching (indoctrination) rather than upon learning. The imitative teacher-disciple relationship and the sense of security in belonging to an influential "school of thought" and joining a "push" are rewarding. On the other hand, independent exploration meets discouragement or outright veto when it challenges the sacred tenets of the prevailing "school" and/or leads across the barbed-wire entanglements erected and patrolled to protect artificial compartments of knowledge from encroachments by outsiders. The survival rate for the maverick is not high and is approaching zero.

The spread of compulsory "education" and the extension of education to the higher levels, primarily in public institutions, has promoted uniformity of indoctrination favorable to the welfare/illfare state. Experimental tests of the effect of the prolongation of schooling seem to demonstrate conspicuously that the longer the schooling, the higher the score in terms of stereotyped answers to standardized tests. The customary interpretation of these facts, however, has represented them as proving that the higher scores meant a higher level of thinking intelligently about public questions. The "joker" in that conclusion lies in the nature of the questions and of the "correct" answers. Certainly the "correct" answers were suspect. In one such study cited, they reflected the prevailing "liberal" sentiment in academic circles during the period immediately preceding the experiment. The outcome reflected, not independent thinking, but conditioned reactions to a stereotype. In terms of the "gifted" student program, high scores on the tests would place the candidates among the elite, in the highest brackets of standardized responses. Emphatically, the high scores were not an index of capacity for independent thought, and, of course, possessed no necessary relation to capacity for creativeness or originality.[3]

The competition among ideas for survival in a free market is a concept that is always superficially attractive. If an idea possesses value, its merit would seem to insure its victory. The delusive element in the supposed process lies in the nature of the market and in access to it. The selective process may suppress the original or creative ideas before they actually reach the market place. If the teacher is deprived of his opportunity to teach at all, or to teach freely, no competition occurs. If an author's manuscript cannot be published promptly and as written, no competition occurs. The supposed freedom of a publisher to issue a book without government censorship—in other words, conventional freedom of the press—along with denunciation of book-burning, only diverts attention from the real issue—the barriers to publication at all. Many excuses are given for the shortage of teachers and for the dearth of productive scholarship, but few are willing to face the facts. Scepticism, uncertainty of knowledge, and subjective relativism are not conducive to either freedom of opinion or of action.

Only men inwardly quite sure of themselves can be truly tolerant.

Nothing in the references to hypercritical attitudes is intended to advocate that the rigor of proof be relaxed or that any effective methods be abandoned or that the search be curtailed for more adequate modes of making intelligence and verbalization effective. They may be pursued in a constructive spirit. Important is more adequate differentiation among the several aspects of relativism. Relativism of measurement of quantity and mere incompleteness of evidence are quite different from the philosophical relativism that challenges the capacity of the mind to know. The problems associated with the concepts of the infinite and the finite need reconsideration. The role of emotion, of the irrational, needs attention. For example, to the extent that emotion entered as a causative factor in explaining the outbreak of the American Civil War, quantitative modes of measurement are inapplicable. Emotion is not a quantity, with space-time properties. It is a state of being, where intensities may bear no apparent quantitative relation to the stimuli, if, indeed, the stimuli can be identified.

Concentration upon method of proof may become an end in itself apart from subject matter and, as such, is delusive in any department of knowledge. In the case of the historian, for example, a mastery of methods alone without subject matter is no more effective than methods of "education" without subject matter. One may be as barren or even as destructive as the other.

What is a creative mind, and how is an original product of the creative individual's mind and skill to be identified? Not by standardized tests. Probably that is the only absolute answer that can be given. Originality and standardization are irreconcilable. Only standardized imitative minds can be measured by standardized tests. Standards are static. Originality and creation defy the statics of standards because they are unique in the absolute sense. In so-called "gifted" student programs, the method of selection insures the choice of those most highly standardized in terms of the tests. Again, how can the unique, original mind and its product even enter the market, which is organized to deal only in standardized types and grades of commodities?

Obsession with the idea of producing something great as the deliberate act of creation, or the discovery of greatness, is a product of delusions of grandeur. Whatever of greatness there may be in an individual or in his work is an unconscious by-product of the commonplace, of his effort to perform the daily task so well, according to the medieval German mystic, John Tauler, "as to be a pattern for all." Not the workman or his contemporaries, but survival through time pronounces the verdict upon what is permitted to compete.

Quality is a state of being and is not measurable according to standards of numerical magnitude. Man's value derives from his quality, something beyond mere space-time properties, even though expressed through finite media. The quality of man and his work is what surmounts the limitations of space and time.

The theme of field-theory mysticism may be appropriately introduced by a quotation from Höffding's commentary on Nicolaus Cusanus (1401-1464): "Our knowledge seeks to rise above the oppositions and contradictions exhibited in experience." [4] Some ideas, or possibly most of them, about life as a conflict between two principles, or opposites, have their origin in the dim beginnings of man's primitive self-consciousness. They cannot be discarded at once, but somehow, somewhere, some time, the effort to surmount them must be undertaken.

Toward the middle of the twentieth century several academic disciplines have undertaken to define more adequate methods for the explanation of phenomena. The one most favored apparently is "field theory," a term given currency particularly by the mathe-

matical physicists, some of whom themselves carried the term
over into the social field. Strictly speaking, such usage was unwarranted, because no real analogy existed between man, possessing will, and atoms. Social scientists sometimes adopted the term
under the mistaken assumption that an analogy existed, and a
certain prestige accrued to the social sciences by its use. What was
actually being done was neither the mode of mathematical physics,
nor was it new. As the present writer understands the matter,
Aristotle was the first philosopher to formulate a highly significant
statement of the complex, but unified, concept of space-time-
motion. His entelechy was a version of it. But because of mis-
interpretations that are current in terms of determinism, the
reminder is in order that Aristotle frankly confessed his inability
to verbalize the concept successfully. The difficulty is inherent in
any attempt to reconcile the Infinite and the finite—in more particular terms, space-time and simultaneity.[5]

The positivist who is moderate in his formulations and doubts,
but does not deny that actuality may exist outside of the actuality
that he can "explain" operationally, tacitly admits that his positivism is not wholly valid. His agnosticism is an admission that
he has omitted something. He does not exclude, rather admits,
that the Infinite, of which his tangible and measurable finite is an
integral part, may, if it does not inevitably, exert a causative
influence upon the events he is trying to explain operationally.
Such an implicit admission means that his operational explanation is incomplete and does not explain entirely. The simultaneity of the Infinite (immensity and eternity) are always present
in the spatial and temporal causation of the finite. But the reverse
cannot be true. Therefore no concept of space and time is possible
but it comprehends this simultaneity.

Traditional cause-effect reasoning is based upon a naive assumption about space and time and the sequence in which duration is
implicit. Yet space and time are nothing more than devices or
instruments constructed by the finite mind as a means of organizing sense phenomena in a finite world—quite convenient and
useful, to be sure, so long as they serve their limited purpose of
making finite intelligence effective. But they become a barrier to

the extension of knowledge beyond the more elementary limits of needs associated with man's emergence from the cave environment. When this cave animal became sufficiently self-conscious to call for something beyond those simple requirements, he undertook to make a place in his space-time construct to accommodate a concept of simultaneity, together with all of its implications and consequences, as they slowly emerged into his consciousness.

When the human mind can effectively conceive of so-called cause and effect in terms of complete simultaneity without space connotations, something momentous happens to the thinker and to his attitude toward the relations of the self to the phenomenal world and toward phenomenal relations within that world. The cause *is* the effect, and the effect *is* the cause, and the actor in the historical event is included or involved. These relations are not conventional space-time sequences in which duration is implied between cause and effect, regardless of whether single or multiple factors are being considered. In order to verbalize them in conventional language, the device of interaction, or reciprocal action, is customarily employed, or the process is sometimes described as circular—cause produces effect, and in turn, effect becomes cause, all of which implies duration in both directions. This is nonsense. The whole field of causation is simultaneous at the decisive instant. Simultaneity transcends finite space-time, and by whatever linguistic name or conceptual label the process is designated for purposes of identification in communication among persons, the phenomena involved partake of the Infinite— something beyond the naive space-time of the *Homo sapiens* who has just emerged from the cave.

Possibly the conventional brand name for this conception of cause and effect would be mysticism. If so, make the most of it, instead of dismissing it as something forbidden and fit only for ridicule by twentieth-century scientific rationalism.[6] What the mid-twentieth century is calling field theory is essentially this mystical phenomenon, even though the user is unaware of the implications and formulates the idea crudely as something new.

The equations of Einstein defy any truly intelligible verbalization. Also, they defy three-dimensional Euclidian geometry and are not verifiable by direct tangible evidence of the senses. They are mental constructs, not tangible things in themselves. To the present writer nothing would appear more natural than for a mathematical physicist to become a religious mystic, a twentieth-century Neoplatonist.

Unwittingly, much of what is professed by modern science is a modernized version of the Neoplatonic negative road to a definition of the One, the Infinite—by stripping Him, one by one, of all finite properties as attributes that He does not possess. The One is indefinable, because any definable attribute assigned to Him becomes a limitation and deprives Him of His Infinity. To be Infinite, He must be No-thing—a thing is finite. He is No-thing, He is Nothing, Infinite. That is not a paradox; it is truth. The finite is an emanation from The One, assuming space-time properties as a measure of His finiteness, but striving always to free itself of finite limitations in order to return to the Absolute.

Verbalization of thought is necessarily a space-time device. To speak, to write, or even to arrange thought in an orderly fashion in the mind for purposes of communication, is to act within a space-time frame of reference. In consequence, any abstract idea that in any manner partakes of the Infinite must necessarily be released from space and time. If such a state is at all possible to the human mind, it may be in terms of mathematical theory or of some type of symbolism that transcends both space and time. But any attempt to verbalize an operation of that sort abandons by that act any hypothetically Infinite properties and assumes space-time properties. Einstein's first attempt to explain relativity for a popular audience by verbalization met with embarrassment to him on even cruder grounds. In the controversy with Henri Bergson, Einstein was worsted and was made to appear ridiculous. His blunder was not in his mathematics, but in his verbalization.[7] Of course, the question must be left open whether or not even the mathematical theory had actually transcended space-time in the sense pertinent to the problem of the Infinite and the finite. Whether or not consciously declared to be such, it is an attempt in that direction. The goal of such an operation is not to vindicate relativism as such, but, admitting an objective relativism as a property of finite space and time, to transcend it, to experience the undefinable Absolute.

In their philosophy of science, unknown to most of them apparently, scientists are crushing the old grapes of mysticism. The vintage is that usually labeled Neoplatonic. At least two things are essential to the education of those indifferent or hostile to religion: first, to break the mold of twentieth-century prejudices and bigotry about religion; and secondly, to induce them to steep themselves in the history and writing of Plato and his successors, usually known as Neoplatonists.[8] As a prelude to modern philosophy, Nicolaus Cusanus was the first to analyze explicitly the problem of the Infinite and the finite. Further attempts were made a major theme of modern philosophy.[9]

In the history of religious mysticism, grounded in prehistoric social experience and magic, primitive peoples developed archetypes of religious ideas that are inherent in human culture. Different eras and areas of culture have produced variants in typology and have clothed them sometimes in strange superficial masks and practices, but the forms are still present. In ostentatiously pretending to repudiate religion and all things supernatural, some scientists have only succeeded in backing themselves into some of the most naive forms of supernaturalism. They should try to discover the typological parallels and identities of their own bungling philosophy of science with the historical typological models. They would soon realize that instead of inventing or paying homage to a philosophy of relativism, they are actually desperately trying to escape from the relativism of spacetime and to find intellectual and emotional security in something probably best described as similar or comparable to what the candid mystics called unition with the One, the Absolute, as of Plotinus, Iamblichus, and Proclus. This twentieth-century scientific mysticism, as thus far developed, however, is a poor substitute for non-Christian mysticism and Christian mysticism, which Dean Inge characterized as "largely an intellectual movement." Also, he emphasized that the latter combines the mystical with the practical and the commonplace.[10]

Relativist "man-afraid-of-his-mind" does not have the courage to face and to explore adventurously the unknown realm of the supranatural (more than the supernatural) toward which his thought leads him and which tradition labels mysticism. His secular scientific conditioning has taught him that such premises are "off limits" and that only the mentally abnormal could be so deluded as to believe in direct revelation from God, in unition with the One, or the Absolute, beyond space and time.

William James, in his *Varieties of Religious Experience* (1902), was sympathetic toward mysticism—a certain faith as essential to the completion of truth—but the rather general interpretation of most readers has been to consider it a study in abnormal psychology, which virtually reduced religion to delusion. In spite of his attitude toward mysticism, which can have no meaning except in unity with the One, the Indivisible, James developed a philosophy of pluralism.[11] This appears as illogical as that of the American philosopher-historians Charles Beard and Carl Becker, also pluralists, who invoked Benedetto Croce, an extreme idealist, in support of their subjective relativism.

To be sure, this essay is not a proposal to revive Neoplatonism as such, but a thorough knowledge of the history of that mystic archetype affords a perspective upon what twentieth-century scientists are actually doing.

Furthermore, to a greater extent than they seem to realize, scientists are operating upon the premise of "revelation" as the basis of their philosophy of history. Nothing can be accepted as truth unless it is "revealed" by scientific experiment. Nature's behavior or laws are revealed as truth and become the standard by which all other knowledge is verified. All that has been previously accepted as truth is vindicated or rejected according to its conformity with that "revealed truth"—verified by experiment. In Communist Russia, however, all knowledge, as well as science, is verified by reference to "revelation" according to Marx and Lenin.[12]

Many of the problems which academic people expend so much energy in "solving" are created by definitions. The direct, simple, and economical manner of solving—really solving—such problems is to discard the definitions that created them. But that would be disastrous because the academic world would be obliged to find something to do. The dichotomy between the tradition of "verification" by scientific experiment and other forms of "revelation" would dissolve into thin air. If all forms of revelation were candidly accepted for what they are, an intelligible differentiation among them might possibly be effected. A certain courage is necessary to defy the prejudices and bigotry of the long tradition about a particular kind of conflict or warfare between science and religion. More truth than is likely to be admitted is contained in the generalization that in the twentieth century science has displaced religion as the chief source of error.

If the concept of a new order of magnitude of thought is in any degree valid, then the present is a transitional stage and period, in which the old has been outgrown so far as effectiveness is concerned, and the new has not yet been formulated sufficiently for us to be sure yet just what forms it may take, and certainly not adequately to implement reliable current use. The best that can be done now is to state things very much in the old framework of Infinite-finite explanation, but introducing something of the new point of view and the necessity of absolute difference, regardless of the adequacy of the present conceptualization and verbalization. A completed restatement of the problem is impossible at this stage, if for no other reason than that the transition is not yet complete. Probably a long period of transition is yet required. On the other hand, a sufficiently original mind may crystallize the whole process almost overnight, and with startling clarity. All this lies in the realm of the unpredictable.

Possibly the word "simultaneity" is not the proper term, nor is the traditional Neoplatonic Infinite exactly the concept necessary to the situation. One aspect is certain, neither is adequate, and they may even be frustrating rather than helpful. So many people of high intellectual attainments, in the traditional sense, are so prejudiced and ignorant about Platonism, Neoplatonism, and especially the word "mysticism," that the mere mention of any of them may cause a complete mental block that will render impossible even a passing consideration of the matters presented here. In the very nature of the case, however, no existent word or concept expressible in language can meet the requirement. If it did, it would no longer be finite; but it is finite and therefore cannot express the Infinite. In the attempt to transcend the space-time of the physical senses, as Plato and Neoplatonists chewed on that bone and "wooled" it round and round, the only thing they could say in words (which are finite) was what the Infinite is *not*. Whether or not men are in any better position now is doubtful, but it must be recognized that merely imitating the Neo-Platonic tradition is not sufficient. Something absolutely original is called for, but no response has come in anything positive. The attempt to be independent has been made in this paper, or sufficiently so, to recognize that the answer is not yet available, and, that being the case, there is little choice but to follow along the explored paths, hoping to find the basis for a genuine breakthrough in thought to an understanding of what is over and beyond space-time, or transcendent of space-time.

The Einstein tradition has associated relativism with this beyond, or seems to do so, and certainly his imitators do, those who try to ride to intellectual distinction upon his coattails. Of course, they do not put it in the perspective here outlined, but beyond conventional space-time there is talk of "the fourth dimension," of "curved space," or recourse to other terminology that is intended to verbalize something that is not comprehended within the garden varieties of ideas about Euclidian geometry and something that is expressible only in mathematical equations. The expounders of the Einstein tradition insist that his equations prove relativism.

The contention of this paper is that the opposite of this Einstein tradition is true.[13] Relativism lies within the space-time frame of reference, is inherent in it, which is finite. To escape this relativism, the mind must transcend completely this space-time frame of reference. That is the significance of Einstein's work on relativism. Traditionally, what is beyond space-time is the Absolute, the One. Possibly, that terminology is confusing in this context, especially upon first acquaintance and to those not fully saturated with the newer scholarship dealing with Plato, Aristotle, and those who have traditionally been labeled Neo-Platonists.

The older traditions and prejudices about these matters are fatal to such intellectual operations as are proposed here. But, again, words and concepts are lacking, except as they can be constructed essentially *de novo* in new contexts of scholarship and by talking all around the subject, stripping the tradition of the things to which there is legitimate objection, leaving bare the new conceptualization toward which the main argument is directed. The firm and constant truth of existence, etc., is in this realm beyond space and time. It is not subject to the five physical senses. *Life* is more than something physical and tangible; because it is *life,* it is beyond the five senses. Life must possess other senses than the five senses of the physical body.

Natural rationalism is based upon the five senses, utilizing physical phenomena. A monopoly is assumed upon the channels through which knowledge may be acquired. Natural rationalism ignores life, which is not derived from the physical senses, or from merely physical processes in the conventional tradition. Life is a concomitant of all organized, physical, sensory organisms; it is over and above them, and the door cannot be shut upon the possibility that life may exist independent, separate, and apart from all things physical. Any one of the five senses may be destroyed without injury to life itself; possibly all may be lost without destroying life itself—effectiveness of life is not the issue in the preceding sentences, only the fact of life as existence.

Reasoning capacity is not explained by the senses; it is associated with life, whatever that is, and uses the physical senses as instruments for gathering phenomenal material. This accumulated material, with memory, is utilized, analyzed, sorted, and synthesized by mental processes associated with the mind, the reasoning power, and the logical processes invented or discovered by the mind and reason—life.

John Locke recognized the necessity of this certain capacity of the mind to know as the prerequisite of the accumulation on the white blank tablet of all experience. This admission was fatal to all major conclusions misdrawn by Locke himself, and even more erroneously by his imitative disciples—to the effect that all knowledge is derived from experience, and nothing is to be believed unless it is verified by experiment, the data being channeled through the five physical senses. This "modern" attitude of verification by experiences goes back explicitly to Nicolaus Cusanus and in the earlier archetype to Greek philosophy or beyond.

The certain capacity of the mind to know and to receive sensory data was the heart of the whole human situation and owed nothing to the five senses for its existence or to the sensory phenomena in a sequential relation. Here, apparently, occurs that necessity which philosophers have totally ignored—simultaneity, which transcends space and time and is the key to all knowledge, that is, processes through which knowledge eventuates. The capacity of the mind to know and the phenomenal data supplied by the senses meet each other, not in space-time sequences that involve initial duration necessary to the concept of cause-and-effect, but in simultaneity—life and data in relations beyond the finite space-time frame of reference.

Scientists boast about the rapidity of scientific discovery, about new knowledge outmoding earlier knowledge, about the era of the specialist, who, according to the current witticism, knows more and more about less and less and is unable even to keep up with the new knowledge essential to his specialty. But what of it? In what way is this knowledge new? In details, or in basic ideas? Relativism thrives on the emphasis upon rapid change, which is the pride of modern scientism. The basic archetypes of thought formulated by primitive man prior to writing are not ephemeral, and obsolescence is not conspicuous.

The general and the particular occupy different perspectives. What of the individual man, as differentiated from the human animal in general? For each and every human being, his life experience is new—new to him absolutely. (This is true within the limits of present knowledge, but Dr. Carl Jung's major contention about the "collective unconscious" cannot be ignored.) Man's uniqueness—absolute—is the basis of his claim of right against all comers to work out his own destiny. The warning sign that he has so often forgotten to keep in sight and focus is that this momentous fact of absolute novelty to him personally must not mislead him about the whole race experience in creativity of thought and invention of technology. The latter is not the work of one man or one generation. A fundamental change, no doubt, will try the patience of man for a considerable number of generations, centuries, or milleniums.

The magic of primitive peoples formulated concepts of good and evil and set them off against each other as opposites, along with natural phenomena, light-dark, male-female, action-reaction, as antagonistic principles. The Greek philosopher Heraclitus is credited with making the warfare of antagonistic principles the basis of his system. Either/or logic and the dialectic formula (thesis, antithesis, synthesis) are manifestations of this principle or archetype.

But attempts to split the difference, to reconcile, compromise, or synthesize opposites are both a logical and a practical impossibility. That is why all systems of thought that derive from any form of assumptions about opposites must necessarily lead to scepticism and relativism.

Of course, to complete the longer term behavior within this formula, a reaction eventually arises against the inadequacies of sceptical relativism, and a return is attempted toward absolutes. In a rough way, this appears to have been the course of the history of thought from the heroic period of Greek history. through the Sophists, through the era of Socrates, Plato, and Aristotle, etc.—fluctuations, not cycles. These fluctuations did not involve human culture as a whole, which lacked a unity that would have made such a thing possible. Neither did these fluctuations involve at one time all the people living under the Greek heritage. Both phases of the phenomena were probably always present, and only at particular times and places did one or the other dominate to such an extent as to lend character to a period in some geographical area.

It is in this perspective and context that twentieth-century relativism of the Dewey-Becker-Beard sequence is associated with self-styled progressives and self-appointed liberals. Of course, the self-styled neo-conservatives of the mid-twentieth century are also relativists, only using different criteria, but just as intolerant.

They are now in a hopeless minority, but should the balance of power shift, they would be as insufferable as their liberal opposite numbers. Too much emphasis cannot be placed upon the point that neo-conservatism is fully as relativistic as the Dewey-Becker-Beard relativism with the progressive or the liberal label.

All of this leads to the conclusion that if these historic abuses represented in such fluctuations are to be overcome, it must be through some means of breaking the "eternal recurrence" archetype of thought. It must also be something more than the ten-thousand-year opportunity of escape invented by the Greeks, the archetype of which is still embodied in European folklore and only recently revived in modified form in the musical show, "Brigadoon." The eschatology of the theologian belongs to this escape archetype along with the secularized twentieth-century theories about revolution or the "science" of social change.

The concept of a new order of magnitude of thought is introduced with a view to the formulation of something to supersede the historic archetype. The term "field theory" has been used, but, at the same time, other methods in the sciences that do not go by that name might be cited. Until the breakthrough in thought actually occurs, no other course seems available. If and when such a breakthrough occurs, then all these clumsy fumblings will be brushed aside, and a new simplicity of method, terms, and communication will emerge, as in the case of breakthroughs in other technologies that the mind uses as instruments to implement its operations.

Returning to the mathematical physicist's equations and their form of relativism, so called, we observe that in reality they were trying to achieve the reverse, in other words, to escape from relativism—the relativism inherent in finite space-time. Mathematical physicists by means of mathematical equations not dependent upon verbalization are seeking to state truth in a form not subject to distortions of space-time and to effect a correction independent of, or beyond, space and time limitations. They are not trying to achieve relativism, but to escape from it. To be sure, this is not the conventional interpretation, but once the mold of conventional formalism is broken, the logic of the facts and the interpretation seems unmistakable.

Relativism of the twentieth century, or possibly the matter should be put in the plural, relativisms, are a phase in intellectual change that has achieved a major position for the time being, but this vogue should sooner or later be outgrown, along with the associations with progressivism and liberalism as evidences of sophistication. To fluctuate in the opposite direction, however, and no more, is of no intrinsic value, but only of temporary value in the sense that it might tend to redress the balances super-ficially by neutralizing one extreme with the other. The only basic change would be an escape from relativism in both forms of associations, left and right, through the achievement of a new order of magnitude in thought that may transcend the limitations of space-time, at least partially, if we remember how little man has learned since he has learned to write and how long a time was required (finite space-time) between the cave and writing. A true escape from relativism requires something more than repudiation—negation. Certainly the mathematical physicist has penetrated a beyond, where the evidence of the five senses, in a space-time context, cannot actually follow.

Possibly, even probably, the outcome of this discussion leads only to the conclusion that the whole subject of Infinite-finite is due for a fresh reconsideration and a complete redefinition, an original conceptualization in all particulars, that could lead twentieth-century culture into a new order of magnitude of thought about being, becoming, existence, and causation. Pos-sibly, even probably, the creative thought involved could put man in a new relation to reality that would afford new powers, hitherto undreamed of, at this emergent level of magnitude and introduce him into a quite original and different culture. The value judg-ment that would be involved in the word "higher" level, etc., has been excluded purposely. The level would be different, but to speak comparatively in terms of higher and lower would be a gross error.

The problem of the Infinite and the finite and their meaning to midtwentieth-century knowledge is obviously more than a theologian's quibble, more than a delusion of abnormal psychology, and more than a facetious game to be played by a logician clever in the manipulation of words at the expense of man's faith in his own intelligence. The meaning of revelation needs a fresh examination. The mathematical physicist's preoccupation with difficulties arising out of the limiting factor of finite space and time and his devices for transcending them by methods other than verbalization certainly require a new orientation that may be significant for all knowledge. He is not advocating relativism or resorting to relativism, but is trying to escape from it or to nullify the space-time limitations that restrict his creative thought. Aspects of the old concepts of the Infinite and the finite may not only be valid, but may be essential to a modern restatement and to a reassertion of a sense of confidence in man's capacity to solve his problems in their novel contexts.

To adventure into the unknown in any significant manner must be for the thinker to find himself beyond his depth. To say that a man is beyond his depth is a favorite mode of ridicule that may be turned into a compliment. No significant thinking can be done until the thinker does adventure beyond his depth.

The hypercritical characteristics of Western culture have produced a "man-afraid-of-his-mind." He is sadly mistaken when he assumes that this is a commendable token of sophistication. Adventure into the unknown beyond the boundaries of proven knowledge requires the assumption of the risk of being wrong, the courage to admit error; all as the price of the possible breakthrough to some new order of magnitude of thought. The only reward of originality is in the doing. If enough men within the ranks of Western culture possess this property, this individual urge to adventure, it may survive. If not, then the responsibility for failure lies within.

NOTES

1. Edwyn Bevan, *Symbolism and Belief* (1938; Boston: Beacon Books, BP 42, 1957).

2. Thomas Robert Malthus, *An Essay on the Principle of Population,* 1st ed. (London, 1798), pp. 155-172.

3. Seba Eldridge, *Public Intelligence. A Study of the Attitudes and Opinions of Voters,* Humanistic Studies, Volume V, No. 1 (Lawrence: University of Kansas, 1935).

4. Harold Höffding, *A History of Modern Philosophy,* trans. by B. E. Meyer, 2 vols. (London: Macmillan, 1900), I, 86.

5. The present writer has discussed different aspects of these problems explicitly in *The Contriving Brain and the Skillful Hand in the United States. Something about History and Philosophy of History* (Lawrence, Kansas: the author, 1955), chap. 11, "Open End Modes of Thought and Formalism." The psychologists' use of field theory and history was discussed in *On the Nature of History: Essays about History and Dissidence,* (Lawrence, Kansas: the author, 1954), chap. 3, "History in Relation to Aspects of Field Theory." Citations to the pertinent literature are given in connection with these discussions and need not be repeated here.

6. As early as 1914, Bertrand Russell, in "Mysticism and Logic," *Hibbert Journal,* XII (July, 1914), 780-803, reprinted as the title essay in *Mysticism and Logic and Other Essays* (London and New York: Longmans, Green and Company, 1918), declared: "But the greatest men who have been philosophers have felt the need of both science and mysticism."

7. Charles Nordmann, *The Tyranny of Time: Einstein or Bergson?* trans. from the French by E. E. Fornier d'Albe (London: T. Fisher, Unwin, Limited, 1925).

8. The writings of Werner Jaeger and others on Plato and Aristotle change substantially the perspective not only on them and their period, but also on the following, the so-called Hellenistic period, and later. See especially Werner Jaeger, *Aristotle: Fundamentals of the History of His Development,* trans. by Richard Robinson, 2nd ed. (Oxford: Oxford University Press, 1949); *Paideia: The Ideals of Greek Culture,* trans. by Gilbert Highet (Oxford University Press, 1939), 3 vols.; Harry Austryn Wolfson, *Philo: Foundations of the Religious Philosophy of Judaism, Christianity, and Islam,* 2 vols. (Cambridge: Harvard University Press, 1948); *The Philosophy of the Church Fathers* (Cambridge: Harvard University Press, 1956).

   For the Neoplatonists, *see* Philip Merlan, *From Platonism to Neoplatonism* (The Hague, The Netherlands: Martinus Nijhoff, 1953). Merlan belongs to the revisionist school that insists that no gap existed between Plato and Aristotle and the so-called Neoplatonists. The late nineteenth-century writers had emphasized discontinuity.

9. Among the most elaborate attempts at exposition of the Infinite and the finite is that of Emanuel Swedenborg (1688-1772), in his scientific and theological works.

10. W. R. Inge, *Christian Mysticism* [c.1899] reprinted (New York: Meridian Books, 1956), 11, 22. Inge's comment was limited to Christian mysticism. Inge quoted John Tauler (ca. 1300-1361): "One can spin, another can

make shoes; and all these are gifts of the Holy Ghost. I tell you, if I were not a priest, I should esteem it a great gift that I was able to make shoes, and would try to make them so well as to be a pattern to all."

11. One of the strangest facts about James' book was that he did not mention Emanuel Swedenborg, a most significant example of a form of Christian mysticism. Swedenborg was the major inspiration of William James' father, Henry James, although neither William nor his brother Henry shared their father's enthusiasm.

12. An explicit history of the revelation philosophy of history is needed. The present author has collected some significant notes on the subject that await elaboration at another time and place.

13. Immediately after World War I, when the Einstein "relativism" equation was the vogue, along with others, the present writer accepted the extension of the mathematical-physical verbalization of relativism in its extreme form. With regrets, that experience must be listed among the mistakes of intellectual adolescence.

10

Relativism and Social Control

JOHN W. TIETZ

> It seems to me, therefore, that the principle of relativity is a philosophical principle which. . . . is destined to give us a new world view.
>
> H. Wildon Carr [1]
>
> It seems that for about three hundred years, Nature has destined the middle of each century to be the period of a revolution in the mind of man.
>
> D'Alembert—1759 [2]
>
> We live in a relative and contingent universe.
>
> Gruber—1958 [3]
>
> To quarrel with the world is attractive, but dangerous.
>
> Amiel—1872 [4]

This paper attempts to trace the rise of current relativism in thought to the confluence, in the nineties, of four streams of thought: scientific thought and its application to human behavior; the emergence of scientific humanism; the flowering of sociological thought; and the spread of the concept of relativity in physical science to other areas of thought. This spread into two "sensitive" fields of social controls and sanctions—education and jurisprudence—is then sketched to show the revolutionary effects produced by relativistic thought in these fields.

The all-pervading relativism, presently seen in many areas of our thinking, referred to above by Gruber, is really an emergent

197

derived from streams of thought going back more than two millenia at least. Harold Faulkner, in the opening words of his *Politics, Reform and Expansion—1890-1900,*[5] probably was right when he wrote: "The 1890's separated not only two centuries but two areas in American history." This seems particularly so in such fields as scientific, social, educational, and jurisprudential thought. Relativistic thinking probably had its greatest effect in the field of social controls and sanctions—education and jurisprudence.

Louis Blanc[6] said: "The true history of our century is the history of its ideas." Would then the history of education not be, above all, a history of the ideas of various cultures? Can we trace the origin, evolution and mutation of ideas, or even isolate the seed idea in many cases? Perhaps. Any area of thought resembles that of an atomic field in which ideas originate and develop, collide, and jostle each other, ricochet and "feed-back" to re-enforce others, and split and recombine to form new patterns, in endless and restless fashion. Yet one can notice during the so-called "gay nineties" (which really were not so gay) at least four emerging streams of thought contributing distinctly to a *Zeitgeist* of relativism. These are (1) a steadily rising tide of scientific methodology and its projection into the study of human behavior, (2) the flowering of the sociological thinking of the previous decades, (3) the ever-increasing political overtones of social democracy, and (4) the mushrooming concept of relativism with, of course, a corresponding de-emphasis on the concept of "absolutes."

However, just as ideas have consequences, so also these very ideas themselves are consequences of other antecedent and earlier ideas. G. T. W. Patrick (1888) says, "To Heraclitus we trace the notion of relativity."[7] The scientists of the nineteenth century were slowly becoming aware that the crust of the earth had changed and was changing and that the species of living things upon that earth had also changed and were also changing—that a process of "an unrolling" or evolution was going on. The capstone of this line of thought was Darwin's great work of a century ago, *The Origin of Species*. He showed that of the many variations (individual differences) occurring in all groups of living things, those that were best fitted to survive in their environment would be perpetuated and were so "naturally selected" and gave rise to a new species. A slight shift in thinking could remove the emphasis from both the organism and its environment and place it upon the adjustment between them, i.e., a "relationship." Although those who accepted this idea took life as a basis for the evolutionary process, many theologians of that day, already alarmed at the growing materialism of the times, noting the denial of a special creation of each species as well as the absence of the mention of God, called the book atheistic or agnostic. At any rate, one could search in vain for any statement of the indicated origin, purpose or goal of the evolutionary process. The starting premise, however, was that of individual variations or differences among the living things in a group, a condition that made for the "relativity of individuals" in that group. This was to be objectively demonstrated before another generation had passed.

In 1879, Wilhelm Wundt established in Leipzig the first experimental psychological laboratory, which was to become a beachhead for the invasion of scientific study of human behavior. Here he introduced the methods of physical science into the study of sensation, a frontier where the physical and the psychological meet. Some five years later, Galton, who had published his *Hereditary Genius* (on the inheritance of the human variation called "genius"), set up at his own expense at the International Health Exhibition in London (1884) an anthropometric laboratory where he measured seventeen physical and certain psychological characteristics of some nine thousand visitors. After the closing of the exhibition, he continued this scientific invasion into the study of individual differences at South Kensington. In order to handle and digest this mass of data, Galton invented his "novum organum"—the correlational calculus—the basis of our modern mathematical theory of the statistics of variables.

It was, however, Cattell who, after studying with Wundt and Galton, returned to America and devised tests of a more psychological character. Here, then, the study of intelligence had its inception. It opened up the vast field of psychological testing in all areas of human behavior. Masses of data, often showing great individual differences, were derived by the use of carefully devised new instruments, used under controlled conditions, and correlated by the mathematics of statistics.[8] Before long this "relativism" among capacities, aptitudes, kinds of knowledge, skills, and personalities began to impress the educators.

Humanism, with its premises of relativism, unfolded in Greece as the result of many factors. About eight years after the victory of Cimon in the Persian Wars (468 B.C.), Pericles came into the leadership of Athens, hoping to build the Athenian empire of which Themistocles had dreamed. Athens became a "vibrant city"[9] of untold prosperity with a leadership in trade similar to that of England before 1914, a city of beautiful architecture, sculpture, and paintings, of sparkling conversationalists, of great social activity in this Golden Age of Pericles. Because of its new social, intellectual, and political needs, there arose a new class of teachers, largely drawn from among foreigners from Ionia and Greater Greece, who, because of the easy requirements for citizenship, had come to Athens to live upon and to enjoy its great prosperity. Naturally, one would find among this group of Sophists, as they were known, many unscrupulous ones who would bring disrepute upon the name. Many of their teachings did start with the Heraclitian idea of constant flux [10] and the materialistic sensualism of Democritus, who taught that there is nothing but atoms and space, knowledge of which is to be arrived at through the senses.

Added to these ideas were the ethnological observations of the much-traveled Greeks, which showed them all too clearly the conflicting and relative differences in political institutions, social usages, religious beliefs, moral standards, and philosophies of life —even through successive generations. As a result, it was easy to accept the Sophist philosophy. The contemplation of the nature of the universe, started by Thales, was replaced by a focus on the universe centered around man. We see this in one of the two fragments left to us by the first man to call himself a Sophist (or wise man), Protagoras of Abdera (490-421 B.C.): "Of all things the measure is Man; of the things that are, that they are; and of things that are not, that they are not." [11] Gorgias of Leontinum (470-375 B.C.), the second most eminent Sophist, contended that virtue is many, not one, and differs with age, temperament, occupation and sex. He first developed a theory of moral relativism. Implications ripple outward from these, some of which could read: that an individual's perceptions and judgments are relative; universal truth valid for all men is denied, each man being the sole judge of what seems so, and therefore true to him; there is no authority higher than man to weigh and decide between conflicting opinions; and since man is constantly changing his mind, truth is not only a matter of the individual, but of the individual at that moment.

The next major manifestation of this man-centered philosophy was the Renaissance. Again, the attention of man shifted from the things of the spirit to discoveries of things material. Thus, finally, we come to the beginnings of science as we know it today. It was not, however, until soon after the beginning of the nineteenth century that we begin to see the initial merging of the streams of science and humanism to form a positivistic or scientific humanism. The French Revolution had been a deep-going socio-political disturbance based upon a materialistic and naturalistic philosophy of an excessively radical, liberalistic type that had torn up all social, political, and religious sanctions of any importance. Many French thinkers regarded it as having failed in its mission, and some sought to meet the problem with a formula for a new society for mankind, a social revolution to be achieved through enlightenment and education that would adjust the inequalities of property, power, and happiness in man.

This new system was to be based, not upon "impossible metaphysics," but upon a positive (i.e., scientific) study of objects of sense experience, because these latter alone could be known. Of the thinkers engaged in such endeavors, two seem to stand out: Saint Simon (1760-1825) and Auguste Comte (1798-1857).[12] At first they collaborated, but Saint Simon, trying to retain his admiration of the spirit of medieval times, sought a new system of a Christianity based upon love of the poor and lowly. Comte rejected the idea, alleging that the philosophy and theology of the Middle Ages represented primitive thought and that metaphysical thought substituted abstract powers and entities for human beings. His new social science was to be patterned after the natural sciences with their positivistic, real, useful, certain, and exact knowledge derived from observation and experience.

This concept of Comte's can easily be considered the archetype of the modern scientific humanism that interprets man as "a biosocial organism," "capable through the use of intelligence of directing his institutions and creating a human civilization. This humanism also emphasizes the universal application of methods of experimental inquiry and holds that truth, reality, etc., are human values to be judged by reference to consequences humanly expressed." [13] Not a few texts in psychology today are patterned upon this concept. Besides designating the study of the associated life of humanity as "sociology" (1838), Comte also seems to have been the first person to have projected a new society planned upon scientific lines rather than on metaphysical considerations (or abstractions). Like Comte, the later formulators also left out the religious and spiritual side of man. This can be seen in the scientific-socialistic society of Karl Marx, the scientifically motivated society of Lester F. Ward, and the one to be achieved by an education that was projected by John Dewey early in this century. In all of these there is the refusal to consider any "absolutes" outside of man. In its "constant reconstruction of experience," Dewey's educational philosophy is definitely Heraclitean in character. The results of following this educational philosophy are coming under fire today after two generations.

Closely allied with the humanism of the nineteenth century was the sociological movement of the later half of that century. This alliance still prevails. The movement was given impetus by a series of chain reactions in the form of many humane and religious movements beginning early in the nineteenth century and was fed by a deep concern about the miserable conditions of the working classes. Albion Small considered the sociological movement a "child of its time." This growing sense of "social" concern and the effort which accompanied it were widespread in Western societies around 1900.

There are three major successive, somewhat overlapping, phases of the sociological movement: a benevolent, an academic, and a philosophical phase, each making its peculiar contribution. Considering our country, one can place the first period between 1865 and 1885. Some writers even feel that the Civil War had suggested or even demonstrated that life in the United States was not the success it had been believed to be. An increasing number of people, agitated by what Small had termed "social consciousness," engaged in an amateurish benevolence groping for the solution to "social" problems. And, to judge from any collection of college textbooks on "social problems" in the United States of 1959, it seems that little clarification and verification of what "social" problems really are have yet come about. This growth of a "social consciousness" was new in the history of man. Hardly any similar phenomenon had ever appeared in human history. It became the new motive to shape and foster the sociological movement. During that period the American Social Science Association was founded, patterned somewhat after Lord Brougham's National Association for the Promotion of Social Science. The preface to the first issue of the journal of the American Social Science Association in 1869 reads: "Social Science or the Science of Society treats man as a social being. It fulfills its function just as other sciences fulfill theirs by collecting facts, applying principles and reaching laws which govern social relations." [14] A later volume called for an objective approach in such a study. This marks a scientific, and not a philanthropic, approach, which so often starts from an impulse of the moment and solves the need of the moment, but never seeks causes upon which to plan prevention.

While the need for an organized study of social problems, at a more intellectual level, had become apparent, the organized academic study of society upon which to build such an accumulation of needed data was to wait for nearly a decade and a half

longer. The appearance of Lester F. Ward's *Dynamic Sociology,*
in 1883, may be considered the beginning of such an academic
movement. Although very provincial and preoccupied in its out-
look, biological and not psychological in its analogies, the book
asked the basic question of the meliorism of its day: "Is it possible
for society to improve its character?" Ward thought so. To him,
society is the highest point of evolution. It depends for its evolution upon the mind, which is the highest property of matter.
Man is a psychic agent capable of psychic causation and organization. Social evolution toward the gaining of happiness is therefore
a psychic process. Consequently, Lester F. Ward could foresee the
building of a new society through a process of a new education,
which he outlined. Ward held a materialistic naturalism. He was
antagonistic to all forms of religion and supernaturalism. And he
was, by the way, reprimanded by Small for his gratuitous and
illogical depreciation of Christianity.

The nineties saw the building of the second and third phases
of the movement. Sociology entered the academic curriculum.
President Harper, in staffing the newly constituted University of
Chicago, gathered a galaxy of sociological thinkers: Small, Dewey,
Henderson, and Taylor. Similar thinkers (Ely, Ross, Jordan,
Giddings, and Kidd) came to occupy social science chairs in other
universities.

A discipline takes form in formulating a purpose and a procedure of investigation, of accumulating and organizing data.
Eventually it must have a philosophy. When Small wrote a code
of thirteen points, concepts, and postulates for sociological
thought, the academic or content phase had given rise to the
philosophical phase. Similar to the corpus of relativistic ethnological facts gathered by the Greeks during the Golden Age of
Pericles, this philosophic phase of sociological ideas contained
many relativistic elements. These, in turn, were introduced to
the fields of sociology, psychology, and education in our century.

The ideal material for sociology was to be drawn, in a scientific
manner, from an objective observation of the realities of human
experience. And since causation extends throughout the whole of

man's social experience and achievement, these facts are viewed always as part and parcel of the realm of cause and effect. Seemingly, nearly all sociologists agreed with Dewey's condemnation of the supernatural and the absolute in human affairs. For all was "in flux" and hence relative. In this, they followed their forerunner of the previous decade, Ward. Kidd was the "one voice crying in the wilderness" of relativists when he emphasized the religious motive, the function of idealism and supernatural sanction in social progress, the inestimable service of religion in determining individual will to truly social conduct—in short, contending that religion is a factor in social evolution and progress.

The central construct to be studied was the group, since human life is a constant interaction of social processes, and relationships within the group are brought about by participation in social life.[15] In this group, man had his being and *raison d'être*. Spencer had some years before called man a social organism, that is, an organism operating in a social "field," i.e., a group of participating individuals. We can easily cull from the literature such expressions as: "One man is no man"; "man himself is largely a social product"; "we have our being one with another"; "individualism is a superstition"; "except as a member of society, no man, however endowed, can become human in the best sense." Odum said: "We can understand social life as a whole and that each part can be understood *only by its relationships*." [16] Here we have the "makings" of what we have come to call the "field theory," which was soon after to receive support from the scientific field of physics. There are also signs of a continuing Messiah-complex among the sociologists from Comte on down. In one place we find it stated: "The individual who can grasp the structure of society and adapt it can become the helmsman for the future." Since then we have had many examples of this arrogant assumption.

So far the concept of relativity had had but limited circulation. It stayed more or less within the walls of philosophy. However, as we scan the indexes of philosophical papers of the time, we see an increase of titles referring to "absolutes" and, above all, "relativity," as the decade moved along. In the meanwhile, science, during the last half of the century, had been growing because of discoveries and courageous thinking. Science acquired even more prestige because of its many gifts to man. Physical science, with its neat formulae and seemingly complete organization of its data, was accorded great authority. When, in 1905, Einstein announced his "Theory of Special Relativity," it was as if King Science had spoken.

All of the previous scattered relativistic ideas of the "lesser" disciplines gathered with raised hands to receive the royal warrant of approval. One can epitomize the concept of relativity by saying that a thing derives its nature not so much by its isolated essence as from its relationships to other things in its frame of reference. The Newtonian theory of classical physics that "simultaneity is merely the function of two events" is replaced by Einstein's statement that is succinctly stated by Alonzo Church [17] as: "Simultaneity is the function of two events and *a coordinate system* or frame of reference." The addition of a conditioning frame of reference to the phenomenon in the Newtonian concept shifted attention from the intrinsic forces themselves to a relationship in a frame of reference in which they were operating.

In Einstein's student years he was inspired by Maxwell's theory.

What made this theory appear revolutionary was the transition from *forces* at a distance to *fields* as fundamental variables—the incorporation of optics into the theory of magnetism with its *relation* of the speed of light to the electric and magnetic absolute units as well as the *relation* of the refraction coefficient to the dielectric constant— the qualitative *relation* between the refraction coefficient and the metallic conductivity of the body—it was like a revelation.[18]

Einstein set to work upon his theory of relativity. He gave his initial paper on "Special Relativity" to the world in 1905, and ten years later his more comprehensive "General Relativity," which really crowned the philosophical concept of relativity in the world with the sanction of science.

At the opening of our century, we had the four streams of

thought merging and then emerging as a mighty current of an ideology of relativity in the world. Each stream contributed to or re-enforced the ideas of the others. Science contributed proofs of the idea of great individual differences among men in physique, mentalities, aptitudes, emotional life, and personalities, as well as the proof of a changing and evolving world. Humanism focused its attention and thought away from the natural universe and upon man and his problems, the differences among men throughout the world as well as the changing character of man and his society. The sociological movement introduced the objective study of the social group and its structures, which it came to regard as a "field of interacting processes," thereby shifting the emphasis away from man onto the "field" (or his social environment). It also picked up the ideas of the positivistic humanists in particular and explored the application of these scientifically derived data to the building of a new man and a new society.

Through all of this was woven the method of objective observation, but above all a thread of relativity that definitely crowded out the metaphysical, the supernatural, and the religious thought of earlier times with their acceptance of absolutes. The "relative" was replacing the absolute as a frame of reference, incorporating itself into the thinking of man, and giving rise to a growing *Zeitgeist* of relativism. All absolutes were being discarded. Science, in demonstrating objectively the great differences among men in all fields, physical, mental and social, was demonstrating that men, because of varying equipment and ability, were not equal, but unequal, in their potentialities and achievements. It also demonstrated their relative progress and position in the framework of society. Humanism pointed out, from philosophical observation, the relativity of man's customs, beliefs, institutions, and standards, as well as the changing of these in a given man at different times and down through time. These ethnological facts showed man as relative to his former self and to his former group. Sociological thought brought in the concept of man in a field of fellow men (i.e., society) and of social forces to which he is "relative" at all times and to which he must always be referred.

This "climate of relativity" is well summarized by Znaniecki in his article of 1915.

Not only is modern philosophy unable to find any foundation for absolute system-building in scientific results, but, on the contrary, its own relative character is reflected in the whole domain of knowledge. The unavoidable conclusion forces itself upon us that every truth is only a temporary and partial view of some artificially limited side of experience, that it is valuable only from the chosen position, on the ground of accepted assumptions. On the other hand, every error is also only temporary and partial, because it is an error only in relation to some truth.[19]

Knowledge is neither black nor white but only an uncertain and foggy grey.

Znaniecki continues: "The same relativity which appears in the domain of knowledge can be asserted also in the domains of morality, art, religion, economics" where "it was observed at an earlier period and more clearly demonstrated by means of historical and ethnological researches." The first half of our century has seen this idea of relativity fan out like the distributaries of a river delta, invading all areas of our thinking, some of which should be closed to it. We must remember that Einstein was concerned only with the phenomena of the world of physics. The late Hans Reichenbach queried this diffusion when he said: [20]

What has been called the philosophy of relativity represents to a great extent the fruit of misunderstandings of the theory rather than its physical content. Philosophers who regard it as an ultimate wisdom that everything is relative are mistaken when they believe that Einstein's theory supplies evidence for such a sweeping generalization; and their error is even deeper when they transfer such a relativity to the field of ethics, when they claim that Einstein's theory implies a relativism of men's duties and rights. The theory is restricted to the cognitive field. That moral conceptions vary with the social class and [with] the structure of civilization is a fact not derivable from Einstein's theory; the parallelism between the relativity of ethics and that of space and time is nothing more than a superficial analogy

which blurs the essential logical differences between the fields of
volition and cognition.

In the half-century since Einstein's famous paper of 1905 and
1915, the philosophical climate of relativity has permeated our
thought in practically all social institutions. The institutions that
are particularly "sensitive" and strategic to our culture are, of
course, its religions, its homes, its education, and its jurisprudence. They carry important controls and sanctions of the culture.

The social institution most affected by the sociological and
scientific trends described earlier, with all their philosophical
overtones of relativistic thinking, is education, for into educational thought went, in some measure, every phase of the "new
thought" of the nineties.

John Dewey sought to synthesize and integrate all the postulates and concepts of the scientific-humanistic and sociological
movements into a scheme of education to build a better man and
a better social order. He felt that European philosophy originated
under the direct pressure of educational problems. Following the
cue that he took from the Athens of the Sophists, he felt that the
pressure became greatest under changing conditions, such as
attended the rise of Athens as an imperial city. The Sophists who
rose to meet these problems became the first professional educators in Europe to instruct the youth in virtue, the political arts,
and in city management and economy. He pointed out that under
the Sophists philosophy became a philosophy of relationships:
of individual to individual, of individual to some comprehensive
class or group, of man to nature, of tradition to reflection, of
knowledge to action, and of theory to practice. This was certainly
not a philosophy of "essences," but of "relationships," of "relativities." Dewey, who detested pluralisms even more than he did
dualisms, held that since philosophical thought arose as a theory
of educational procedure, the intimate connection between philosophy and education was axiomatic.

Moreover, Sophist philosophy dealt with the conduct of human
life, and the phenomenon of this human life was largely social.
Therefore, philosophy should be social in its character. Dewey

integrated these pluralisms as follows: [21] "The reconstruction of philosophy, of education, and of social ideals and methods, thus go hand in hand." This integration had been made necessary by the changes in society brought about by the advance of science, the industrial revolution, and the development of democracy. "Education" is to be "the laboratory in which philosophic distinctions become concrete and are tested."

This new education is, however, not an education in the pedagogical sense, but a growth in sociality. In a review of a book of his time, Hyslop made the following somewhat cryptic comment: "It [education] is the means of securing greater equality among individuals than will exist without it, though it widens the inequality between those that succeed and those that do not." [22] Here is added the equalitarian democratic overtone to the social concept. In addition to this idea of equalitarian democratic sociality, the new education has absorbed into it many ideas from science, such as the concepts of objectivity, measured quantities, the experimental approach, and tentative findings, along with a relativistic philosophy. This syndrome has become the basis of educational theory and practice today, appearing in the philosophies of curriculum, methodology, and class procedures. The results have not always been happy ones, and some critics feel they have led to chaos. The field theory, with its stress upon relationships, has turned the aim of education in the United States to one of "adjustments" and has relegated to a distant second place the development of knowledge and skills—even the basic ones.

Standards (or absolutes for striving) do possess many values, instructional and ethical. The title of the report of the Carnegie Corporation in 1958, "The Pursuit of Excellence—The Education and the Future of America," is just one sufficient and significant comment indicating the loss incurred through this phenomenon of the "vanishing absolute."

One can also welcome, in fairness, the wise attempts to utilize the knowledge of individual differences, as revealed by forms of mental and psychological tests appropriately administered and evaluated, for the setting up of homogeneous class groups or "educational tracks" of curricular material for the different patterns of ability, as has been developed by the "child-centered philosophy" of education. However, many kinds of knowledge, and with them many values, necessary for survival and full living that have been so painfully, so patiently accumulated by man, at the expense of thought and effort during his presence on earth, possess integral and intrinsic dignity and great usefulness. It would seem wise to conserve these. The adjustment of content to ability had reached such a point even fifteen years ago that Krutch, speaking before an English teachers' convention, felt forced to say we should endeavor to bring the child to the curriculum instead of bringing the curriculum to the child. Should we not also question the procedure of having the child simply compete with his own potential ability, and then marking him, so that an "A" for one child is not the "A" for another? Another example of the same "relativity" in marking is seen in marking a class of students on probability curves allotting "A's" to 7%; "B's" to 24%; "C's" to 38%, etc. By the method of intrinsic relativity, two classes of quite different distributions of ability or grades become incomparable because of failure to refer to some extrinsic standard.

In jurisprudence, based upon sociological relativity, Protagoras' famous phrase now reads: "Man is the measure of all law." Somewhere toward the end of the nineteenth century, a revolt arose in the field of jurisprudence, here and abroad. In our country, the names of Holmes, Pound, and Cardozo stand out. Just as John Dewey had come to feel that education had become separated from life, so these jurists had come to feel that law had become a "sealed system of concepts, mutually interacting and using only internal criteria—producing a lawyer's law." [23] They felt that life, not logic, should determine law, for law was a social phenomenon, a functioning social science in a functioning civilization. Since humanity, like all other aspects of nature, changes as it floats on the stream of life, civilization is a dynamic phenomenon in constant flux. Hence law should not be a system of immutable concepts, but a fluid reality subject to change and growth.

Holmes laid the groundwork, contending, among other things,

that an ideal system of law should draw its postulates and its legal justification from science—"not from tradition and vague sentiment": "premises must be tested by critical analysis." [24] Holmes rejected absolutism in any shape and along with it the "fetish of mathematical deductivism"—"not logic but experience is to determine the law—not deductivism but good sense." "Logical method and form flatter the longing for certainty and for repose of the mind. Certainty is generally an illusion and repose is not the destiny of man." The notion that overemphasis on certainty leads easily to a rigidity of law seems to be the consensus today, yet an old English jurist has been quoted as saying that worse than an unjust law is an uncertain one.

Naturally, precedent must go. Cardozo, in his "Growth of the Law," says: [25]

"Our law stands indicted for uncertainty—disorder has been brought about by a too faithful application of *stare decisis*—we are lost in a wilderness of precedent."

He was firm in his criticism of errors of unrestrained pursuit of precedent. "Law must be stable and yet it cannot stand still." In 1945, President Gannon of Fordham aptly remarked that, judging by the way the United States Supreme Court had functioned of late, "Law must not stand still long enough to become stable," [26] and Judge Roberts, about the same time, compared the Court decisions to "a railroad excursion ticket—good for one day only." Pound agreed in holding that law is something relative and not set forever.

When made, the new laws were not to be referred to as an a priori metaphysical spectrum of authoritarian precepts, but as an extralegal norm derived from a sociological analysis of the mores in the cultural life of the community that it supports. This analysis is to be done by naturalistic-humanistic methods, the law being considered as an inductive, relativistic, pragmatic one, deriving its sustenance from the social sciences. By "relativistic" is here meant varying according to the changing circumstances of time and place. By "pragmatic" is meant that the law should strive for the attainment of a working agreement between conflicting partners, endeavoring to maintain the merits of both sides while ironing out their differences in a practical way. Cardozo adds that this is never perfectly successful. Let us note that again we meet the idea of what is "practical, not perfect."

Rather rapidly the jurists of the sociological school moved from the idea that sociological jurisprudence finds its incentive in public law, which is closely related to the group rather than the individual, to the idea of social control by the courts. So the way is open to move from "man as the measure of the law" to a group of men and then to one man as "the measure of the law." One of the oft-repeated criticisms of the absolute is its tyranny. Yet here a system based upon relativism could attain to a similar tyranny.[27]

In summary, we see how the relativism of the sociological movement, with its idea of man as relative to a field, moved from the focus on man as "an essence" in his own right, first to a focus on his relations in a field, and then to the field or environment to which he must adjust. Slowly the field assumes such importance that it is blamed for everything. Thus, all sense of responsibility is taken from man. In this condition man loses his dignity and his sense of any responsibility. He becomes completely expendable to his environment, of which he becomes either a slave or a victim. Again, in the field of ethics and conduct, relativism leads to an oscillation among goals, an ambivalence in thought and feelings, or even worse, an ultimate confusion because ends are not clearly seen.

NOTES

1. H. Wildon Carr, *General Principle of Relativity in Its Philosophical and Historical Aspects* (London: Macmillan, 1920), p. 160.
2. D'Alembert, Jean de Rond, "Essai sur les eléments de philosophie," *Oeuvres complètes de D'Alembert* (Paris: Behn, 1821), I, 121. D'Alembert describes the "revolution" of the middle of the eighteenth century as one of rationalistic philosophy. We can extrapolate the idea, making that of the nineteenth century the one marked by the evolutionary theory and even making that of our country one of a beginning of a reaction to relativistic thought.
3. Frederick C. Gruber (editor), *Aspects of Value*, Brumberg Lectures, 1958 (Philadelphia: University of Pennsylvania Press, 1959), Preface, p. 11.

4. Frederic H. Amiel, *Private Journal of F. H. Amiel,* trans. by the Brooks (New York: Macmillan, 1935), p. 359.
5. Harold U. Faulkner, *Politics, Reform and Expansion—1890-1900* (New York: Harper and Brothers, 1959).
6. Louis Blanc, *Révolution Française—Histoire de dix Ans—1830-1840* (Paris: Pagnerre, 1843), III, 89.
7. G. T. Patrick, *The Fragments of the Work of Heraclitus of Ephesus* (Baltimore: N. Murray, 1889). Reprint from *American Journal of Psychology* (1888). In the Introduction, p. 74: "To Heraclitus we trace the notion of Relativity, the central point of the Sophists which, by withdrawing every absolute standard of truth, threatened to destroy all knowledge, all faith, and which sent Socrates searching for something permanent and fixed in the concepts of the human mind and so led to the finished products of Plato and Aristotle."
8. The development of psychological testing can be found in many books. Brief sketches will be found in: S. S. Sargent, *The Basic Teachings of the Great Psychologists* (Philadelphia: Blakiston Co., 1944). See especially chaps. II, III, and VII.
9. C. A. Robinson, Jr., *Athens in the Age of Pericles* (Norman: University of Oklahoma Press, 1959).
10. Kathleen Freeman, *Ancilla to the Pre-Socratic Philosophers* (Cambridge: Harvard University Press, 1948). Translation of Diel's *Fragmente der Vorsokratiker,* ed. by Walter Kranz, 5th edition, 1934-1938. Heraclitus wrote one book containing all knowledge, metaphysical, scientific, and political, in oracular style: No. 12, p. 6—"Those who step in the same river have different water ever flowing over them." No. 91, p. 31—"It is impossible to touch the same mortal substance twice, but through the rapidity of change they scatter and recombine."
11. Freeman, *op. cit.* Protagoras wrote two books, *Truth or Refutatory Arguments on Being* and *On the Gods.* The quotation, "Of all things Man is the measure," is from *Truth.*
12. Amiel, *op. cit.,* p. 566 (4), referring to Comte's positivism: "This sham doctrine, so meagre in new perceptions, as in interesting results—had only one idea, spun it out with unbearable prolixity, and this idea is not exact, it is not new, it is not great. When one takes away from Comte what he has taken from Hume, from Broussais, Saint Simon, Turgot—nothing is left but the diffuse, pretentious letter of vulgar empiricism."
13. Carter V. Good, *Dictionary of Education,* 2nd edition (New York: McGraw Hill, 1959), p. 275—definition of scientific humanism.
14. *Journal of Social Science,* I (June, 1869), 1.
15. The history of the sociological movement is to be found in the books and articles of Small, Odum, Vincent and many others.
16. Odum in his *Masters of Social Science,* p. 151; compare Small in his *General Sociology* (Chicago: University of Chicago Press, 1905), p. 507. "We live and move and have our being as parts of each other. There is no such phenomenon within the range of our knowledge as an

absolute individual. Every member of the human race gets his personality through direct and immediate partnership with other members of the human race and through direct contact with all the human family."

17. Dagobert D. Runes, *The Dictionary of Philosophy* (New York: Philosophical Library, 1942). See definition of "Relative," p. 269.

18. Paul Arthur Schilpp, *Albert Einstein—Philosopher-Scientist* (New York: Tudor Publishing Co., 1949-51), p. 53.

19. Florian Znaniecki, "Relativism and Absolution," *The Philosophical Review*, XXIV, 150-164.

20. Hans Reichenbach, *The Philosophical Significance of the Theory of Albert Einstein*, Schilpp, *supra* (note 18), p. 289.

21. John Dewey, *Democracy and Education* (New York: Macmillan, 1916), p. 386.

22. James H. Hyslop in his review of Vincent's "Social Mind in Education," *Book Reviews*, V (January, 1898), 207-210. Quotation on p. 209.

23. Moses J. Aronson, "Cardozo's Doctrine of Sociological Jurisprudence," *Journal of Social Philosophy*, IV, No. 1 (October, 1938), 10-11.

24. Moses J. Aronson, "Tendencies in American Jurisprudence," *The University of Toronto Law Journal*, IV, No. 1 (1941), 93-94.

25. Moses J. Aronson, re: Cardozo, *op. cit.*, pp. 15-16 from Cardozo, "Growth of the Law."

26. Rev. Robert I. Gannon S.J., "The Moral Law," *Fordham Law Review*, XIV, No. 1 (March, 1945), 6, paragraph 2.

27. Rev. Robert I. Gannon S.J., *op. cit.*, p. 6, paragraph 3.

11

Relativism in Linguistics

MARIO PEI

Relativism in the field of linguistic studies may be said to have had its inception with the ancient Greeks.[1] In Plato's *Cratylus*, one of the disputants, Cratylus, argues in favor of the view that language is a natural phenomenon *(physis)*, bestowed by the gods upon man, and that the names of things are not mere symbols, but an inherent and essential part of the objects they stand for. The other participant, Hermogenes, presents the view that language is a matter of convention *(nomos, thesis)*, and that a thing or action has a given name only because men have agreed to accept the name as the symbol of the object in question. Here we may have the beginning of the relativistic idea as applied to language.

Aristotle later sponsored what may be described as the relativistic position by presenting the idea of language as a social contract; this, of course, implies that language is subject to human variations and to different interpretations.

Among the Roman grammarians, Varro, in his *De lingua Latina*, expresses the opinion that language is basically utilitarian. This is relativistic, since what is utilitarian is implicitly subject to change in accordance with the changing needs of its users.

It must, however, be remembered that, generally speaking, the view of language, and particularly of grammar, held by the ancients was a static, prescriptive, and consequently antirelativistic

216

one. The Greek and Latin languages were presented by their respective grammarians in accordance with a timeless, unchanging pattern. Other languages of antiquity were thoroughly neglected and seldom referred to, and the Greeks even coined the word *barbaroi,* "barbarians" or "babblers," to describe speakers of other tongues. The only comparisons ever attempted were between Greek and Latin. The grammatical principles of both languages were set, and anyone who for any reason whatsoever violated their canons was deemed incorrect. We may therefore define the classical position with regard to language as basically antirelativistic, despite the philosophical digressions of Plato and Aristotle.

Yet the spirit of relativism crops up when least expected. We find a hint of it in Quintilian, a Roman grammarian of the first century C.E., who states, *"aliud esse latine loqui, aliud grammatice"* ("It's one thing to speak Latin, another thing to speak grammatically").[2] This reveals, if not a condonation of divergences from the standard, at least a consciousness that they existed. Probus, another grammarian of the third or the fourth century C.E., has left us a precious testimonial in the Appendix of his Latin grammar,[3] in the form of well over three hundred words and expressions that he heard currently mispronounced or otherwise mishandled. To the linguist, the value of his contribution is that he gives us both the "correct" and the "incorrect" forms (sometimes he actually reverses them), and the "incorrect" forms are often the direct and immediate forerunners of later Romance forms. To the philosopher and the student of social phenomena, his contribution lies in his awareness, even though coupled with condemnation, of the divergences from the standard. Relativism apparently existed, but was deplored.

The early Christian Middle Ages were almost barren of linguistic consciousness. The problems that interested the minds of this period were otherworldly ones. Languages existed, and people were conscious of them and their diversity; this is proved by the numerous Bible translations and language aids for pilgrims and travelers, some of which are forerunners of the modern tourist or military phrase-book; there are also numerous glosses, interlinear and marginal translations into the current spoken language, of words and phrases in an older Latin text the language of which was beginning to be forgotten and was often no longer understood.[4] Relativism, in other words, existed in practice, but no one seems to have directed any conscious thought toward it since the beginning of the fifth century, when Saint Jerome had stated that *"ipsa latinitas et regionibus quotidie mutetur et tempore"* ("The Latin language itself is changing daily, both region by region and with the passing of time"),[5] and Saint Augustine had said that *"melius est reprehendant grammatici quam non intellegant populi"* ("It is better that the grammarians should condemn us than that the people should not understand us").[6] This statement, made in justification of his deliberate use of vulgarisms, is perhaps the most relativistic pronouncement we have from the entire era.

It is only in the thirteenth century that we begin to find a new interest in philosophical speculation about the nature of language. It begins with the concept of a universal grammar, valid for all tongues, though with minor variations. Roger Bacon expressed the concept in these words: *"Grammatica una et eadem est secundum substantiam in omnibus linguis, licet accidentaliter varietur"* ("Grammar is one and the same in all tongues, as far as substance is concerned, but it may vary in particulars").[7] Here we have the first clear-cut medieval statement of an antirelativistic position. If the grammatical concepts are basically the same in all languages, and the latter display only accidental variations, there is little room for relativism.

The subsequent three centuries have much to interest the linguist, but rather little in the language field to interest the philosopher. The concept of a universal grammar into which all languages must be fitted prevailed almost universally, along with a generally held belief that all the world's languages stem from the Hebrew of the Old Testament.

It was not until the middle of the sixteenth century, following the West's rediscovery of Greek as a result of the fall of Constantinople and the invasion of western Europe by refugee Greek scholars, that renewed interest in ancient Greek texts and their dialectal variations led Henri Estienne to formulate, in his *Thesaurus Linguae Graecae* of 1572, the principle that what we must seek in words is objective truth rather than esthetic beauty. This theory of objectivity and the search for truth rather than fancy was furthered in the same century by Mabillon [8] and Du Cange,[9] who established the rules for determining the authenticity and approximate dating of ancient texts. Language as reality, not language as a vehicle for esthetics, might be the summation of this antirelativistic position. It may be remarked that the battle is still being waged, though under disguised forms, today, between those who look upon language as primarily a vehicle for communication and those who regard it as predominantly a vehicle for poetic and literary expression. One picturesque ramification of this conflict in the seventeenth century is the Italian *Questione della lingua*,[10] where the Tuscanists may be said to represent an esthetic, or relativistic current, the anti-Tuscanists an objective, or antirelativistic one (the former held that the literary Italian tongue stems from the "beautiful" Florentine dialect, the latter that it is a conglomeration of forms from various dialects, not all of which can be described as esthetically pleasing).

The great contribution to the science of language in the eighteenth and the nineteenth centuries lies in the development of the comparative method created by the joint efforts of Rask, Pott, Grimm, Bopp, von Humboldt, William Jones, Diez, and Schlegel.[11] Here we have an extension of the objective, antirelativistic position, since the new methodology consisted in laying side by side forms taken from the oldest Indo-European languages, and from their comparison deriving the "laws" of their separate development, along with the reconstruction of the hypothetical Indo-European parent language. But what may be described as a mildly relativistic attack was in the offing, for Schleicher [12] soon suggested that the true basis for our study should be not the dead, static early tongues, but the living languages, which are subject to change and fluctuation, and in which the linguistic processes may much better be observed and made the basis for our conclusions.

Another field of battle was opened in the course of the nineteenth century, when the Neogrammarian School,[13] headed by such renowned figures as Brugmann, Paul, and Leskien, propounded the theory that language change operates in accordance with phonological "laws" that have the same stringency as the laws of physics; that in a given area and at a given period, if an innovation occurs, that innovation will work universally and without exception, save insofar as it may be interfered with by such extraneous factors as analogy, or foreign and learned borrowing (this is the same as saying in physics that a given substance will expand uniformly when heat is applied, provided other factors, such as pressure, are kept constant). Opposition to this iron cogency of the *Lautgesetz* was voiced first by the Neolinguists of the Schuchardt-Bertoni group,[14] then by a philosopher, Croce. Rejecting, in his *Aesthetics*,[15] the view that language can be subject to any rigid laws of change, he offered instead the proposition that language is sound for the purpose of expression rather than of communication; that it is the individual, in his creative urge, who is the arbiter of change and innovation, and that just as the individual cannot be regimented, neither can language. This struggle, still continuing today, between a school that is predominantly mechanistic and one that may be called mentalistic, definitely reflects an aspect of antirelativism vs. relativism.

Further phases of the controversy are illustrated by de Saussure's definition [16] of one of the purposes of general linguistics as "to seek out the forces operating permanently and universally in all languages" and "drawing up general laws from particular phenomena," which smacks of antirelativism. The structuralism first put into vogue by the Prague School of Trubetskoi [17] and Jakobson [18] deals with the study of the linguistic phenomena of a given language within the framework of that language's general structure rather than in isolation (the changes in a language, that is, are dictated by the total pattern and do not occur at random; a language that possesses the series *t-d, p-b,* and *k* but not *g* will eventually tend to produce *g* or discard *k*). All this is highly controversial; it also tends to bring into the picture an element of antirelativism.

Among the most recent developments in the field may be mentioned the highly relativistic doctrines of the American anthropological school, led by Boas,[19] Sapir,[20] and Bloomfield.[21] Here we have several facets, some of them highly controversial. The studies of this school in American Indian languages objectively proved the existence not merely of numerous different languages, but of enormously divergent language types, having no seeming common denominator with the universal grammar postulated by the medieval philosophers. Language, in the view of the Americanists, is therefore an extremely relative phenomenon; those language features which are fundamental and indispensable to one type of language may be quite irrelevant and nonexistent in another, and the old grammatical categories and parts of speech have no reality as universal phenomena.

A curious extension of this doctrine is the one presented by Whorf,[22] who asserts that not only does the type of culture influence the language and its development, but that the converse is true; in other words, we are influenced in our mode of thinking and our behavior by the type of language we habitually speak (a language whose verb has clear and precise tense distinctions, for instance, will induce in its speakers a keen consciousness of time values and punctuality, while a language in which the action is represented merely as occurring, without reference to time, will create in its speakers a sense of timelessness that will lead them to shrug their shoulders at time clocks and due dates). Yet, strangely enough, Whorf himself hints at a new type of universal grammar which, while altogether different from that of the Middle Ages, will nevertheless cover all linguistic types.[23]

Perhaps the most important contribution made to relativism by the American school is the doctrine of permissiveness or usage in language. According to this school, language is "what people speak, not what someone thinks they ought to speak." [24] At the minimum, this proposition gives full recognition to the historical truth that the slang of yesterday is often the correct language of today (classical Latin, becoming vulgar and slangy, gives rise to the Romance languages, which ultimately become vehicles of cultural thought equal to their ancestor). At the maximum, it sanctifies "usage" and makes it paramount over prescriptive grammar, giving full currency and encouragement to all innovations, slang and dialectal forms, and making them equal in practical value with the standard language. It tends to discredit the written form of the language as an archaic survival and to revere the spoken tongue as the only "true" language. This is relativism at its peak and goes hand in hand with other relativistic manifestations in present-day American life, particularly permissiveness in education and the relaxation of standards of both expression and behavior.

A secondary feature of what might be styled neorelativism in the field of language is the tendency to regard all languages as of equal importance, regardless of their size, extent, or the contribution their speakers may have made to the world's civilization.[25] This is a carry-over from the field of anthropology, where "cultures" are viewed as being on a par, whether the culture is that of a group like the French or the Italian, which has a millenary tradition of progress and achievement in art, literature, science, and political institutions, or that of a savage cannibal group in New Guinea that still lives in the Stone Age. Since this form of relativism is also at the root of certain concepts of "democracy," "equality," "tolerance," and other similar notions, we leave it to other members of this discussion group to delve into the ideologies that may motivate it. Suffice it to say that in the purely linguistic field it leads followers of the school to favor, for purposes of a campaign to promote literacy, the teaching of pidgin English, in preference to ordinary English, to the natives of Melanesia,[26] and of Haitian Creole,[27] in preference to standard French, to the population of Haiti, regardless of the fact that English and French are world languages that would give their new speakers access to Western culture.

In summing up this survey of the manifestations of relativism and antirelativism throughout the history of linguistic thought, we may present the ten basic oppositions that have become manifest in which a relativistic or antirelativistic aspect may be discerned, with the further consideration that it may perhaps be possible to reduce them to five fundamental propositions. At various times, language has been viewed as:

(relativistically)	(antirelativistically)
1. arising by convention	arising by nature, or divine fiat
2. primarily utilitarian	primarily esthetic
3. beautiful or ugly	true or untrue
4. free to respond to the whim of the individual	bound by quasi-physical laws
5. operating freely, spontaneously and at random	subject to forces operating permanently and universally
6. a series of isolated phenomena	a system operating in accordance with a pattern within a language
7. to be studied primarily in its living forms	to be studied primarily in its dead forms
8. subject only to usage	subject to authority
9. what people actually speak	what the grammars say they should speak
10. neither correct nor incorrect	correct or incorrect

Proposition 1 stands by itself, since it deals with the mysterious origin of language; there is, however, a distant link with 8, 9, and 10.

Propositions 2 and 3 seem at first glance contradictory, since the view of language as esthetic is described as antirelativistic in 2, while the view of language as beautiful or ugly appears as relativistic in 3; but here we must consider the esthetic view of language in the light of the qualities to which it is opposed, utilitarian in one case, true or untrue in the other.

Propositions 4 and 5 are basically one and the same, and 6 may be said to bear a certain relationship to both. Proposition 7 has links with both what precedes and what follows, though it is largely a question of methodological procedure, and its bearing upon the problem of relativism is slight. Lastly, 8, 9, and 10 are aspects of the same general proposition.

Any judgment passed upon these aspects of linguistics must of necessity be subjective. Granted a sufficient technical background to permit a rational stand, each individual will arrive at his own answer. My own opinions are here offered, not for the purpose of convincing anyone to take identical stands, but merely as an example of one man's line of reasoning.

Proposition 1 (language by nature or language by convention) deals primarily with the origin of language, something concerning which no one has any assurance. In the final analysis, language by nature means language created and bestowed upon man by a higher Being; language by convention means language originating through one of the many picturesque methods envisaged in the bow-wow, pooh-pooh, heave-ho, and similar theories, or through a blend of all of them.[28] The former involves a metaphysical belief not subject to scientific demonstration; the latter postulates a primitive language structure which seems at first glance plausible, but which no known language, ancient or modern, exemplifies. Proposition 1 may safely be dismissed as a fruitful source of relativistic discussion.

Whether language is primarily utilitarian or primarily esthetic depends largely upon points of view, tastes, and leanings. But there is nothing to prevent the acceptance of both features, at different stages of language and for different purposes. No one can deny that language is man's primary tool of communication, a tool without which no fruitful human collaboration is really possible (witness the Biblical episode of the Tower of Babel); as language develops, it is also used to give voice to man's desire for beauty and self-expression, a desire which seems to be common to all groups. I would cast my vote for the utilitarian facet as primary, the esthetic as secondary but very important. In connection with modern needs, I would approach the problem of language, language learning and language teaching first and foremost from the standpoint of communication (stress on the conversational rather than the literary language, stress on both spoken and written language for purposes of everyday use), later as a vehicle for creative thought of the literary, philosophical, scientific, and political variety.

Views of language as beautiful or ugly vs. true or untrue do not, to my mind, constitute a real point of controversy, because beautiful and ugly can apply equally to what is true and what is untrue. But beauty is highly subjective, while truth is objective. In linguistic research, truth should always be the first consideration. It is undeniable that Melanesian pidgin exists and is spoken, whether I like its form of expression or not. My own esthetic taste, on the other hand, may dictate that I spend my time on Italian rather than on Melanesian pidgin.

Whether language is subject to forces operating permanently and universally or whether it is free to respond to the whim of the individual is perhaps the most controversial point in historical linguistics. Creators of the *Lautgesetz* and compilers of tables of phonetic correspondences were quickly forced to bring in the factor of analogy to account for deviations from their rigid "laws." [29] Analogy is, of course, the play of individual human factors. Analogy is capricious and unpredictable, appearing in one language and not in another, in one form and not in another, or working in two opposite directions in similar forms. Cases of analogy (and here I include such phenomena as assimilation, dissimilation, metathesis, and all sorts of deviations that cannot be circumscribed by "laws") are often so numerous and widespread that they tend to crowd out the "law" to which they are exceptions. Nevertheless, the "law" is seen to operate, in one fashion or another. If for the word "law" we substitute the word "tendency," we shall have a much clearer picture of what happens in language. Language is, after all, a human activity, subject to human vicissitudes. Human beings are often forcibly regimented, and as often tend, of their own accord, to behave like sheep. But there are always exceptions, rugged individualists, who stand out against the common herd and sometimes succeed in reversing a trend. Why not accept this fact and cease to view the operation of language as purely mechanical? On the other hand, the position of the ultramentalists, who refuse to recognize any regularity whatsoever in linguistic change, is just as extreme as that of the language totalitarians, because a general pattern in language change is clearly discernible, however much it may be obscured by irregularities. A healthy compromise between dictatorship and anarchy, with reasonable allowance for individual freedom, seems to be in order.

The question whether we should view language change as a series of isolated phenomena or as a system operating more or less regularly within a language is tied up, in my opinion, with the broader question of the regularity of phonetic laws. Here again I should prefer to take a middle-of-the-road stand. Exceptions to the regular patterns postulated by the structuralists are numerous and striking and cannot be altogether ignored.

Should we study language primarily in its living or in its dead forms? This is somewhat like inquiring whether a physician should study physiology or anatomy. Why not both? The living tongue certainly illustrates certain language processes as they occur. But just as you cannot cut up a living body and expect it to stay alive, neither can you fully analyze language by observing it merely at one point of time in the course of its existence. A historical (diachronic) as well as a descriptive (synchronic) study is necessary to produce a fully rounded picture.

This brings us down to the last group of propositions, which is in many ways the most important from the standpoint of relativism. There are several reasons for its importance: (1) Even though it has its roots in the past, it is in its acute phases distinctly a present-day problem and therefore affects our generation vitally; (2) It is not a matter of methodological procedure or higher philosophy, affecting only a few specialists, but reaches down into the life and language of everyone; (3) It has intimate connections with similar problems in the fields of general education, economics, sociology, even international relations; (4) By the same token, our views on this problem tend to color our thinking in those related fields and form part of a single over-all pattern of modern thought; (5) For what concerns the specific topic under discussion, namely relativism, we have here the particular field of language in which relativistic and antirelativistic positions are most definite and clear-cut, and in which a head-on collision is not only fully possible, but almost inevitable.

To begin with, there is no use in denying that language change exists, always has existed, and always will exist; language reflects the general history and progress of mankind, which never has been and never will be static. Neither is there any point to denying that there is infinite variety both in language generally and within the same language.[30]

Having made these concessions to relativistic thought, how much farther ought we to go? Ought we to accept the proposition that language is subject, not to authority, but to usage alone, that language is what people (all people) actually speak, rather than what someone in authority thinks they ought to speak, that there is no such thing as correct or incorrect language, but only language, which is correct by virtue of the fact that someone uses it?[31] Ought we to view all languages as being substantially on the same plane, regardless of their history (or lack of history), of their development as tools for the expression of higher thought, whether of the literary or the scientific variety, of their number of speakers, distribution, political, and economic importance?[32] Ought we to view the spoken language as basic and all-important, and the written language as merely an annoying holdover from the past, hindering our understanding of the "true nature" of language, getting in our way with its antiquated forms of spelling and grammar, restricting our freedom of self-expression?[33]

In this particular gathering, I may perhaps be forgiven for pointing to the parallelism that appears between this linguistic philosophy and the broader philosophy of thought and action that prevails in our so-called democratic way of life, where questions of vital policy are decided by the nose-counting process and that is assumed to be right which a majority of those polled say is right, regardless of whether they may or may not be qualified to pass expert judgment on the point at issue; where behavior is deemed right merely because it is fashionable or practiced by the majority or even by a loud minority; where all are given equal importance and equal rank, regardless of their natural equipment, background, qualifications or achievements; where the traditional is discarded, not because it has outlived its usefulness, but merely because it is traditional, and therefore old-fashioned, and therefore undesirable, while innovations are accepted, not on their merits, but merely because they are something new.

It is my opinion that progress, to be true progress and not retrogression in disguise, must be (1) carefully thought out; and (2) orderly, even to the point of being slow. If progress is ill-considered and haphazard, it will inevitably slide back into the worst form of retrogression. This is amply proved by those regimes in which appeals to liberty and freedom have been coupled with forms of repression worthy of the most obscurantist Middle Ages, and the divine right of kings, after an interlude of permissiveness and relativism, has been replaced with the divine right of the state.

This tendency is also clearly visible in the field of linguistics, where we have, on the one hand, the sort of permissiveness shown by the doctrine of usage, and, on the other, a fanatical intolerance of all opposing currents of thought that finds expression in such formulas as "the superstitions of the past,"[34] sweeping away all previous or nonconforming ideas and research as not merely irrelevant and useless, but as "an active danger in the hands of the public to which it is addressed" and "potentially harmful."[35]

Examples of the first of these tendencies, which particularly interests students of relativism, could be multiplied *ad infinitum*. So could examples of its far-reaching results.

Spelling should be abolished, says one of the greatest minds in the field of linguistic science.[36] Spelling has already been abolished, as indicated by "Why Johnny Can't Read." One of the many results of learning to read and spell by induction (osmosis would perhaps be a better word) came to this writer's notice recently, when he was informed by an official of one of the big TV broadcasting corporations that after interviewing hundreds of supposedly qualified candidates for various writing posts in his organization, he had been forced to reject all of them because none of them could write a page without making numerous errors, both in spelling and grammar.

Reject the grammatical superstitions of the past, advocate some of the leading figures in linguistic science.[37] They have already been rejected, and traditional grammar, as such, is no longer taught in the majority of public schools. One of the results is the uniform complaint voiced by high school and college teachers of foreign languages, almost without exception, that the first semester of foreign-language instruction has to be spent teaching the students those grammatical concepts and that grammatical terminology without which the work cannot proceed.

"Everyone who is not deaf or idiotic has fully mastered his native language by the end of his fifth year, no matter how difficult or complex it may seem to strangers."[38] This principle, which seemingly does away with the need for any and all formal study of one's native language, has apparently been interpreted by the more permissive branch of the educational profession in the sense that there is no point in imparting instruction in English grammar, spelling, composition, etc., to the children who presumably come to kindergarten with a full mastery of their native tongue. The time once devoted to these outworn subjects can more profitably be spent on courses in "life adjustment" and similar trivia.

The relaxation of language standards advocated by the members of the anthropological school of linguistics has strange applications and even stranger results; of the latter, some are deliberately sought, others quite accidental and unplanned.

During the late war, the writer was asked by a government agency to revise a booklet designed to impart some knowledge of English to French speakers. Coming across the phrase, "I laid on the bed," he corrected it to "lay." Somewhat to his surprise, the error was restored by the man in charge. "That's the way ninety percent of the G.I.'s say it," was the explanation.

"Educated or cultured informants are by no means preferable, and often inferior."[39] In accordance with this principle, during the early days of the Army Language Program, native informants were taken from the lower strata of the population. This was assumed to be conducive to the greatest good to the greatest number. The principle backfired when soldiers who had been taught "Italian" by illiterate Sicilian barbers discovered that their Sicilian dialect was incomprehensible on the Italian continent. At this point, the policy was quickly revised, and cultured speakers of Italian were brought in, whose language, if it lacked the merit of coinciding with that of a local peasantry, was at least comprehensible to most of the population everywhere in Italy.

Elsewhere in the Foreign Language Program conducted by the linguistic scientists, we find a massive display of pessimism for what concerns the rank and file of language learners, in the form of an oversimplified, and therefore highly confusing, system of grammatical terminology.[40]

The culmination of the debasing process is reached in the pronouncement:[41] "To get an easy command of a foreign language one must learn to ignore the features of any and all other languages, especially of one's own."

It is a fascinating question whether the twin doctrines of unrestricted usage in language and of permissiveness in education are a cause or an effect of the general relaxation in social, political, economic, moral and ideological behavior, whether they contribute to the changes that plague modern times, or are only a symptom of an underlying frame of mind.

It has been the writer's observation, made at a time when he taught high school classes, that sloppiness of language leads to sloppiness of thought and general behavior. Students with a high I.Q. have been observed to go into a deliberate imitation of gangster talk in their normal conversation, debasing their language standards by a conscious process; whichever be the cause and the effect, there was an attendant deterioration in their standards of politeness and conduct, their school work, even their walking and standing postures.

Historically, the situation is not without parallel. Christian authors of the late Empire, such as Tertullian, remark upon the general demoralization of the social structure in their days, which coincided with the relaxation in linguistic standards. Then, as now, both phenomena were viewed with approval by some of the community's intellectual leaders (the example of Saint Augustine, cited above, is particularly cogent).[42]

It is quite true that the downfall of the Roman civilization and language paved the way for the new modern cultures and the Romance tongues; but the transition occupied a period of nearly ten centuries, during which the general standards of civilization were considerably lower than they had been under the Empire. It is possible that present-day Western civilization, particularly of the Anglo-Saxon variety, is destined to undergo something similar and that the general lowering of our linguistic and educational standards is a symptom, if not a cause, of the coming debacle.

At all events, the methodological and even the ideological excesses of the relativists in linguistics, which are in part a reaction to earlier excesses by their opponents, ought not to blind us to what is positive and historically true in their thinking.

The truth, as usual, lies somewhere in between. Usage alone will never solve the problem of language, for usage is basically anarchy. A measure of law and order must prevail in language as in everything else. The basic purpose of language is the transfer of meaning from one human mind to another. Excessive permissiveness tends to destroy this basic purpose and bring about the conditions said to have prevailed after the Biblical episode of the Tower of Babel, when everyone went off in a different direction, each speaking his own language, which no one else understood. Language and language change must be kept under a measure of intelligent control. There must be certain standards which, within reason, must be fairly uniform at a given time and in a given area.[43] Strangely enough, even the relativists admit this when they speak of "standard" and "substandard" speech. Too many substandard forms (and substandard forms inevitably tend to proliferate and multiply) lead to mutual incomprehension and consequent chaos. A measure of regularization and standardization is not only desirable, but necessary. It should never, however, assume the aspects of a straightjacket.

Are we to view all languages as being on the same plane? In the abstract, yes, just as we view all men as being fundamentally equal. But this basic equality does not imply equality of development or effectiveness.[44] There are different stages of physical or intellectual development. The untrained child of four can be given theoretical, but not practical, equality with the grown man, in the logical supposition that he will eventually attain maturity. The same may be said of racial and cultural groups and of their languages.

The written tongue is the major depository of the past records of human civilization and as such is entitled to respectful handling. At our present stage of civilization, it is something more: a practical, utilitarian tool of everyday communication rivaling the spoken tongue. It is quite possible that in the future it may be replaced in the latter function by various mechanical devices for aural communication, though this development is somewhat difficult to envisage (note that in the conflict between radio, which appeals to the ear alone, and TV, which appeals to both ear and eye, radio is losing). But our mechanical devices may reach a stage where both a visual and an auditory record are produced, and this combination may effectively do away with the need for a written language. This is on a par with saying that some day the combination of plane, helicopter, and rocket will entirely do away with the train, automobile, and ship, which does not warrant our scrapping our cars, railroad lines, and transatlantic shipping while we wait for the change to take place. Neither should the written language be neglected at a time when it is more generally in use than ever in the past. And even if some day the combination of mechanical, audio-visual methods of communication render the written language superfluous, this development will apply only to the future, not to the past. Unless the human being of the year 2000 chooses to become completely oblivious and ignorant of all that went on before 1900, practically his sole source of information regarding his past will continue to lie in written records.[45]

If there is one basic conclusion that may be reached from our survey of relativism in the field of linguistics, it is that relativism must be accepted and applied with caution, circumspection, and conservatism—in other words, with numerous and large grains of salt.

NOTES

1. R. H. Robins, *Ancient and Medieval Grammatical Theory in Europe* (London, 1951).
2. *See also* A. Monteverdi, *Manuale di avviamento agli studi romanzi* (Milano, 1952), p. 4.
3. Monteverdi, *op. cit.,* pp. 40-44.
4. W. Foerster and E. Koschwitz, *Altfranzösisches Uebungsbuch* (Heilbronn, 1884), pp. 1-43.
5. Monteverdi, *op. cit., Pauli epist. ad Galatas II,* prol.; p. 47,
6. Monteverdi, *op. cit., Serm. in Psalm CXXXVIII, 20;* p. 36.
7. Robins, *op. cit.,* II.
8. *De re diplomatica* (1680).
9. *Glossarium ad scriptores mediae et infimae Latinitatis* (1678).
10. T. Labande-Jeanroy, *La question de la langue en Italie* (Strasbourg, 1925); R. A. Hall, Jr., *The Italian Questione della Lingua* (Chapel Hill, 1942).
11. L. H. Gray, *Foundations of Language* (New York, 1937), pp. 435-440.
12. A. Schleicher, *Compendium der vergleichenden Grammatik der indogermanischen Sprachen* (Weimar, 1861).
13. Gray, *op. cit.,* pp. 443-444; I. Iordan and J. Orr, *Introduction to Romance Philology* (London, 1937), pp. 15-19.
14. Iordan and Orr, *op. cit.,* pp. 15-19, 86-143.
15. B. Croce, *Estetica come scienza* (Bari, 1912); *Filosofia del linguaggio,* (Bari, 1924). *See also* Iordan and Orr, *op. cit.,* pp. 115-120.
16. F. de Saussure, *Cours de linguistique générale* (Paris, 1916).
17. N. S. Trubetskoi, *Grundzüge der Phonologie* (Prague, 1939).
18. R. Jakobson, *Kindersprache, Aphasie, und allgemeine Lautgesetze* (Upsala, 1942).
19. F. Boas, *Handbook of American Indian Languages* (Washington, 1907-1911).
20. E. Sapir, *Language* (New York, 1921).
21. L. Bloomfield, *Language* (New York, 1933).
22. B. L. Whorf, *Language, Thought and Reality,* ed. J. Carroll (Cambridge, 1956).
23. Whorf, *op. cit.,* "Grammatical Categories"; "Language: Plan and Conception of Arrangement."
24. B. Bloch and G. L. Trager, *Outline of Linguistic Analysis* (Baltimore, 1942), p. 9; L. Bloomfield, *Outline Guide for the Practical Study of Foreign Languages* (Baltimore, 1942), p. 16.

25. This view is generally implied rather than expressly stated; see L. Bloomfield, "Philosophical Aspects of Language," *Studies in the History of Culture* (Menasha, Wis., 1942), pp. 178-184.

26. *The Use of the Vernacular Languages in Education,* UNESCO (Paris, 1953), pp. 103-115; R. A. Hall, Jr., *Hands Off Pidgin English!* (Sydney, 1955).

27. UNESCO, *op. cit.,* pp. 25, 54.

28. Gray, *op. cit.,* p. 40.

29. Iordan and Orr, *op. cit.,* pp. 15-19.

30. M. Pei, *The Italian Language* (New York, 1932), p. 4; *Language for Everybody* (New York, 1957), pp. 107-110.

31. R. A. Hall, Jr., *French Review,* May, 1944, p. 377: "In itself, and apart from all considerations of social favor, one form of speech is as good as another." See also, by the same writer, *Leave Your Language Alone!* (Ithaca, 1950).

32. M. Pei, *The Story of English* (Philadelphia and New York, 1952), pp. 140-141.

33. Bloomfield, *Outline Guide,* p. 8: "After one has some command of the language, and providing its alphabet and mode of writing are not too different, one may learn the conventional writing in order to read." Bloch and Trager, *op. cit.,* p. 10: "When the student has mastered the pronunciation, he may find it convenient or necessary to learn also the foreign system of writing; but until he has a thorough practical knowledge of the pronunciation, any preoccupation with the written form of the language is likely to be confusing and ineffective." B. Bloch, *Language,* XXI, 2 (1945): "The German and Russian forms are disguised by appearing in the native alphabets."

34. C. C. Fries, "Meaning and Linguistic Analysis," *Readings in Applied English Linguistics* (New York, 1958), p. 113; McC. Barnet, "Structural Syntax on the Blackboard," *ibid.,* p. 349.

35. B. Bloch, *Language,* XXI, 2, pp. 108-113. *See also* Bloomfield, *Language,* p. 1: "Our schools and colleges teach us very little about language, and what they teach is largely in error." See also R. A. Hall, Jr., *AAUP Bulletin,* Summer, 1945: "They" (language teachers who resist the inroads of linguistic science) "fear that their jobs, income from textbooks and prestige will be swept away."

36. E. H. Sturtevant, *Introduction to Linguistic Science* (New Haven, 1947), p. 25: "It may perhaps be suggested that the most efficient as well as the easiest way to remedy the situation would be the complete cessation of the teaching of spelling."

37. J. B. McMillan, "A Philosophy of Language," *Readings in Applied English Linguistics,* p. 209: "The traditional superstitious identification of the 'rules' of English grammar with the 'rules' of a mythical 'good English' must go."

38. Bloch and Trager, *op. cit.,* p. 7.

39. Bloomfield, *Outline Guide,* p. 4.

40. A German language manual composed by members of the linguistic

science school uses such terms as "general form" instead of "infinitive"; "unreal" instead of "subjunctive"; *"ich* and *er*-forms" instead of "first and third singular"; *"der, die* and *das*-nouns" instead of "masculine, feminine, and neuter"; "the object in form 2 and 3" instead of "the accusative and dative," or "the direct and indirect object." As an example of the incomprehensibility that may arise from this supposed simplification of terminology, we have: "Form 3" (what traditional text-books would call the dative) "is used for the person in regard to whom a statement is made." Language students, apparently, are not to be trusted with such terms as "infinitive," "subjunctive," "accusative," "dative," or even "direct and indirect object." Their ability to learn and apply such forms is denied. They must forever remain grammatical illiterates and linguistic morons, while their teachers, fortified by "exocentric constructions," "sandhi alternants" and "compound junctures," tower above them like Brahmins over the pariahs.

41. Bloomfield, *Outline Guide,* p. 1.
42. *See also* J. Schrijnen, *Charakteristik des altchristlichen Lateins* (Nijmegen, 1932).
43. K. W. Dykema, "The Grammar of Spoken English: Its Relation to What Is Called English Grammar," *Readings in Applied Linguistics,* p. 96, cites such expressions as "I seen the bothen of 'm," "Them dogs are us'n's," "I'll call you up, without I can't," and asserts that these expressions perform for him the function of communication and are accordingly part of English speech. The question arises: How many English speakers would understand them? At what point does a sub-standard form, however native, cease to form part of the common language?
44. Pei, *Story of English,* pp. 140-141.
45. Pei, *Story of English,* pp. 278-281; Sturtevant, *op. cit.,* p. 7.

12

Relativism and the Use of Language

RICHARD M. WEAVER

Nor do I think it a matter of little moment whether the language of a people be vitiated or refined, whether the popular idiom be erroneous or correct. . . . It is the opinion of Plato, that changes in the dress and habits of the citizens portend great changes and commotions in the state; and I am inclined to believe that when the language in common use in any country becomes irregular and depraved, it is followed by their ruin or their degradation. For what do terms used without skill or meaning, which are at once corrupt and misapplied, denote but a people listless, supine, and ripe for servitude? On the contrary, we have never heard of any people or state which has not flourished in some degree of prosperity as long as their language has retained its elegance and its purity.

—Milton to Benedetto Bonomatthai,
September 10, 1638 [1]

The epigraph from Milton is included here to represent a rather general feeling that a society cannot remain harmonious and healthy unless its use of language remains pure. "Pure" in this sense means stable, because fixed with respect to semantic references. More precisely, the feeling is that people cannot express the same idea or take the same attitude toward the same thing or agree on a policy which all will follow alike unless there is a certain minimal identity in the signification of the signs they employ, and the most common of these signs are linguistic. Confusion and conflict may result when the people engaged in any enterprise, which would include, of course, the maintaining of a state, find that their words are no longer reliable communicators of ideas and feelings. In such cases, where words have ceased to be a fixed medium of exchange, each party that feels misunderstood because its meaning was not received in the form intended may react with passion, and this can be the beginning of internecine strife. It will be recalled that the United States Senate debated for thirty years whether the term "constitution" could be translated "compact." This difference was eventually settled by a bloody civil war. In our own time we have had ample occasion to notice how words of critical importance are used in varying and even conflicting senses. For the people of most Western countries, "democracy" means "government by the people"; for those in the communist world, it means "government of the people" by an elite presumed to be wiser than they are. "Liberalism" has been so twisted and perverted that it may be beyond any hope of rehabilitation in our time. Even a term like "peace," whose referent used to be a certain idea of order, now seems hard to match consistently with any idea. "Peace" and "war" have become hard to disentangle, and there seems to be a rather widespread mentality today that understands "peace" as the successful imposition of one's will upon resisters.

In opposition to this is another view, generated by the popularity of modern relativism, which is that semantic reference must be a relative affair. It is not easy to state this in the form of a precise theory, but the general sense seems to be that language, like every other phenomenon, has to be viewed as part of a changing world. There are, accordingly, no fixed significations. The meaning that a word has will depend upon the time and place in which it is used and the point of view of the user. Meaning is thus contingent and evolving. There is no absolute position from which the application of a word can be judged "right" or "wrong." There can be only shrewd estimates as to what the majority of men will accept. As the world changes, meaning changes too, and we can only hope that the two will proceed *pari passu.* The relativist is, of course, pleased rather than otherwise that language offers no exception to, or way of escape from, his world of relativity.

An awareness of the problems growing out of man's dependence upon words for communication is at least as old as the Greeks. It led Plato, in the *Cratylus,* to ask, with the typically Greek direct approach, whether there is not a natural rightness to the names of things. Does every object that bears a name have a kind of proprietary right to that name because of a definite (and possibly iconic) relationship between the two? Cratylus appears in the dialogue as the upholder of a doctrine that "everything has a right name of its own, which comes by nature, and . . . a name is not just whatever people call a thing by agreement, just as a piece of their own voice applied to a thing, but . . . there is a kind of inherent correctness in names, which is the same for all men, both Greeks and barbarians."[2] After a long discussion in which Socrates puts this theory to a number of tests, the idea that names have an essential rightness because they are imitations of the realities named is given up as inadequate, and the necessity of some element of convention is admitted. I believe that no serious student of language today, with the exception of a few advocates of "semantics" who are not very well grounded in language study, argues as a general thesis that there is some aboriginal iconic connection between a word and what the word stands for. (A few indisputable examples of onomatopoeia may have to be excepted.) Plato could not prove it for the Greek language, in spite of many ingenious attempts in this dialogue, and the immensely greater knowledge of linguistic variety that we have today seems to remove the problem from consideration.

The obscurity of the whole matter of semantic relationship, however, continues to create illusions. Some of these are due to the work of popular writers offering easy solutions, most of whom seem to take vaguely relativist positions. The sum of their doctrine appears to be that if we will simply adjust our vocabulary to changing external reality, most of the world's ignorance and prejudice will be removed. This might do no more harm than other nostrums, except that it finds reception among people whose use of language has a very practical bearing upon society. For in addition to permeating the public mind to an appreciable extent, it seems to have influenced some of our jurists, whose very prerogative makes them "definers," and whose definitions are, of course, binding in a legal sense. Here are two examples. Mr. Justice Holmes is on record as saying, "A word is not a crystal, transparent and unchanged; it is the skin of a living thought and may vary greatly in color and content according to the circumstances and time in which it is used."[3] Chief Justice Vinson observed: "Nothing is more certain in modern society than the principle that all concepts are relative: a name, a phrase, a standard, has meaning only when associated with the considerations which gave birth to the nomenclature."[4] The first of these pronouncements stresses the relationship between a word and the circumstances under which it is used. The second states outright that all names and phrases are relative to the situations that gave birth to them and introduces a further difficulty by maintaining that this principle has special application to modern society. I would not deny that some element of truth could be extracted from both observations, yet it would have to be hedged about very cautiously. Taken as a philosophy of language without careful interpretation, such statements are insufficient and misleading. In these instances, the source causes them to pass readily into popular thinking.

The difficulty of the whole problem makes us wonder whether some help cannot be found by investigating the ultimate origin of language. Yet this turns out to be a subject of the utmost perplexity. None of the theories of language thus far propounded impresses us as convincing, and some of them appear almost childishly naive. Attempts have been made to show that man first learned to speak by imitating the sounds of nature. Other attempts have been made to trace language to instinctive cries. Still other attempts have been made to show that the roots of words found in cognate languages express certain temporal and spatial relations. But why these root forms were chosen for these particular perceptions, why they are not found in all languages as well as the Indo-Germanic, and how they were elaborated upon to produce words capable of complex signification are questions that go unanswered.[5]

About all that can be affirmed with confidence is that language is a very ancient creation of man. Edward Sapir is of the opinion that it "antedated even the lowliest developments of material culture, [and] that these developments, in fact, were not strictly possible until language, the tool of significant expression, had itself taken shape."[6] He furthermore believes that not even interjections are merely instinctive; he thinks that they express some feeling about the occasion molded or transformed by a mentality that is qualitatively human.[7]

It therefore seems impossible to arrive at any theory of the "rightness" of the meaning of words by studying their first origin and by tracing their early evolutionary development. The origin remains wrapped in mystery, and there are those who will say that language is a divine gift to man, like his soul. The best resource left to us is to look at its constitution and function to see what light these shed upon semantic change and upon the social and cultural problems connected with this.

Language, as I conceive it, is a social and cultural creation functioning somehow within the psychic constitution of those who use it. The scope of the reference of words is accordingly determined by forces within the psychic constitution and not outside it. The question of stability in language cannot be considered apart from the psychic stability of the cultural group. And by the same inference the reason for changes in language, whether of the kind we approve or disapprove, will have to be sought in that prime source. All this may seem to border on a mystical account of what, after all, is an empirical fact, subject in several of its aspects to direct observation. Yet the problem of meaning remains elusive after observations of this kind have been made.

I am inclined to agree with W. M. Urban, in his *Language and Reality*, that the situation is the reverse of what is usually conceived.[8] It is not that things give meaning to words; it is that meaning makes things "things." It does not make things in their subsistence; but it does make things in their discreteness for the understanding. Extramental reality may itself be a nameless flow of causality, but when we apperceive it, we separate it into "discretes" such as "house," "tree," "mountain." And naming follows hards upon this, if, indeed, it is not an essential part of the process itself. Communication and cognition thus seem very closely related. To know a thing is not to arrive finally at some direct perception of a property, as Locke suggests, but to form some ideal construct of it, in which meaning and value are closely bound. Theories of meaning that include only the symbol and the thing symbolized leave out of account the interpreter. But there can be no such thing as meaning, in the sense of understanding, unless there is a third entity, the human being, who brings the two together in a system of comprehension.

The central point of this essay is that language cannot be viewed as a merely naturalistic phenomenon, subject only to forces that have their source in the objective world and, therefore, varying simply according to time and place.

As a starting point for the analysis of language, a statement which Shelley makes, in his "A Defence of Poetry," seems better than anything I have found in the writings of the scientific linguists. In the course of a passage dealing with the relationship of language and poetry, he says: "Language is arbitrarily produced by the imagination and has relation to thoughts alone."[9] This is equivalent to affirming that language is a humanistic creation, whose function cannot be understood except with reference to the realm of the mind. I shall qualify this later on, but taken as it is, it leaves us in position to deal with one of the paradoxes about language, which is (1) that there is no "natural" relationship between a word and the thing it stands for, and (2) that, nevertheless, the meanings of words cannot be changed by an individual on his own motion. An effective change cannot be made unless it is endorsed by that part of humanity to which one belongs linguistically. But since change is a fact of language, this leaves the question of who the real arbiters of a change are when it is made. I would answer that they are those who share most fully in what Shelley referred to as the imagination. I would here borrow an analogy that Croce uses in speaking of art when he says that all men are artists, but that some are great and some are small ones. In the same way, all men are "imaginers," but some men are small ones and some are great. Those who have the greatest insight into what words should mean are those with the greatest imaginative power.

Imagination in the sense used here is an absolute faculty. Not in actual cases, but ideally, it is commensurate with humanity itself. It is capable of telling us theoretically exactly what every word must mean because it is the imagination that holds in contemplation all the various meanings that have to remain discrete and yet have somehow to function together in coherent discourse. Just as those who have the best judgment in art approximate absolute taste, so those who have the best judgment in words approximate absolute imagination. All of us have had the experience of finding a particularly felicitous phrase in poetry and of feeling: "This is what the word really means; he has hit it closer than anyone has ever hit it before." I assume that we could not have this feeling unless two things were present: (1) our everyday, more or less obtuse understanding of the word, and (2) an awareness that there is a meaning beyond this, which our own imagination had not permitted us to attain. It is the man of greater imagination who helps to raise our imagination toward the absolute correctness of meaning.

The problem of deciding upon the correct meaning of words, then, is not one of external measurement, but one of internal receptivity or capability. If we share to a large extent in that mutuality of spirit which makes meaning possible, we are receptive to true meanings; if we do not, we may accept wrong or perverted ones. And since there is no way of getting outside the human imagination to decide otherwise what a word should mean, we are compelled to realize that the most imaginative users of language are those who are going to have the greatest influence upon vocabulary in the long run. We realize further that the ones who name things in this way have a great influence in determining how the things will be regarded by our customs and laws. This is why Shelley, in that famous concluding sentence of "A De-

fence of Poetry," could call poets "the unacknowledged legis-
lators of the world," a claim which might seem a bit of chauvin-
ism in a poet, but which is capable of the most sober kind of
defense.

Some such concept of language is required by the undeniable
fact of its conventional function. And since words do function conventionally, they must function as deductive instrumentalities.
Let us note here that one type of critic today tends to attack
language as a means of communication on this very ground—
the ground that words are conventional in their meaning and are
therefore falsifying. The point of the criticism is that a convention
is something abstracted and, therefore, untrue, a generalized
sign of the thing itself, which we use because we are unable or
unwilling to render the thing in itself in its fullness. A word in
this conception is nothing but a stereotype, and "stereotype" is
here an expression of disparagement, because it is felt that "typ-
ing" anything that is real distorts the thing by presenting it in
something less than its full individuality and concreteness. Let us
suppose that I make reference to a tree standing in my yard.
The term "tree" does not designate the object with any degree
of particularity. It does not tell whether the tree is young or old,
low or tall, an oak, pine, or maple. The term is, therefore,
merely a utility symbol, which I employ in communicating because in my laziness or incompetence I cannot find a fuller
and more individualizing way of expressing this tree. If I were
really communicating, the argument goes, I would reject the
falsifying stereotype and produce something more nearly like the
picture of the tree.

But if the analysis I have offered earlier is correct, these critics
are beginning at the wrong end. They are assuming that individual real objects are carriers of meaning, that the meaning
is found in them as redness is found in an apple, and that it ought
to be expressed with the main object of fidelity to the particular.
What they overlook is that meaning does not exist in this sense,
that it is something that we create for purposes of cognition and
communication, and that the ideal construct has the virtue of
its ideality. [10]

Hence it appears that they misconceive the function of the word as conventional sign or "typifier." For if it is true that the word conveys something less than the fullness of the thing signified, it is also true that it conveys something more. A word in this role is a generalization. The value of a generalization is that while it leaves out the specific features that are of the individual or of the moment, it expresses features that are general to a class and may be lacking or imperfect in the single instance. What "tree," therefore, expresses is the generic nature of the tree, and so with "house," "city," "man," and all other such terms. In order to make statements that will have applicability over a period of time or in the occurrence of many instances, we have to avail ourselves of these classifiers. Obviously there are many situations in which we wish to say more about a thing than a specific image would convey. To do so, we abstract the common features of many such images, (i.e., we arrive at a general meaning) and use the result as an index to a class of things. I repeat that if something is sacrificed in this process, something is also gained. Those who object to the word because it "stereotypes" are refusing to consider what may be the prime reason for the invention of language. They are forgetting that oftentimes we need to refer to a class of things, to those now out of sight as well as those before our eyes, to those that are past as well as to those that are now existing, and especially to those of the future.

At stake is nothing less than the whole body of general ideas. If we insist upon a point-by-point resemblance of word and particular thing signified, language would have to limp along at a very slow pace. Even ideographs are not really pictures of the things they represent; they are generalized depictions of objects and actions. It must be clear that the very business of a people and the continuity of a cultural tradition depend upon an acceptance of the agreed-upon sign in its extensive application. It is the imagination that sets the bounds of that application and has the privilege of widening and narrowing them.

One of the most interesting criticisms of the conventionalizing property of language, which I desire to notice at length, was made by the late Benjamin Lee Whorf. Whorf became interested in linguistic problems as the result of work he was doing as investigator for a fire insurance company. In was his duty to find out and report the circumstances surrounding the outbreak of fires. In the course of this work he became impressed by the way in which people are misled by what he calls "verbal analogies." He found that accidents sometimes resulted from the fact that people behaved in response to the conventional meanings of words when attention to the actual conditions would have produced a very different kind of behavior. Behavior dictated by the actual circumstances would have prevented an accident.

Here are two incidents he uses to illustrate his point. A group of men were employed around some gasoline drums which they had been told were "empty." Now "empty," just because it conventionally signifies the absence or privation of something, suggests at the same time an incapacity to cause harm (as it would if applied to a gun). But actually "empty" gasoline drums, because they contain vapor, are much more likely to explode than filled ones. Acting on the assumption that these drums were empty and therefore harmless, the men were careless about lighted matches and burning cigarettes and so allowed an explosion to occur. They had been betrayed by the general meaning of "empty" into misinterpreting the actual situation. The second example involves a wood distillation plant, where metal stills were insulated with a composition made from limestone.

No attempt was made to protect the covering from excessive heat or contact of the flame. After a period of use the fire beneath one of the stills spread to the "limestone," which, to everyone's great surprise, burned vigorously. Exposure to acetic acid fumes from the stills had converted part of the limestone (calcium carbonate) to calcium acetate. This, when heated in a fire, decomposes, forming inflammable acetone. Behavior which tolerated fire close to the covering was induced by the use of the name "limestone," which, because it ends in "—stone," implies incombustibility." [11]

Now these seem to me very interesting, if unfortunate, exceptions to the utility of the generic sense of terms. But my point is that they can be regarded only as exceptions. For every occasion on which the use of a term like "empty" or "stone" leads to misguided action, there must be hundreds or thousands on which it guides the action correctly. In other words, the "class" meaning saves us incomparably more often than it harms us or causes us to have accidents. The analogizing function that these instances are used to deprecate is something we are unable to do without. Numberless necessary actions of our lives are predicated upon assumptions that "empty" does not mean "more dangerous than ever" but less dangerous and that "stone" means "fire-resistant." To the extent that these situations have to be faced as practical problems, I would merely point out that the user of the language had not been as specific as the language easily permits one to be. What was said was true up to a point, but beyond that it was not qualified in the right way. The gasoline drums were empty of liquid, but they were not empty of vapor, and the insulating material was stone in a sense, but it was stone in the process of chemical transformation. This is a problem that arises at every turn in the use of language. It does not call for denying the predictive "analogizing" function of words, but for making the prediction a little fuller by expressing additional meanings. The meanings that were given needed to be supplemented by other meanings. But these meanings are no more physically attached to the objects than were the other "erroneous" ones. The real task is always to find the right construction for the real order in the logical order.

Believers in the value of language as a convention (and in the connection of this with preserving cultural tradition) are, for such reasons, suspicious of those who take a complacent attitude toward semantic change. They feel that change of meaning is somehow a sign of ignorance or laxity. It represents to them a breaking away from some original standard of "rightness" owing to the user's failure to inform himself fully about the word or to irresponsibility. They wish language to remain pure, and "pure" means in accordance with the old standards of signification. I share the moral impulse that makes them take this stand, but I believe some way will have to be found to take into account more of the realities involved. It seems an irre-fragable fact that meanings do shift over a period of time, with a movement hardly more to be resisted than a glacier's. Is there any way of reconciling the ideal of semantic purism with this fact? Is it possible to visualize a kind of gold standard of semantic reference, from which illegitimate departures could be detected? I think it might be possible if we could find some basis for distinguishing between those changes which are "natural" and therefore must be conceded and those which are perverse and should be put down in the interest of intellectual and cultural integrity.

We can begin by noting what some students of language call "linguistic drift." This is a change, occurring usually over a long span of time, which affects such features as inflection, syntax, and usage. "Drift" suggests some kind of irrational, direction-less change, whereas the striking thing about this change is that it seems to manifest direction. It is not an accumulation of ran-dom divergences, but a change occurring according to a pattern, which will accept some innovations and reject others. Sapir observes that "linguistic drift has direction. . . . The drift of a language is constituted by the unconscious selection on the part of its speakers of those individual variations that are cumulative in some special direction."[12] In brief, the change is selective and not simply accidental.

Now, there seems to be something corresponding to this that might be denominated "semantic shift." Over a long period of time words will change their references in ways that are not haphazard but are consonant with changes in the general mind. Just what the ultimate cause of the change is seems difficult to ascertain. Perhaps it is the result of an aging of the cultural group that speaks the language, of a sophistication or an assimila-tion of experience, of the accumulating of past history that in-evitably brings with it a change of perspective. Nor do we understand the law of this change. The changes may follow our insights into reality, or they may reflect epiphanies of experience.

Usually as the word changes, the meaning keeps polarizing around some idea. The word "dress," in the earliest meaning that can be traced, meant "to make straight." (Hence, "to dress food"; "to dress hides.") It is apparent that something of the core meaning survives in our phrase "to dress oneself." The word "write" traces back to an earlier word meaning "to cut, scratch." Since writing, after its many metamorphoses, is still a process of making an impression upon a surface with a pointed instrument, I would say that the original denotative meaning survives. These are examples out of ordinary vocabulary showing that while processes may change, the essential idea of the process may be conserved in the word used to signify it. This sort of change does not play havoc with codes of behavior or institutions.

But I think we can recognize two types of semantic change that are inspired either by false reasoning or by motives that are objectionable. The first of them I shall call "rhetorical substitution"; the second, "rhetorical prevarication." (I leave out of account those changes that are the result of simple ignorance of lexical meaning on the part of a few, such as the use of "fortuitous" to mean "fortunate" or of "thus" to mean "therefore.")

The first of the improper changes keeps the old word but applies it to a new thing (the user not being aware that in the world of language words create "things.") Evidently, this has its source in the old iconic fallacy. One finds in the writings of modern semanticists a persistent tendency to refer to language as a "map" of what it stands for.[13] I say that this seems to go back to the iconic theory of meaning because a map is a small-scale configuration of the territory it plots. Language, on this supposition, must follow the outline of what it symbolizes. Now if a territory changes (e.g., if a river alters its course), the map has to change too. Otherwise, there will be a growing disparity between map and terrain, between language and the realities of the world, and we shall end in hallucinations. Words whose referents no longer exist are of no more use than outdated maps. Always, of course, the referent, as a shaper of meaning, is supposed to be something "out there." But since the word continues to exist (and since it may have agreeable overtones), the trick is to take it and apply it to a new situation. One writer revealingly calls this adjusting language to "life facts."[14]

I believe it can be demonstrated that this is what has happened to the word "liberalism." In the nineteenth century, this word referred to an ideal of maximum individual liberty and minimum state interference, to put it generally. Today, it is being used to refer to something like the ideal of the welfare state, which involves many restrictions upon liberty. Now if those who use the word thus could be brought into a semantic disputation, I think they would argue that the new meaning is justified because the old meaning is no longer possible. And if we pushed them to explain why it is no longer possible, I think they would answer that "circumstances have changed." I would want to ask them next what changed circumstances have to do with an ideal construct. What they have done is to take the old term "liberalism," whose meaning polarized around a concept of personal liberty, and to use this to mean something like philanthropic activity through the machinery of the state. The two ideas are manifestly discrete, but they have used the word for the second idea because it carries with it some of the value connotations of the old one. The second idea is, according to them, the only context in which a benevolent man can now operate. In fact, however, liberalism in the old sense is still there as a viable ideal if the mind is disposed to receive that ideal. When they say that the old meaning is no longer possible in the circumstances, what they are really indicating is that they prefer the new circumstances. Then they make the substitution, in disregard of the transcendental basis of language.

I believe that this is a very general truth. When a person blames a change of meaning upon changed facts, he is yielding to the facts and using them to justify a change that should not be made except by "ideal" consent. He is committing the fallacy of supposing that the reason for such change can lie outside the realm of discourse itself—that meaning must somehow tag along after empirical reality. All of this seems to reflect a purely materialist or "physicalist" view of the world. But if one believes that physical reality is the sole determinant of all things, including meanings, one collapses the relationship between what is physical and what is symbolic of meaning and value. It is another evidence of how the modern mind is trying to surrender its constitutive powers to the objective physical world.

The second kind of improper change, rhetorical prevarication, does not allege the excuse that the world has changed. It is a simple attempt to impose a change in the interest of an ideology. (I here use "ideology" in contradistinction to "philosophy." A philosophy, having a much wider circumspection, will have something to say about a word's meaning that connects with the larger work of the imagination. An ideology works to serve particular ends, and therefore the changes in meaning that it produces will not be circumspective and must result in a degree of injustice.) For example, when the modern leftist applies the term "reactionary" to everyone who will not accept the Marxist concept of economic and social organization, I would regard this as an ideological perversion. The Marxist is using the word to ascribe an impulse to "go backward" to people whose political views may reflect nothing more than a nonmaterialistic concept of man.

My next example is a more insidious and, therefore, more dangerous instance of prevarication. We mark a growing tendency among certain groups of people to refer to alcoholics, moral delinquents, and even criminals as "sick" people. The violence that this does to the legitimate meaning of "sick" is easily seen. We have always thought of a sick person as a man who is a victim of things beyond his control and who, therefore, deserves sympathy and assistance from his family and perhaps from society. If he becomes exposed to bacteria, which, of course, he cannot see, and contracts a disease, or if he suffers from some degeneration of tissue or bone, we regard him as undergoing a misfortune to which he did not in any conscious way contribute. He may become more or less a burden to his family and society, but not through any act of will.

Now the attempt is being made through this rhetorical prevarication to edge the delinquent and the criminal into this category. The result, it is almost too obvious to point out, is to remove the idea of moral responsibility from delinquency and crime. It has always been thought that society is the victim of the criminal. But now it is being implied, through a tendentious use of language, that the criminal is the victim of society, which did not take appropriate steps to keep him from getting "sick." By this verbal trick, what was formerly considered worthy of punishment is held up for indulgent sympathy.

This line of false reasoning probably begins with sentimentality. It certainly ends by denying the power of self-discipline. For what it says is this absurdity: Every man is conditioned, but the criminal is more conditioned than others; as a result, we are supposed to pity him and show him more solicitude than the person who is behaving himself and working hard at his job. Society has not agreed, and it cannot agree and maintain its own health, that those who have willfully done wrong belong in the same category and should be treated with the same commiseration as those who are afflicted with physical illness. It is, therefore, nothing less than scandalous to spread the view that alcoholics, criminals, and others who have adopted evil courses are merely "sick" people.

But to return to my earlier characterization: this is a designing shift, a deliberate misapplication in the interest of a special program. The users do not fall back on the excuse that reality has changed and that verbal usage must change with it; they simply take the word out of one context and put it in another in order to advance an ideological point of view. The ideology that is seeking to advance this prevarication is utterly hostile to the idea of freedom and the concomitant fact of responsibility. Such perversions have to be fought by a noetic and dialectical examination of the contents of the words involved.

This essay has attempted to relate the modern concept of relativism to language and, more particularly, to semantic reference. I shall emphasize, in closing, that the findings must be read in the light of one very important distinction. There is a

difference between saying that language is relative because it is
a convention and saying that because it is a convention it may
be treated or used relativistically. If language is a more or less
local convention, then its meanings are relative to those who use
it. It clearly does not follow from this, however, that those who
speak it may use it with unrestricted license. Here one might
usefully paraphrase a statement that Burke makes about civil
government: "If language is the product of convention, then
that convention is its law." Now, when we say that that convention is its law, we accept the idea of prescriptive meaning.
I would prefer to describe the fact with a word of stronger implication: language is a covenant among those who use it. It is
in the nature of a covenant to be more than a matter of simple
convenience, to be departed from for light and transient causes.
A covenant—and I like, in this connection, the religious overtones
of the word—binds us at deeper levels and involves some kind
of confrontation of reality. When we covenant with one another
that a word shall stand for a certain thing, we signify that it is
the best available word for that thing in the present state of
general understanding. The possibilities of refinement toward a
more absolute correctness of meaning lie within and behind that
convention. But as long as the convention is in effect, it has to
be respected like any other rule, and this requires that departures
from it must justify themselves.

Language, therefore, must be viewed as nonrelative in two
ways. Meanings cannot be judged as relative simply to time and
place; hence, in our dialectical vocabulary there is a theoretical
absolute rightness of meaning. (Another distinction, which I owe
to the members of this Symposium, is the difference between
knowing an absolute and knowing an absolute absolutely. We
posit, without knowing, an absolute correctness of meaning; how
we attain toward that I have indicated in my remarks on poetry
and imagination.) In the second place, the convention or covenant
of language must be treated as absolutely binding upon us, as
far as our human condition permits, until a change is authorized
by right reason. These two considerations prevent the anarchy
which an unconditional permissiveness—itself a pernicious abso-

lute—would allow. They are all the defense that is needed for those who believe that both effective and right ways of saying things can be taught the student who is entering the universe of linguistic discourse.

NOTES

1. *The Prose Works of John Milton* (London, 1806), I, xi-xii.
2. *Cratylus,* 383 b.
3. Quoted in Clinton Rossiter, *Conservatism in America* (New York, 1955), p. 4.
4. In his opinion upholding the conviction of eleven Communist leaders. See *New York Times,* June 5, 1951.
5. For a survey of theories regarding the origin of language, *see* Mario Pei, *The Story of Language* (Philadelphia, 1949), pp. 18-20.
6. Edward Sapir, *Language* (New York, 1921), p. 23.
7. *Ibid.,* p. 4.
8. W. M. Urban, *Language and Reality* (New York, 1939), pp. 105-106.
9. Percy Bysshe Shelley, *Prose Works* (London, 1888), II, 6.
10. The author is aware that in these paragraphs he is going over ground that was well trodden in the Middle Ages. The great controversy over the status of universals, in which Abelard, Aquinas, and William of Ockham were prominent contenders, concerned questions with which the modern student of language and semiotics still has to deal. The position taken in this essay, which perhaps comes closest to that of Abelard, represents an attempt to answer the following question: What is the relationship between words and the extramental order that they symbolize? It is impossible, for reasons we have already seen, to assume a simple correspondence between the two. But, on the other hand, if we say there is no relationship, we abandon the objectivity of knowledge and leave the door open for pure subjectivism or skepticism. This is where Shelley's dictum has to be emended: words do not have relation to thoughts alone; they have relation to the real world *through* thought. The relationship between a word and whatever it stands for is thus an *imputed* relationship, which is the same as saying a relationship in thought. According to Abelard, what is expressed by a general term is in the thing symbolized (and hence the term has objective reference), but it is not in the thing in the form in which it is conceived by the mind. This distinction enables one to affirm that words do have relation to the real order, but that this relation can never be explained by simple analogies based on correspondence, contiguity, or other ideas involving that order. When I say that meaning creates things, I am saying that the mind conceives things in its own way for purposes of communication. It is the logical content of a word that is predicated of a percept, and this brings us back to the fact of language as a closed

system, into which the extramental world has no direct mode of ingress. Prior to a more definitive epistemology and metaphysics, it seems impossible to say anything more definitive about the nature of reference.

11. Benjamin Lee Whorf, *Four Articles on Metalinguistics* (Washington, D.C.: Department of State, 1950), pp. 75-76.

12. Sapir, *op. cit.*, pp. 165-166.

13. Irving J. Lee, *Language Habits in Human Affairs* (New York, 1941), pp. 17-22.

14. *Ibid.*, p. 83.

Index of Authors

Index of Subjects

Due 28 Days From Latest Date
